THE MIRACLES
OF SAINT JAMES

EX RE SIG NA TVR
IA CO BVS LIBER ISTE VOCA
IESVM SCRI BEN TI —
SIT GLORIA SITQ: LE GEN TI

Incipit ep̅l̅a̅ beati calixti pape:

ALIXTVS epl seruus seruorᵱ dei.
sanctissimo cōuentui cluniacensis basilice:
sedis aplice. sue electionis: herois; q̆ famo
sissimi a̅ uiltino patriarche hierosolimita
no. & didaco cōpostellanensi archi epo:
cunctisq; ortodoxis salutem & aplicam be
nedictione ī xp̅o. Quoniam incunctis
cosmu climatib; excellentiores nob herves
dignitate & honore reppiri nequeunt:
hunc beati iacobi codicem. paruitati uᷢ
misi. qᷢ z̅ mul siquid cōrrigendum ineo inuenire poteris: aue
torital uᷢa amore apti diligenter emendet. Verūtamen innu
meras ᵱ hoc codice passus sum anxietates. Dum uero cēm sco
laris. ab infancia aplin diligens: quatuordecim annoᷢ spacio.
ᵱ ambulans terras & puincias barbaras: que de eo scripta inue
niebam paucis etiam utilib; & irsutis scedulis diligenter scribe
bam: ut ī uno uolumine ea comprehende potuissem: quatin̅
sci iacobi amatores apcius simul inuenirent. que necessaria sꝝ
festis diey; legenda. O mira fortuna; Inter preclones cecidi. & rap
tis omibus spolijs meis codex tantum ī remansit; Ergastulis tꝛi
sus fui & ꝑditio toto censu meo. ī tantū ī codex remansit; Inpe
lagis multaru̅ aquaru̅ crebro cecidi ꝓim̅ morti & euasit co
dex minime infectus: me exeunte; Domus qua era cremata. &
consūptis reb; meis. euasit codex mecū inustus; Qua propter

THE MIRACLES
OF SAINT JAMES

TRANSLATIONS FROM
THE LIBER SANCTI JACOBI

First English Translation,
with Introduction,
by
Thomas F. Coffey
Linda Kay Davidson
&
Maryjane Dunn

ITALICA PRESS
NEW YORK
1996

Italica Press, Inc.
595 Main Street
New York, New York 10044

LIBRARY OF CONGRESS CATALOGING-IN-PUBLICATION DATA

Codex Calixtinus. Liber 2. English.
    The miracles of Saint James : translations from the Liber sancti
    Jacobi / first English translation, with introduction by Thomas F.
    Coffey, Linda Kay Davidson & Maryjane Dunn.
        p. cm.
    Includes bibliographical references and index.
    ISBN 0-934977-38-0 (pbk. : alk. paper)
    1. James, the Greater, Saint--Legends. 2. James, the Greater,
Saint--Cult--Spain--Santiago de Compostela. 3. James, the Greater,
Saint--Sermons. 4. Christian pilgrims and pilgrimages--Spain-Santiago
de Compostela. 5. Catholic Church--Sermons. I. Coffey, Thomas F. II.
Davidson, Linda Kay. III. Dunn, Maryjane. IV. Title.
BT685.5.C6413 1996
263'.0424611--dc20   96-14801
                                                                CIP

ISBN 0-934977-38-0
Printed in the United States of America
5 4 3 2 1

Cover Illustration: Saint Jacques de Compostelle, nineteenth-century en-
graving. Musée Paul Dupuy, Toulouse.
Frontispiece: *Codex Calixtinus*, Folio 1r, Cathedral Archives,
Santiago de Compostela.

St. James the Apostle, eighteenth century, Museo Colonial, Quito, Ecuador.

Stone on which St. James' body landed, Iria Flavia, Galicia, Spain.

CONTENTS

ILLUSTRATIONS

PREFACE

On a cold July 25, 1993, Saint James' feast day, the first Holy Year in eleven years,[1] the plaza in front of the cathedral in Santiago de Compostela was overflowing with people. Many came to gawk: King Juan Carlos, Queen Sofía and other important politicians were there to honor Spain's patron saint. So were about a thousand cameras to record the event. The pilgrims, who had traveled the Route from as nearby as one hundred kilometers (the minimum distance in order to receive the *Compostela*[2]) and from as far away as the Americas and Scandinavia, wandered the plaza, easily identified by their worn boots, backpacks and often unkempt appearance. The townspeople, all snuggled in coats, made a contrast to those who had walked during hot days and had not come prepared to meet winter in July.

The archbishop and the bishops, the military, the king and queen; bright colors, music, horses; all the pomp and circumstance: the official procession left from the Hostal de los Reyes Católicos, proceeded across the plaza, up the stairs and into the cathedral to begin the holy mass to celebrate the saint's day. So many people were there that we[3] could not enter the church. Movie cameras were strategically placed to capture this moment: important for the Catholic Church as a celebration of an apostle's special day; important for Spain, as it venerated its patron saint; important for the Council of Europe that in 1987 had named the pilgrimage roads to Compostela as the First European Cultural Itinerary; important for Catholic believers; and important to the pilgrims who actually walked the road sometime during 1993, because it signified the official end, the official goal of 100 to 1500 kilometers of exertion, sweat and struggle. Records indicate that more than 99,000 pilgrims from Spain, Europe, and the Americas made it to Compostela sometime during 1993.[4]

When one thinks of pilgrimage, one often pictures other, non-Christian religions. Most of us are aware that Moslems are required to travel once in their lifetime to Mecca to pay homage. Many know that Buddhists often wish to travel to see a holy relic of Buddha and that Hindus go to the Ganges River for ritual cleansing. But many times in Western, European culture when one pictures a Christian pilgrimage, it is Chaucer's famous lines that first come to mind:

> Whan that Aprill with his shoures sote
> The droghte of Marche hath perced to the rote,
> And bathed every veyne in swich licour
> Of which vertu engendred is the flour;...
> And smale fowles maken melodye,
> That slepen al the night with open yë
> (So priketh hem Nature in hir corages):
> Than longen folk to goon on pilgrimages....
>
> *(Canterbury Tales,* ll. 1-4, 10-13)

It is the "medieval" aspect of the Christian pilgrimage that one thinks of: the Chaucerian scenes, the knight, the miller, the merchant, the prioress, the parson and his tale, the wife of Bath who had been to Jerusalem three times, and to Rome and to Bologna and to Compostela and to Cologne.

Yet Christian pilgrimage is not just medieval. The numbers of persons awaiting apparitions of the Virgin in Medjugorje, in former Yugoslavia, bespeak a yearning for miracles, for a contact point on this physical sphere with the holy, the ethereal. Newspaper headlines tell us of specific instances: "Crowds Gather at Billboard for a Glimpse of Light or Vision"[5]; "'Crying' Statue of Virgin Set for R.I. Tour."[6] A New Jersey man reported that the Virgin Mary would visit his backyard on a certain evening and 28,000 people came.[7] The first Saturday of every month, an unpaved narrow road which snakes its way to an altitude of nearly 15,000 feet in the Ecuadorian Andes is filled with buses and cars traveling to a new shrine where a young girl named Patricia Talbot has seen and communicated with the Virgin.[8] So many people come in search of this connection that sometimes public safety is put into jeopardy. On December 3, 1993, a judge banned public vigils in the New Jersey backyard.[9]

Pilgrimage is in vogue. New sites and new places where persons may receive some direction and blessing and sense of connectedness are emerging. "Old" sites also are experiencing a resurgence of interest. In 1974 a small academic group walked from Roncesvalles to Santiago de Compostela.[10] Along the way priests were surprised to see the group, and villagers hastened to empty a barn for everyone to sleep in. In 1979, repeating the venture,[11] the American group was guided one day by a friar in Roncesvalles, Father Javier, who marked the trail with spots of green paint for other, occasional pilgrims to follow. And follow they did, such that in 1993, when Davidson walked the route for the fourth time, if there was no room to sleep in the inn, it was because literally hundreds of other pilgrims had arrived there earlier in the day. One youth group, for example, came from Madrid and had nearly 1,700 walkers. The pilgrimage to Santiago de Compostela is recovering importance. Some people walk for the exercise, others for religious reasons, others for curiosity, others out of boredom, others to study medieval art and architecture, others to fulfill a vow, and still others to fulfill a penal sentence. For whatever reason, they are walking to a holy shrine, and thus making a pilgrimage.

With the heightened interest in Compostela and the route (routes) to this site, have come at least two diverging emphases: religious and scholarly. Before 1990 few local Spanish churches would undertake the difficulties of taking adolescents on long walks that included sleeping out in tents. Now, however, with the goal of making a pilgrimage to Compostela, these long walks, supplemented by devotional studies in the evenings, have become activities that many Spanish religious youth groups support. For larger groups there is an entire corps of cooks, aides, drivers, and health-care providers to accompany the pilgrims. While the honorary religious fraternity that supports devotion to Saint James and his pilgrimage, the

Archicofradía of the Compostela Cathedral, looks with excitement at the increasing numbers of pilgrims on the road, it looks with some misgivings at the kinds of pilgrims making the trek. In the summer of 1993, for example, the pilgrims were very noticeable at mass: in their boots and spandex walking shorts and sleeveless tops, they stood out from the rest of the residents attending the service. The *Archicofradía* is attempting to ensure that the experience be a Christian, Catholic one. In November 1994, at the first meeting of the confraternities allied with the Compostela Cathedral, the topic of maintaining the religious experience was an important one.[12]

Similarly, scholars' interest is turning to pilgrimage. The boom in pilgrims is mirrored in the boom in books about the pilgrimage to Compostela.[13] We sought in our comprehensive bibliography (Dunn and Davidson) to give, at a minimum, adequate bibliographical citations to everything written before July 1993 that contains a reference to the Santiago pilgrimage in its title. We amassed 2,941 items, and we missed more than a few. Since then, in an effort to maintain our data base, we have continued the bibliography, at least annotating titles. Between July 1993 and March 1995, we logged nearly 500 titles more. Obviously there is plenty of material around, more and more of which is in English.[14]

The scholarly emphasis has moved beyond the strictly historical-archaeological. For sociologists and anthropologists, the numbers of pilgrims afford tremendous research possibilities. Psychology professor Dosil Maceira at the University of Santiago has a corps of students evaluating interviews taken with the 1993 pilgrims. The February 1995 issue of *Peregrino* contains a supplement with similar kinds of evaluations about the 1994 pilgrims, based on interviews conducted under the auspices of the Federación Española de Asociaciones de Amigos del Camino de Santiago along with the financial support of the Ministry of Culture.[15] Scholars in other areas are adding their information: about local cults, about excavations of long-disappeared hospitals along the routes, about known routes through places like Italy, Germany and Switzerland, about the economics of travel, about jurisdictional rights and laws (both canon and civil) that affected (and affect) the pilgrimage.

Amid all of this interest, both secular and religious, our experiences along the road have shown us that we must come to terms, individually and culturally, with the biography of Saint James the Apostle and his place in the development of medieval Spain and medieval civilization; for, whether one's motives for making this trek are religious, scholarly or strictly personal, one needs to know the background of the phenomenon. How did the cult of Saint James develop? How far was his "reach"? What did the medieval pilgrims who walked to Santiago know and believe of him? Where did those who walked these roads come from? Why did they come?

The pilgrimage to Compostela is graced with an exceptional witness from the early days of the route: the *Liber Sancti Jacobi*. This twelfth-century manuscript offers a compendium of individual items that collectively compose an encyclopedia of the pilgrimage and cult of Saint James, and that separately display the nascent stages of several literary forms. Book V, the Pilgrim's Guide, for example, is a walker's or horseman's guide to the route, with appropriate cautions and important vocabulary. It is a unique twelfth-century travel guide, often likened to the Fodor of the twentieth century.[16] Book IV, once thought so spurious that it was removed from the manuscript, contains an early version of the Roland and Charlemagne story, with material not found in the other early versions that have come down to us.[17] Books I, II and III deal directly with the cult of Saint James, offering forms for masses and other liturgies, miracle texts and a story of the translation of his body from the Holy Land to Galicia.

Until 1993 there were only three routes of access to read the entire *Liber Sancti Jacobi*: travel to Compostela and ask the cathedral authorities to view the manuscript; read the transcription of the Latin done by Walter Muir Whitehill and published in 1944 (approximately a dozen copies are available in the United States)[18]; or read the Spanish translation done by A. Moralejo, C. Torres and J. Feo published in 1951 (fewer than a dozen copies are available in the U.S.A.).[19] Individual books of the *Liber Sancti Jacobi*, have an uneven history of publication. Book IV, the Turpin Chronicle, has been edited, translated and commented on in detail many times. Incomplete versions of the miracles, the nucleus of the attraction to Saint James, have appeared irregularly.[20] Book V, the Pilgrim's Guide, was practically ignored until the twentieth century. In the last sixty years it has been re-edited and translated into Dutch, English, French, Galician, German, Italian, and Spanish.

Fortuitously, 1993 saw the publication of a facsimile of the *Liber Sancti Jacobi* manuscript in Compostela, called the *Codex Calixtinus*.[21] We have been able to secure a copy of the facsimile for our work; and this acquisition has richly enhanced our translation, for, in the course of our work, it became evident that the Whitehill transcription of the Latin is replete with errors. This fact could have serious consequences for the many scholars who have not had access to the manuscript itself.[22]

We have undertaken the project of translating into English three important portions of the *Liber Sancti Jacobi*: the Introductory Letter to the entire manuscript; chapter 17 of Book I, a sermon generally referred to by its first two words, "Veneranda dies" ("A day to be honored"); and Book II, the collection of the saint's twenty-two miracles, the heart of the saint's work. These sections of the *Liber Sancti Jacobi* give the reader a good understanding of the saint's miracles, as the compiler would have his audience know them. They indicate the importance, popularity and dangers of the pilgrimage to the Compostela Cathedral. They are reflective of the significance of the entire work. They link important persons and places to the saint, not only in the salutation of the Introductory Letter, but in the references to and quotes of other medieval writers and saints. It has been our goal to render the passages into readable, modern English and to make them even clearer through copious annotation.

As scholars of the pilgrimage and walkers along the road to Santiago for nearly two decades, Dunn and Davidson have watched the increase in the numbers of pilgrimage studies and interpretations as well as in the number of pilgrims. Coffey has brought a background in medieval philology to bear upon the text. This fortuitous combination of talents, abilities and interests have benefited the project which involved the knowledge of Latin and vernacular literary styles and conventions, a knowledge of the geography and history of the period and a familiarity with the road itself.

NOTES

1.   Holy Years occur when July 25 falls on a Sunday. This follows a regular patterns of occurrence of 6, 5, 6, and 11 years. The next Holy Year is 1999.

2.   The *Compostela* is a document awarded by the Compostela Cathedral confirming that the bearer has arrived as a true pilgrim. This certificate originally granted the bearer three days' free room and board at the Hostal de los Reyes Católicos near the cathedral. In 1993 the Holy Year "true pilgrim" was defined as traveling on foot, by bicycle, or a horse at least 200 kilometers and in the true Catholic spirit (the concluding rite of the Catholic pilgrimage is confession and communion). Because of the large numbers of pilgrims now, only a select few receive lodging at the Hostal, which is now a five-star hotel. Other pilgrims are allowed to stay at hospices *(refugios)* run by the Church or the Galician government *(Xunta)*.

3.   Linda Davidson was part of a group that walked to Compostela in 1993.

4.   Records from studies by the Compostela University personnel and the number of *Compostelas* awarded.

5.   The billboard shows the face of a young girl, Laura Arroyo, who was abducted and killed in June 1991. *New York Times* (July 28, 1991).

6.   The "first pilgrim statue blessed by the bishop of Fatima, on May 13, 1947," this statue is the pilgrim who visits congregations around the world. *Providence Sunday Journal* (May 28, 1989).

7.   Joseph Januszkiewicz on Aug. 2, 1992 [*Providence Sunday Journal* (Sept. 6 1992): A5]. For these examples and others, see "Do You Believe in Miracles? If you do, you're not alone. From a vision of the Virgin Mary on a hilllside in Yugoslavia to the face of Christ on a billboard in Georgia, signs of a divine presence are touching millions," *Life* (July 1991): 28-41.

8.   Ms. Talbot experienced several visions between 1988 and 1990 in a desolate area, now a national park called El Cajas, near Cuenca. Occasionally more than 100,000 pilgrims have visited the site on a single day.

We refer here to religious-centered pilgrimages. In modern civilization visits to other, special, places are replete with emotional impact: historical places such as the Washington Monument or secular sites such as Graceland and even Woodstock. Lately the unlikely spot of Lake John D. Long in South Carolina is a place that many people visit, leaving toys and other mementos, to commemorate the deaths of two children who were killed there. See the article in the *New York Times* (Jan. 23, 1995): 10. It is becoming an increasingly more difficult task for twentieth-century theologians, anthropologists, sociologists, and historians to discern the exact line or definition that differentiates the religious pilgrimage, the secular pilgrimage, and the curiosity visit. See Davidson and Dunn-Wood 37-39.

9.   *New York Times* (Dec. 12, 1993).

10.   Linda Davidson was a member of this group, which was sponsored by Indiana University; David Gitlitz was the organizer and leader of the trip.

11.   Gitlitz and Davidson co-directed the academic program, under the auspices of the University of Nebraska. Dunn was a student participant.

12.   Members, for example, expressed ambivalence about the gift shop attached to the cathedral. Was it appropriate that the shop have an entrance directly off the cathedral's nave? Was it appropriate that, alongside the religious books about pilgrimage in general, and the pilgrimage to Compostela in particular, certain new-wave, new-age, non-Catholic interpretations of the road to Compostela also be available for purchase there?

13.   Davidson and Dunn are guilty of being part of this boom. More information about the subject of pilgrimage, medieval and modern, general and specific to Compostela, can be found in Davidson and Dunn-Wood, and Dunn and Davidson.

A good indication of the nature of this change can be seen in the Spanish periodical named *Peregrino*. Begun in 1985 by Father Elías Valiña Sampedro, it was a small (approximately 10 half-pages), mimeographed newsletter. Its new version (first issue, Sept. 1987), now edited by Father José Ignacio Díaz in

Santo Domingo de la Calzada, appears 4 times per year in glossy format with exquisite photos, and generally contains 25-30 pages per issue with articles by contributors from all over the world.

14. There has been greater attention placed upon the pilgrimage to Compostela in English-language popular literature: articles in *Conde Nast* and *Smithsonian,* for example (see Dalyrymple and Winchester). The year 1994 saw the appearance of two book-length personal narratives by North Americans who had made the trek on foot (see Hitt and Stanton).

The Confraternity of St. James in Great Britain was formed in 1988 and now has over 1,000 members; Cornwall and Ireland have also begun local societies in this decade. In the United States the Friends of the Road to Santiago (begun in 1989) has more than 200 members.

15. Recent statistics for the 1994 year indicate that nearly 16,500 people requested pilgrim documentation. See "Suplemento."

16. Gerson 9 n.1.

17. "There for the firt time one finds the narration of the loves of young Charlemagne, Maynete, for Galiana" ["Allí se encuentra por primera vez la narración de los amores del joven Carlomagno, *Maynete,* con Galiana" (Blecua 456a); translation ours].

18. See the bibliography under *Liber Sancti Jacobi.* We will refer to transcriptions or other information in this transcription as "Whitehill" for convenience. The work was actually carried out by a number of people over a twenty-year period, and it would be unfair to actually ascribe the numerous errors in the transcription to the named editor. See Hämel and Díaz y Díaz et al. for the complex history of this transcription.

19. See the relevant bibliography under *Liber Sancti Jacobi.* We will refer to information or interpretations found in this Spanish translation as "Moralejo et al." The Spanish translation was reprinted in 1993 to celebrate the Holy Year. It may be that more copies of this work are now available in the United States.

20. See the discussion of the manuscripts and versions in the introduction, xxxiv-xxxix.

21. *Liber Sancti Jacobi,* published by Kaydeda. We refer to this facsimile simply as Kaydeda, to distinguish it from the manuscript and from the transcriptions.

22. See the introduction, xxxvii, for further commentary. The more serious deviations of Whitehill from the manuscript have been signalled in the notes to the translation.

Candle seller shop, 1993, Santiago de Compostela.

ACKNOWLEDGMENTS

We have been working on this translation since 1993. In addition to traversing the now-indispensable internet communications, we have traveled to Santiago de Compostela to view materials associated with Saint James' cult and consulted the resources of several North American libraries. We wish to thank people who have lent their support in a variety of helpful ways: Margaret L. Riley who supported the research in St. Louis; Plinio Prioreschi of Creighton University; the staff of Reinert Alumni Memorial Library at Creighton University; the Pius XII Memorial Library and the Vatican Film Library at St. Louis University; Metropolitan Community College, Omaha; Father José Ignacio Díaz, the editor of the Santo Domingo de la Calzada-based magazine *Peregrino,* who facilitated the purchase of the *Liber Sancti Jacobi* facsimile.

We used the helpful Mediber (Medieval Iberia) internet list to ask occasional questions, especially about a reference to the *Libro de los doce sabios.* Answers were quick and to-the-point, and we thank Professors Charles Faulhaber, Steven Kirby, and Jeremy Lawrance for their information about the *Libro*; and Georgina Olivetto and Daniel Eisenberg for advice on computer texts.

For permission to use a picture taken in 1981 of the first folio of the *Codex Calixtinus,* we thank José María Díaz, the archivist of the Compostela Cathedral. For help and permission to use a picture taken in 1995 of the eighteenth-century colonial painting of St. James the pilgrim, we are indebted to the staff and directors of the Museo Colonial in Quito, Ecuador. Most pictures were taken by David M. Gitlitz during various pilgrimages to Compostela and various trips throughout Central and South America. They are used here with his permission. Other pictures, as noted, were taken by Maryjane Dunn. We thank Robert Dunn for readying our photos for book publication.

We also thank Matthew C. Nicholson of the Environmental Data Center at the University of Rhode Island for taking the information about the various place names in Book II, the Miracles, and plotting them on the map of the Mediterranean. He did so using the *Digital Chart of the World.*

Authors Dunn and Davidson leaving Triacastela, 1979.

INTRODUCTION

> While [the French soldier] was aboard ship, the boat
> began to be threatened by a savage storm, so great
> that…all the passengers…might be drowned. Immedi-
> ately, all…exclaimed in unison, "Saint James, help us!"
> …the Blessed Apostle appeared…, saying, "Do not
> be afraid, my children, because…I…am here with
> you.…" He immediately loosened the cords of the sails,
> cast the anchor, stabilized the vessel, and controlled
> the storm. Then, after having brought about great tran-
> quillity on the sea, the Apostle disappeared.
>
> — *Liber Sancti Jacobi*

Saint James' powers are evident on both land and sea. He
is skilled with ships and helps those who cry to him in
need, no matter where they may be. His appearance during the battle of Clavijo in the late ninth century is one of
his first miracles in his militant aspect. The relic of his
hand, while housed in Reading Abbey, England, wrought
cures during the twelfth century, which are attested to in
a collection of twenty-eight miracles.[1] In 1539 in Tetlán
(Jalisco, Mexico), the saint aided Spanish troops in their
battle against the Indians.[2]

Correspondingly, knowledge of Santiago's miracles
span Europe and the Americas, medieval and later time
periods. One miracle, which in its later versions recounts
how roasted chickens returned to life and crowed the innocence of a pilgrim, is so famous that versions and representations appear as widespread as Switzerland and
England and appear as late as the nineteenth century.[3]
Detractors, on the other hand, retort that the greatest
miracle related to Saint James is that his cult managed to
sustain itself over so many centuries, and that the story of
the translation of his body from the Holy Land to
Compostela, in Spain's northwest region of Galicia, was
capable of generating belief.

Whatever the historical facts might be, the cult of Saint
James flourished throughout the Middle Ages. Although

we do not always have exact tallies of the numbers of pilgrims that visited Compostela, current research indicates numbers in the thousands in ordinary years and perhaps even hundreds of thousands in special years. Even after the Reformation sounded the death knell for certain aspects of medieval Catholicism, apparently the saint's popularity continued unabated in some Catholic regions of Europe. In the sixteenth and seventeenth centuries Saint James was carried by the Spanish to the Americas. His miraculous appearances purportedly helped the Spaniards defeat the indigenous populations from Acoma, New Mexico to Cuzco, Peru. Town after town carries vestiges of his cult in their names of "Matamoros" and "Santiago."

SAINT JAMES / SANTIAGO

The history of the saint known as James the Elder, or the Greater, (*Santiago el Mayor* in Spanish) is a work that evolved slowly during about nine centuries, was authored and embellished by several authors, and spans the eastern and western parts of the early-known world. Whether or not we believe in all or part of this biography has no bearing on his story, nor on the subsequent value of that biography to world history. We do not pretend to offer any solutions to the issues that still remain unsolved. We report here the germane portions of his legend so that readers of his miracle tales can understand their place in medieval religion, history, and culture.

The biography of the fourth apostle to be chosen by Christ is chronicled in only a few places in the New Testament.[4] We read that James, son of Zebedee and brother of John, was a fisherman. When Jesus saw these brothers repairing their nets, He called them into His service. It was James who witnessed the transcendental moments of Jesus' life, for example, His agony in the Garden of Gethsemane and His Transfiguration. At the Last Supper, James and his brother begged to be placed on the right and left hand sides of Jesus in the next world, a request which He soundly rebuffed. It befell James to be the first of the apostles to be martyred, by Herod Agrippa in 44 AD. For some, James' relationship with Jesus was that of a strong arm protecting and supporting the Savior; in this regard, because of his temper, James was called *Boanerges*, Son of Thunder. For others, the references to James and to his temper indicate that Jesus may have regretted his choice of this apostle.[5]

During the early centuries of Christendom, Saint James was not a particularly important figure. For nearly seven centuries, for all intents and purposes, he played no strong part either in the liturgy or in the formation of the Catholic Church. He left no letters and there is no account before the seventh century that documents his activities or sermons. When he is compared to Paul and his numerous writings and status in the early Church, or Peter, whose church in Rome became the locus of the Catholic Church, James played an almost insignificant role. Except for the listing of his name as one of the twelve apostles, he virtually disappeared from the sight of the early Christian community.[6]

Beginning sometime in the seventh century and continuing over the next two hundred years, the transformation was relatively rapid. The additions to this bare-bones biography convert the few early references into a full-blown history. In the early seventh century, the Latin *Breviarium apostolorum* recorded Saint James' death in Jerusalem and his burial in *"achaia marmarica,"* a phrase that has captivated nearly everyone who is interested in the location of the saint's bones. That two-word phrase, which intimates a specific site, is repeated, revised, re-spelled, and reused throughout the Middle Ages. Isidore of Seville (d. 630) may have included it in his description of Santiago's activities, now making the phrase *"intra marmaricam."*[7] Isidore's disciple, Braulio, named this very same Isidore as Saint James' successor to preach in Spain. By the early eighth century, James had become closely and firmly connected to the Iberian Peninsula. Aldhelm of Malmesbury (d. 709), a respected and respectable Church writer, referred to James as the apostle who christianized Spain. Other writers picked up that attribute. The saint had a new chapter in his biography: he traveled to the Iberian Peninsula, Galicia in particular, to preach and convert, although he did so with little success. He returned to Jerusalem and was beheaded shortly thereafter. By about the middle of the ninth century, the biography is clear: not only did Santiago preach in Spain, his grave was located in Galicia.[8] By about 900, the writings of Notker Balbulus of Saint Gall show that the biography-legend of Saint James had acquired most of its parts: James preached both in Palestine and Spain, he died in Jerusalem at the hands of Herod, and his body was brought for burial to Galicia.

In the early ninth century, perhaps around 813, a tomb or crypt was discovered in Galicia. The legends vary but assume supernatural aspects in a literary sense and religious import when interpreted within the framework of the Church. The most popular of the legends relates that some shepherds were guarding their flocks when they saw a bright star in the sky. They dug where the star shone on the ground and found a tomb. The local bishop, Teodomiro of Iria Flavia, pronounced the body to be that of St. James the Elder, and yet another chapter was added to the saint's biography. Additional information was supplied concerning the saint's burial: after his death, the saint's disciples somehow spirited away his body from the Holy City and transported it to the port city of Joppa. There he was placed in a boat and his body was taken westward across the Mediterranean Sea and northward along the Atlantic coast of the Iberian Peninsula where, when the boat landed, other disciples, knowing that he was coming, removed his body from the boat and buried it. It may even be that two of his disciples were buried alongside him. Further elements from folklore attached themselves to the saint's legend: the boat was magical, it had no oars, no sails, no sailors; and permission to bury the saint's body had to be secured from the local ruler (Queen Lupa), a permission granted only after the disciples with the holy body managed several miraculous escapes.[9]

At approximately the same time in the Iberian Peninsula, a land of several small Christian kingdoms and a large area of Muslim control, the battles between the Christians and Moors over territory waxed and waned. Alliances were made and broken but the Christian groups barely edged their frontier southward. According to some historians, the outnumbered and more poorly-armed Christians were especially disheartened during the battles against the Moors because the latter carried the arm of Mohammed with them into battle. What the Christian troops needed was a talisman. Not much later in that century, in the particularly difficult battle against the Moors at Clavijo, Christian troops were aided to victory when Saint James purportedly descended from the heavens, mounted on a (usually, white) horse and brandishing a sword. This miraculous appearance, which may well represent the first of his miracles, afforded him the name *St. James the Moorslayer* (Santiago *Matamoros*).[10]

SANTIAGO DE COMPOSTELA

The discovery of the saint's body took place at a site now called Santiago de Compostela. While it is obvious that the word "Santiago" is derived from the Latin of the saint's name "Sanctum Iacobum," the source of the word "Compostela" is far less certain. Among various suggested etymologies, one finds "Compostela" derived from words meaning "pretty place" or words indicating "burial land" or "cemetery." Some wish the town's name could refer to the *campo de las estrellas* ("field of stars"), but that etymology has been discarded by all but a few.[11]

The city is situated on a hill named Libredón, probably from Latinized Celtic words meaning "hill" or "inhabited place."[12] There may have been a Celtic population there that was Romanized early, as evidenced by the presence of pre-Roman and Roman tombs, moneys and ceramics. There are also Suevic tombs in the area, which indicate later habitation, although excavations indicate that there is a time when the burial site was abandoned in the eighth and ninth centuries. In the ninth century the area may have been abandoned, or there may have been a small population nearby.

The city of Compostela grew quickly in importance and size. Its prominence in medieval history is linked with the fame of the saint himself, the only apostle buried west of Rome. The association between Saint James and the Christians' efforts at reconquest meant the association of Galicia and Compostela with those efforts. The various religious and secular officials who would in turn benefit by this connection completely supported the relationship and gave incentives to the Christians to ally themselves with the apostle. After the discovery, or *inventio,* of the saint's tomb, construction began on a small altar. By 883, a church document gave Bishop Sisnandus (879-920) of Iria Flavia control of the saint's grave. The Sampiro Chronicle relates that Alfonso III (866-910) ordered a *new* church built and made donations for its maintenance.[13] Extant copies of the earliest decrees of donations are fraught with problems and many are now generally considered forgeries, but the fact remains that by the mid-tenth century considerable land was held by the monks who cared for the basilica that housed Saint James' relics.

By the mid-tenth century raiding Vikings were so successful that they simply remained in Galicia from 968-70. In 997 the Moorish army led by Almanzor destroyed important parts of the city.[14] In the eleventh century, Bishop San Pedro de Mezonzo and Bishop Cresconio had to undertake the reconstruction of the city, including the building of fortification walls and two towers. Yet, by the early twelfth century, Compostela had become the Metropolitan See and the archbishop's seat, wrested from the original seat of Iria Flavia by Diego Gelmírez. Larger and more ornate chapels, basilicas, and finally a grand twelfth-century

Romanesque cathedral were constructed, and around the cathedral rose the necessary associated religious structures, such as monasteries, other churches, and the archbishop's palace.

As more and more pilgrims came to the city, their lodging and sustenance could no longer be provided for by the religious groups. Similar to the growth in Lourdes in the early twentieth century, and as we see developing in Medjugorje (in former Yugoslavia), the secular aspects of travel occasion the development of commercial enterprises.[15] In Compostela private homes turned into boarding houses offering lodging to the pilgrims. Candle makers produced more tapers for pilgrims' devotional use. Extra food was sold to the hungry pilgrims. Souvenirs were made available to those wishing keepsakes. Again, as one can see in the area surrounding the sanctuary at Lourdes, vendors placed their wares along the streets so that pilgrims pass by them on their way both to and from the holy site.[16] As the popular emblem of the pilgrimage to Compostela, shells were collected from the sea and sold, and craftspersons began molding other materials into their shape. For all of these purchases, the pilgrim needed the coin of the realm: moneychangers were of high importance, so important that a guild of moneychangers was already a thriving community in the twelfth century.[17]

PILGRIMAGES

The visit to a sacred place is not new or unique to Catholicism nor to the Middle Ages. It was mandated to Old Testament Jews and became a law for Moslems, but for Christians it was not a requirement. In the abstract, the theme of pilgrimage was one that the Church used in its view of earthly existence. It became a cornerstone of the broad view of life as a pilgrimage. Old Testament references to exile and wandering became a prefiguration of the New Testament journey of Jesus Christ here on earth. As such, Adam became the first pilgrim, condemned to earthly exile and wandering, a kind of pilgrimage that the Jewish people would repeat in search of a homeland.[18] This type of pilgrimage would later become a motif for the Celtic journeys in the sixth century. In the New Testament, Jesus' journey into Jerusalem prefigured every Christian's journey toward death and the expectation of eternal salvation. After His death, Jesus journeyed once again on earth, joining his apostles along the road to Emmaus.

In the concrete, Christian pilgrimage is closely intertwined with the desire to see or touch relics.[19] Where a holy body lay, the faithful would visit, whether at local shrines or far-away locations. It was important to be as close as possible to some fragment left on earth by a holy person. Throughout Europe and the Holy Land people sought relics, large and small, ranging from the crown of thorns worn by Christ, to His Mother's milk and her house,[20] to the apostles' bones and their belongings. We have names of and references to persons who, as early as the second century, visited the Holy Land purposefully to see or pray at such places as the site where Christ was born or where events in the Scriptures had taken place. The Catholic superstructure generally did not restrain its flock's impulse to go on pilgrimage, but there was no dearth of sermons on the evils of pilgrimage.[21] Even Guibert de Nogent, who relates tales of miracles at various shrines, was a critic of the idea of pilgrimage. This bipolar attitude is reflected in the twelfth-century sermon in the *Liber Sancti Jacobi*. The author encourages his listeners to make the pilgrimage, stresses the miraculous possibilities and the promise of heavenly salvation, and simultaneously decries the evils found on the route to the pilgrimage site and the sins of and strife among the pilgrims themselves.

Other motives for the medieval pilgrimage were almost as varied as the number of travelers. In general there were three classes of pilgrims. Some pilgrims went to a shrine ex-voto, that is, because they had made a vow to visit a specific shrine in order to ask a special favor or in thanks for the fulfillment of a request. Others, as the author describes in the "Veneranda dies" sermon, were sent, usually by church officials, as penitence for a specific sin (see also Miracle 2). Occasionally, government officials would also exile a criminal from a community by sending him or her to a distant pilgrimage shrine, effectively ridding the community of the troublesome element. A third kind of pilgrim, perhaps best symbolized by those in Chaucer's *Canterbury Tales*, were those for whom pilgrimage was simply an escape — religious or otherwise — from everyday life and a chance to explore new regions.[22]

As Saint James was the only apostle buried west of Rome, pilgrimages to the site of his tomb became very common by the mid-eleventh century. Early documents mention a trickle of pilgrims even earlier. Alfonso III's church in Compostela, consecrated in 899, was a three-aisle structure. In the mid-ninth century revision by Ado of Vienne of the *Martyrologium* of Florus of Lyons, the writer asserts that the tomb of the apostle is "splendorously kept in veneration by the people."[23] Records list specific pilgrims' names for dates beginning about 950, and continuing throughout the following centuries. Gotescalc, a French pilgrim, is known to have visited the tomb in 950. A Viking chronicle relates that a Nordic pilgrim made the journey sometime between 968 and 971. The list for eleventh-century pilgrims is quite long and includes religious and laypeople, commoners and nobles, poor pilgrims and pilgrims with large retinues. The records speak to Italian, German, Spanish, French, and English pilgrims. By the mid-twelfth century Compostela may have become the most frequented of the various destinations for pilgrims, with Rome and Jerusalem in second and third places. Some estimates of the Saint's popularity claim that as many as one million pilgrims a year visited the tomb, although numbers in the thousands seem more likely.[24]

FEAST DAYS AND DATES

Visiting a saint's tomb is an important event, on whatever day one might arrive. However, early in the Middle Ages, the Church began to designate special days when the visit to a specific site took on more importance. Sometimes the Church granted special indulgences. Each saint in the Catholic calendar has a special day or, in some cases, days devoted to him or her, called a "feast day." On that day the mass and other offices of the liturgy celebrate that saint's life and works. Prior to the 1070s the Catholic Church on the Iberian Peninsula used the Mozarabic rite which differed in various details from the Roman rite used in the other parts of Europe. In the Mozarabic calendar, Saint James' feast day was December 30. When Pope Gregory VII and King Alfonso VI caused the introduction of the Roman Rite into the Iberian Peninsula, Saint James' feast day became July 25. For a while there was strong opposition to the change of religious rites, and the Compostela Cathedral celebrated both days. By the time of the composition of the *Liber Sancti Jacobi*, December 30 commemorated both the choosing (or calling) of Saint James and the *translatio*. The Roman date, July 25, was dedicated to James' Passion (or martyrdom). Thus the *Liber Sancti Jacobi* celebrates and has portions of liturgies for both dates. In addition, there is material for a third feast day of October 3 for the miracles of Saint James. A fourth date, March 25, to celebrate the martyrdom of Saint James, is mentioned in Book III chapter 3, but apparently was not as important, perhaps not even celebrated officially.[25]

THE CONTINUING CULT OF THE SAINT AND HIS MIRACLES

By the late sixteenth and early seventeenth centuries, the Reformation had dampened the pilgrimage ardor for much of Europe. Yet at this same time Saint James, or Santiago, as patron saint of Spain benefited from two strong sources of continued support and devotion. The first was colonization of the Spanish Americas: both conquistadors and settlers were taking the Catholic religion and stories of saints there. Santiago went with them and settled in many places: Santiago de Chile, Santiago de Guatemala, Santiago de Guamote (Ecuador), and Matamoros (Mexico). Not every region in the Spanish colonies was awarded a town named for St. James, but many were, and his powers went with him. In New Mexico, Governor Oñate saw the white horse and its rider over the Anasazi village of Acoma during a battle there in 1598.[26]

The second impulse for continued devotion to St. James within the Iberian Peninsula was the threat to his status as patron of Spain. During the early years of the seventeenth century there was a movement to supplant Saint James with the popular Saint Teresa of Avila.[27] Arguments, letters, appeals, and sermons appeared on both sides of the issue until the final debate in 1629, when the matter was decided in favor of Saint James. The result was a rather extensive literature on both sides of the issue. Concerned members of the clergy and of the political realm found it necessary to write long tomes about Saint James: his biography, his *translatio* to the Iberian Peninsula, and accounts of his many miracles on behalf of his devoted faithful. These authors used available texts, other miracle collections, and a great deal of emotion to convince their public not to remove James from his position as patron. Writers such as Hernando Oxea (who wrote a 365-page book in 1615 on behalf of this position), Francisco de Quevedo, and Miguel de Erce Ximenez took the side of Saint James in this struggle. Erce Ximenez is especially relevant to the present work, because he repeated information from the *Liber Sancti Jacobi* and asserted that he believed the twelfth-century work was authored by Calixtus and Turpin.[28] Thus it is obvious that the *Liber Sancti Jacobi* and the *Codex Calixtinus* were works that were known and available for use and consultation.

There continued to be a fascination with the saint's miracle tales throughout Europe, leading to new representations in drama, music, poetry, and art. Numerous confraternities dedicated to Saint James throughout Europe showed their continued faith in the saint in their caring for pilgrims who passed through the area and in celebrating the saint's feast day with the appropriate pomp and ceremony. Their charter books offer details about members, rites, and rules, and occasionally give insight into their own special link with, or a fascination for, the saint as miracle worker. Parma's confraternity's records, in a 1399 manuscript, the *Liber Consort[tii] Sancti Iacobi appostoli de Ga[litia]*, contain, on folio 1v, a miniature of Miracle 4 in which the saint places a dead man on his horse in front of him and a faithful companion rides on the back of the horse.[29] Late-medieval and post-medieval representations of the saint's life bespeak a general interest in the cult of Saint James, perhaps out of devotion to a specific relic. In Pistoia, Italy, where the church claims it houses a part of the saint's cranial bone, the altar was constructed and later remodeled between the thirteenth and fifteenth centuries and is richly covered with silver friezes containing a detailed vita.[30]

Continued representations of the saint's miracles may also be due simply to a desire for a "good story." There are several copies of sixteenth- and seventeenth-century dramatic pieces throughout Europe in various languages. A French miracle play from the late fifteenth century, the *Ludus Sancti Jacobi*, is a version of the hanged innocent miracle (Miracle 5) and includes the innkeeper's daughter. In Italy, a popular rehash of the saint's miracle tales appeared in the form of short dramas.[31] In 1750 another Italian version of a Book II miracle with a known author was circulating.[32] The miracles of the castrated pilgrim (Miracle 17) and the hanged innocent pilgrim (Miracle 5) were particularly popular. In Tafers, Switzerland, a mid-seventeenth-century chapel depicts in clear details the various portions of the hanged innocent story, complete with crowing chickens.[33] In some cases a particular miracle took on a life of its own, leading ultimately to a unique representation that contains only the slightest of connections with the original miracle. The symbol of Barcelos, Portugal, for example, is a beplumed cock, but its link to Saint James' role in the hanged innocent miracle (Miracle 5) is all but lost.[34]

By the late eighteenth and early nineteenth centuries there is apparently less popular literary or artistic output that one can identify as belonging to the long tradition represented by the *Liber Sancti Jacobi*. Pilgrims still visited the tomb, of course, but in greatly reduced numbers. Napoleon's visit in the first decade of the nineteenth century actually served to despoil the cathedral. During the mid- to late nineteenth century, coinciding with the Gothic revival and the Romantic interest in the medieval period, came an interest in inductive, rather than deductive, studies of a wide variety of matters, including the relics of Saint James.[35] Late in 1878 a group of cathedral personnel including López Ferreiro, Fita y Colomé, and Payá y Rica (then archbishop of Compostela) decided to excavate under the altar of the cathedral, expressly to rediscover the tomb of the apostle.[36] After several false starts the crew finally found what it was looking for on January 28, 1879: a sarcophagus filled with earth and what, after more examination, were determined to be the bones of three skeletons.[37] One of the workers on the project, Juan Nartallo, upon looking at the holy bones and smelling the sweet odor emanating from the tomb, was blinded for several days.[38] The fortuitous finding of the saint's relics, along with those of his two disciples led to further study by Vatican officials, and finally, in 1884, Pope Leo XIII proclaimed the bull *Deus Omnipotens*, confirming the *translatio* of Saint James and the authencity of the bones at Compostela.[39] This declaration spearheaded the efforts to return the pilgrimage to Santiago de Compostela to its former, merited, fame and glory. Because of those endeavors and because of the burgeoning fascination in medieval art at the beginning of the twentieth century,[40] scholars turned their investigations toward the *Liber Sancti Jacobi*, and the faithful began to return to the pilgrimage in greater numbers.

THE LIBER SANCTI JACOBI[41]

Sometime in the year of 1172 a monk named Arnaud du
Mont from the monastery in Ripoll wrote to his house
asking permission to stay some length of time in
Compostela in order to copy a portion of a manuscript
that he thought worth having in Ripoll. We call the text of
these manuscripts the *Liber Sancti Jacobi*,[42] and we designate the manuscript that resides to this day in the
Compostela Cathedral library the *Codex Calixtinus* to distinguish it from other copies of the text.

The entire work contains five books, each with a different focus. Book I, the longest portion of the text, contains the liturgical material and music for the saint's feast
days. It also presents some of the earliest polyphonic
musical notations, as well as monophonic pieces. Book II
narrates twenty-two miracles worked by the saint after
his death. Book III, the shortest, narrates the *translatio* of
James' body in its miraculous boat voyage shortly after
his martyrdom in the Holy Land to his preferred resting
place in Galicia. Book IV is narrated by Turpin, Charlemagne's legendary archbishop of Reims, and it describes
Charlemagne's and Roland's battles against the Moors on
the Iberian Peninsula. Finally, Book V, the Pilgrim's Guide
is the only twelfth-century guide to the routes that lead
through France toward Compostela, and to what to visit
on them. It also describes monuments to see and necessary activities to do once the pilgrim has reached
Compostela. Included are cautions about the bad food and
water, and colorful descriptions of local inhabitants.

It is generally believed that each of the *Liber Sancti
Jacobi*'s five books was written at a different time and may
have existed in earlier versions. It appears that the *Liber
Sancti Jacobi* was probably assembled into its final form
sometime between 1140 (the latest miracle placed in the
work is dated 1139) and 1172. The actual compiler's identity may never be determined; even the identity of the
authors of the individual hymns, sermons, and miracles

is doubtful, although many pieces are (probably falsely) attributed to historical figures. The *Liber Sancti Jacobi* opens with the Introductory Letter from Calixtus to Diego Gelmírez in Compostela[43] and William, patriarch of Jerusalem.[44] Although the work is ascribed to Pope Calixtus II, he had died well before the *Liber Sancti Jacobi* was compiled.[45] Toward the end of the manuscript the names of Aymeric Picaud and a companion named Giberga are mentioned as having been the one(s) to carry the manuscript to Compostela. Some scholars ascribe to Aymeric Picaud authorship of the entire work, some just of Book V, while others consider him to be only the scribe or the person who delivered the manuscript to Compostela.[46]

Scholars' opinions also vary widely about the purpose of the *Liber Sancti Jacobi*. Some view it as an exaltation of the saint's cult and propaganda for the pilgrimage route and the aggrandizement of Compostela. Others have pointed to the complex twelfth-century political-religious alliances and relationships on the peninsula, including the pervasive role of the French religious order of Cluny in the establishment of monasteries along the road. Another reading of the text centers on a recurring concern about the reconquest efforts on the peninsula. The importance of feast days and concern for the proper liturgy speak to yet another possible purpose.

THE CODEX CALIXTINUS

The twelfth-century manuscript of the *Liber Sancti Jacobi* housed in the Compostela Cathedral Archives contains 225 folios. It apparently has never left Compostela. It is considered to be the oldest surviving compilation of the various books. The *Codex Calixtinus* parchment evidently has been cut down at least once, and perhaps twice, judging from the loss of folio numbers and the loss of certain letters and numbers along the edges of individual folios. One of those sets of changes probably occurred in the seventeenth century, perhaps as a result of King Philip's ambassador Ambrosio de Morales' comments. When Morales viewed the *Codex Calixtinus*, he reacted with such disgust at Book IV's contents that he convinced the archive and cathedral authorities to rip the Turpin story out of the *Codex Calixtinus*.[47] When they did so, the librarian(s) took pains to change the Guide designation from "Liber V" to "Liber IV." Later, when the Turpin chronicle was reinserted into the *Codex Calixtinus* no emendations were made. Anyone viewing the entire manuscript will now see two "Liber IV" titles.[48]

COPIES OF THE CODEX CALIXTINUS[49]

Three other medieval complete, or nearly complete, copies of the *Liber Sancti Jacobi* are known to exist. They all seem to have been copied in Compostela from the *Codex Calixtinus*. The first transcription occurred in the last part of the twelfth-century and was executed by du Mont for his Ripoll monastery.[50] We know of no complete *Liber Sancti Jacobi* manuscript copy made in the thirteenth century, but two were made in the fourteenth century. Díaz y Díaz et al.[51] avers that although they were both copied in the same century, they were copied in two different shops.[52] There are also a number of partial copies and numerous versions of the Turpin story.[53]

The four most complete medieval manuscripts of the *Liber Sancti Jacobi* contain differing amounts of the three sections that we translate here into English. The Compostela manuscript, the *Codex Calixtinus*, is the most complete. It has the Introductory Letter by Calixtus (fols. 1r-2v), the "Veneranda dies" sermon (Book I chapter 17) (fols. 74r-93v), and Book II's twenty-two miracles (fols. 139v-155v). The Introductory Letter is also contained in the London and Vatican manuscripts, and a portion of it is in the Salamanca and Ripoll manuscripts. The "Veneranda dies" sermon is not in the Ripoll copy but is found in the Salamanca, London, and Vatican manuscripts. Book II's twenty-two miracles exist in all twelve manuscript copies that Díaz y Díaz et al. surveys, although occasionally small portions of the text are missing. Between the twelfth century when it was written and compiled and the end of the sixteenth century there was enough interest in the miracles to prompt the production of copies of the text and compilations in collections as well as artistic and literary interpretations like those mentioned earlier. Such collections as Vincent of Beauvais' *Speculum historiale* and Iacobus de Voragine's *Legenda aurea* contain many of the saint's miracles from the *Liber Sancti Jacobi*.[54]

TWENTIETH-CENTURY EDITIONS AND TRANSLATIONS OF THE LIBER SANCTI JACOBI

THE ENTIRE MANUSCRIPT

In the late 1920s and early 1930s, an American, Walter Muir Whitehill, spent several summers transcribing the Compostela manuscript. The transcription process was fraught with problems, and the Spanish Civil War interrupted the work leading to its publication.[55] The publication of the transcription has been a monumental aid to scholars of the medieval pilgrimage and of the stories surrounding it. It is not without errors, some quite serious, but for twentieth-century scholars who have not had access to any *Liber Sancti Jacobi* manuscript, the Whitehill transcription has been a valuable tool, in spite of the unfortunate errors.[56] Moralejo, Torres, and Feo (see Moralejo et al.), basing themselves primarily on the Whitehill transcription, translated the text into Spanish, and this translation, too, has been consulted by many scholars.[57] The most important boon to scholarly work on the *Liber Sancti Jacobi* came in 1993 when, to celebrate the Holy Year, the Madrid publishing house Kaydeda took on the project of making a true facsimile of the *Codex Calixtinus*. With its publication, scholars everywhere can now more readily consult and work with the text of this twelfth-century manuscript in a useful and faithfully reproduced format.[58]

Partial Editions and Translations

The only complete edition of the manuscript is Whitehill's and the only complete translation is that by Moralejo et al., but partial editions and/or translations exist of some sections of the *Liber Sancti Jacobi*.[59] Outside of these two complete tomes, the Introductory Letter has been quoted in parts, with only one other complete transcription, found in appendix II of Díaz y Díaz et al.[60] At least a portion of the Introductory Letter was translated into Galician and placed as the opening letter to Book II (the Miracles) in the fourteenth-century *Los miraglos*.

Although at least two editions of the music in Book I were produced in the last decade,[61] the "Veneranda dies" sermon itself has never been edited outside of Whitehill. Besides its present translation here into English, we are aware of only one translation, which Herbers made into German in 1986 as a part of his book and study *Der Jakobsweg*.

As for Book II, the history is a bit more complex. There are at least two extant early (thirteenth to fifteenth century) manuscript translations of the Miracles, one into Galician, and one into Spanish, both of which have been edited in this century. Both López-Aydillo (see *Miragres*) and Pensado (see *Miragres*) have published editions of the miracle collection found in MS 7455 of the Biblioteca Nacional in Madrid. This Galician-language collection does not translate exclusively from the *Liber Sancti Jacobi* Miracles, nor does it include the complete text of the *Liber Sancti Jacobi* Book II. Connolly produced an edition of Biblioteca Nacional MS 10252 (from the fourteenth century), *Los miraglos de Santiago* (see *Miraglos*). It is a fairly close rendition of the first twenty miracles of the *Codex Calixtinus*. Connolly notes ways in which the translator has simplified the text and made it audience-friendly (25-29).[62] King made a brief English summary of the miracles as found in the *Acta Sanctorum* in the early twentieth century.[63] The most recent translation of Book II's miracles was into French in 1987. This facing-page Latin-French edition reproduces the Latin from the *Acta Sanctorum* without commentary on either the Latin of the text or on the original source.[64]

THE PORTIONS OF THIS TRANSLATION

The present translation contains the portions of the *Liber Sancti Jacobi* that more commonly typify medieval religious writings than do the famous Turpin Chronicle and the Pilgrim's Guide. In fact, the first two books of the *Liber Sancti Jacobi* are directly concerned with materials proper for reading either in the refectory or in church and are explicitly described as such in the Introductory Letter to the collection. This is certainly not the situation for Book IV's narrative of the exploits of Charlemagne. The three segments translated here are centered on the saint and on the pilgrimage to him — both spiritual and physical.

THE INTRODUCTORY LETTER

The Introductory Letter of Pope Calixtus serves as a glue to hold the various and varied portions of the *Liber Sancti Jacobi* together. The compiler-author uses this Letter to introduce the central figure, Saint James, who serves as the theme for the collection. The Letter carries elements of dictaminal style, which was in its nascent stage at the time of Calixtus and which flowered later in the century. It was introduced to the papal curia by his predecessor, Gelasius II, whose teacher had been Alberic of Monte Cassino.[65] The Letter and the *Liber Sancti Jacobi* are written in a straightforward style, as the author points out in this Letter, although he seems to confess that certain material, excerpted from great authorities, may not be such.[66]

The Letter is explicitly attributed to Pope Calixtus II in the salutation and implicitly in the use of the papal "we" and the place of publication at the Lateran. However, it is highly unlikely that Calixtus had anything to do with this Letter or any significant portion of the manuscript's text. While the Letter as a whole does not jump to the eyes as a forgery, a number of elements combine to indicate that it is, indeed, fabricated. First, the Letter is addressed to disparate people in disparate places almost as a literary appeal to authority. Second, the *Valete,* or "Be well," in the closing of the Letter is more reminiscent of classical than papal expression. Third, with the exception of the one sentence "We have written our sermons...", the entire first section of the Letter, from the end of the salutation up to the passage concerning which texts are appropriate for reading in church, is written in the first person singular, rather than the first person plural, which is the norm for papal communications. Fourth, one is forced to concede, if not apologize, that the pope is relating a dream to explain the ecstatic and exotic story of the book's composition and its ultimate commissioning by Christ. In fact, it appears that the story of the pope's tribulations in writing the book and Christ's approbation of his efforts may have been interpolated into a text that had originally explained the intended use of the readings found in the *Liber Sancti Jacobi* rather than having been originally composed as a papal letter. None of these elements alone provides compelling evidence of forgery. However, there is one inescapable detail that does compel rejection of the authenticity of the Letter: it is clear that the author of this Letter is aware of the majority, if not all, of the work to which this Letter serves as introduction, and it is clear from the contents of the *Liber Sancti Jacobi* that events such as those of Miracle 13 (in 1135) occurred after Calixtus II's death in 1124.[67]

The "Veneranda dies"

The seventeenth chapter of Book I is labeled a "sermon" and is popularly called the "Veneranda dies" ("A day to be honored") in the custom of referring to papal documents by their opening words. This is one of five sermons contained in Book I, two of which are ascribed to Calixtus. In addition, Book I contains three works labeled homilies, nine expositions, two passions and various other liturgical material relative to Saint James. The "Veneranda dies" is the longest work of Book I. It exhibits many aspects of a traditional sermon with several citations of appropriate authorities. While the Latin title is *sermo,* the length and format might well place it more fittingly within the classification of *homilia,* or homily, in harmony with Maigne d'Arnis' explanation of *homilia* as "familiar discussions which were held by Church leaders in holy buildings in which they questioned the people and were questioned by the people and thus distinct from a formal speech."[68] Indeed this sermon is both quite lengthy and makes use of a question-answer format.

This sermon appears destined for use as part of the celebration of the saint's feast day of December 30. Following the tradition of sermons, which were written so as to be understood by the less-educated, the author himself asserts that he writes in "a simple manner," but this must not be construed as "simply." The writer seems to delight in expositions of allegorical truths and symbolic meanings, choosing palms and lilies, for example, to elucidate his text. The treatment of the lily gives us one instance of a simple metaphor extended into an elaborate allegory, with each of its elements symbolically representing an aspect of James' capacities. While there are the usual quotations of apt sections from the New and Old Testaments, the author also refers to tangential items, adapts passages to his meaning, often rather obliquely. This sermon is meta-rhetorical in flavor. Its concern is for the welfare of those being addressed, and its manner of support is citation of scripture and interpretation of the same. When it interprets the world around it, it does so against the backdrop of scriptural precepts. It refers to the Bible and quotes from other revered authorities. It reminds the audience of their sins, it encourages them to mend their ways, and it insinuates into the text the role that the saint can play in helping those seeking his aid.[69] The author's organizational structure is masterful and shows clear progression — chronological, geographical, and general to specific — within each portion.

In general, there are three major areas treated in the sermon. Since it commemorates two important events in the history of St. James (the choosing and the *translatio*), it is typical that it should begin with a factual presentation of events connected with the saint's life and references to the importance of this feast day. After a short description about the importance of this day, the author tells the "truth" about Saint James in a chronological fashion: proceeding from the choosing to his martyrdom, to his *translatio* to the miracles he works after death. There is also a slow shifting from the ethereal to the practical: from allegorical interpretation of the saint's life to an explanation of why and how he performs miracles in places besides his tomb, and then to the peoples who arrive at the shrine to praise him. Finally, there is also a movement from East to West: from Jerusalem and the Holy Land to Spain and Galicia. In a loosely reverse fashion (from West to East, that is, beginning with those closest to Spain) the author enumerates some seventy-four nationalities who arrive as pilgrims to the shrine. This listing serves as a transition to the second part, the one for which the "Veneranda dies" is most famous: its discussion of the practices and malpractices of pilgrimage.

The second portion of the sermon turns to the route itself: "However, since we have dealt above with the various peoples going to him and with the remuneration given to them by the Lord, it remains for us now to treat the pilgrim route of these people." The author condemns the evil customs of both pilgrims and innkeepers, offering valuable insight and intimate detail of the situations to be encountered along the pilgrimage route. The author was well aware of the abysmal state of affairs along the route, for he refers to it in the Introductory Letter when he recounts that as he was writing the sermon, Christ appeared to him and encouraged him to continue with his writing by saying "[correct] the evils of the depraved innkeepers...on the route of my apostle." What appears, at first, as a simple diatribe against evil innkeepers and the frauds they perpetrate on unsuspecting pilgrims, becomes, on closer inspection, a masterful pilgrimage in and of itself, through historical time and real time and from the Near East to the cathedral in Compostela. There is no doubt that the sermon's author is wordy; in an enumerative style (called *synathroesmus*), he inventories the musical instruments heard in praise of the saint in the church, calls out the role of nations — both real and imagined, both Christian and non-Christian — whose inhabitants make the pilgrimage. He recounts the tricks performed by unscrupulous innkeepers and others. The author reminds us that this saint performs miracles, and then he enumerates them, not once, but four times in the sermon. When he discusses economic matters, he makes references not just to money in general, or prices in general, but to the exact overcharging in farthings, oboli and solidi. We are inundated by detail, but within a very organized framework.

From the blessing that the pilgrim receives at the start of the journey to the shells that one brings back as a sign of having successfully made the pilgrimage, the writer describes the appropriate inner journey, the religious experience. By setting the physical pilgrimage against the larger pilgrimage of life and then returning to the daily struggles of the pilgrimage — the pilgrim's vices, the vices of those who take advantage of the pilgrim — the author leads us along the path the listener should elect to take. The author is not just content to preach, but also takes time out to teach: after outlining the ritual departure to begin the pilgrimage and after listing the religious changes that should take place after visiting the shrine, he traces the pilgrimage from its origins: "We must explain how the pilgrim road had its origins among the ancient fathers...." Again the author leads us chronologically: from Adam to Abraham, from Abraham to Jesus, from Jesus to the apostles, and from the apostles to Saint James. In using these examples the author also introduces a geographic framework of Jerusalem, Rome (Saint Peter), and Compostela, the three great pilgrimage centers of medieval Christendom. The author's description of these holy figures' comportment while on pilgrimage leads him to discuss specifics of contemporary pilgrimage.

The author warns specifically against three of the seven vices that are often found in pilgrims — covetousness, wrath, and drunkenness — before venting his wrath at evil innkeepers, moneychangers, false pardoners, false beggars, crafty merchants, and prostitutes. The many details of each trick played upon the unsuspecting pilgrims overshadow those few paragraphs that treat those good hosts and pilgrims who populate the route. This fascination with the sin and sinner mimics a trait often seen in the sculpture of medieval tympana where those at the right hand of Jesus are all blandly and repetitively portrayed, with little or no variation (i.e., perfect), while the sinners at His left fascinate us in their graphic punishments and individualized portrayals. Creeping into these warnings about problems that one might encounter along the route is again a general movement from East to West. The few references to specific places where these evil customs occur begin first in France, but later specific towns in Spain are mentioned (e.g., Barbadello, Triacastela, Palas del Rey), each of which moves the reader closer to the shrine of Saint James. Each individual paragraph closes with either a warning or a possible punishment, but the final paragraph of this section ("If someone then would spurn me...") reminds the listener that those who act appropriately on the route will rejoice.

This reference to the exultation of the pilgrims upon arrival returns the audience to the original theme in this third section: the feast of the *translatio*, the saint's powers, and a calling to all people to make the pilgrimage to Compostela. This final, and shortest, portion describes the benefits apportioned to all "Western people," all people in Jerusalem, and the "favored people" of Spain and Galicia.

Geographically we are transported from the periphery to the center of Saint James' cult — Galicia — where the people are exhorted to "live lawfully" and bask in the honor afforded them in having such a great apostle living among them. The excellence and power of James is recapitulated, and finally, the sermon closes with an invocation to the saint.

THE SAINT'S MIRACLES

An integral part of twelfth-century devotion to a saint is the perception by the faithful that a particular saint is able to perform miracles. This perception is formed and nurtured by hearing stories of miracles performed by that saint. The more detailed the story and the more miracles wrought in more places the more convincing the stories become. When the sick and troubled traveled to a saint's shrine and experienced a personal miracle, the caretakers of the shrine were generally quite eager to have that moment recorded for posterity and dissemination. Thus grew the collections of miracles: some, as records, remained simply a part of a specific church's archives; others were recopied and distributed to other geographical areas. Thus, for example, the miracles performed by Martin of Tours were written down by Sulpicius Severus in the fourth century, and reports of miracles at the tomb of Saint Thomas Becket in Canterbury were recorded. Finucane's study[70] shows that these shrine-based miracle collections were compiled in one of two ways: "If the miracle were accepted it was recorded either by type — usually illness cured — or chronologically; sometimes both systems were mixed...." The same desire to gather the miracle stories still holds true today, as evidenced in the collection of miracles at the tomb of Friar Pedro in Antigua, Guatemala, a collection that the local priests hope will help secure sainthood for him. The church there asks all supplicants to pass by the office to record their miracle.[71]

The preceding helps explain the role of the *Liber Sancti Jacobi* Book II, a collection of twenty-two miracles performed by Saint James. However, distinct qualities begin to emerge when this collection of miracles is compared to other miracle collections. Although Saint James' cult had been in existence, centered around Santiago de Compostela, since about 900 AD, most of the Book II miracles occur between 1100 and 1135 and represent a rather limited period of the two centuries of devotion to James. Book II's twenty-two miracles are a paltry number when compared to the more than two hundred that Gregory of Tours[72] collected about Martin of Tours, for example.[73] The monk Benedict collected more than 250 miracles attributed to St. Thomas Becket between 1171 and 1177 at his tomb or around Canterbury.

Contrasted with the compression in the time frame is an expansion in the geographical area treated. Saint James, like his miracles, is peripatetic. Neither he nor his miracles is centered geographically on the site of the saint's tomb. Indeed, the predominant locus is the pilgrimage route. This saint helps his faithful everywhere, but seemingly in connection with or prior to a pilgrimage. In this he is unlike, and thus his miracles are unlike, those of many other saints. The peripatetic nature of this collection is in direct contrast to another set of miracles associated with Saint James, those miracles wrought by the relic of his hand, housed in Reading Abbey in England.[74] This collection of twenty-eight miracles, datable between 1127 and 1189, compares favorably in number and chronology with the miracles of the *Codex Calixtinus*. But twenty-six of the miracles are cures,[75] whereas in the *Liber Sancti Jacobi* collection only three of the twenty-two can properly be called healing (Miracles 9, 13, 21), and only the last one of these occurs at the shrine.

Not only are the saint and his miracles peripatetic, versions of his miracles are ubiquitous as well. Their versions are found in most European countries and have been recreated over a long period of time. Some subsequent versions of the miracles far outshine the original rendition.[76] Similarly, the twenty-two miracles contained in Book II of the *Liber Sancti Jacobi* do not constitute the entire corpus of the manuscript's miracles. There are, in addition, several miracles elsewhere in the *Liber Sancti Jacobi*: the author narrates in the Introductory Letter several miraculous events that occurred to him while he was writing the *Liber Sancti Jacobi*; in Book I chapter 2 of the sermon for July 24, the author (Calixtus) tells five miracles of vengeance that befell people who did not properly celebrate the saint's feast day.[77] At the end of the Pilgrim's Guide (Book V), three miracles of vengeance occur to those who did not help pilgrims along their way.[78]

Much as one searches, no framework is evident within Book II such as that which one finds in the artistically structured "Veneranda dies." Authorship, chronology, geography, and miracle types all just begin to tease the reader's sense of discovery with a certain pattern when the would-be organizational thread unravels. To aid the reader in understanding the overall structure, each of the following sections is accompanied by a table to clarify the text.

AUTHORSHIP OF THE MIRACLES

Those in charge of collecting reports of miracles at saints' shrines were concerned with the truth of the accounts. Occasionally a miracle was not written down because there was no witness.[79] The compiler of the *Liber Sancti Jacobi* miracles feels the same pressure, and he asserts that the miracles, as well as the entire *Liber Sancti Jacobi*, are true and accurate accounts. His general indication is that these miracles were found written down in a trusted authority (*auctoritas*), or were heard from truthful witnesses, or were witnessed by the compiler himself. The introduction to the miracles, then, is an important starting point for any examination of the miracles. To take the compiler at his word, all of the miracles are from sources that he believes are truthful. Those that he has not seen, he can still testify to since he either heard them from those for

TABLE 1

ATTRIBUTED AUTHORSHIP & DATES OF MIRACLES*

No.	Author	Date
1	Calixtus	"Time of Alfonso" [c. 1065-1109]
2	Bede	"Time of Teodomiro" [9th century]
3	Calixtus	a] 1108; b] 15 yrs later [1123]
4	Humbert of Besançon	1080
5	Calixtus	1090
6	Calixtus	1100
7	Calixtus	1101
8	Calixtus	1102
9	Calixtus	1103
10	Calixtus	1104
11	Calixtus	1105
12	Calixtus	1106
13	Calixtus	1135
14	Calixtus	1107
15	Calixtus	1110
16	St. Anselm	[c. 1093]
17	St Anselm	[11th C.]
18	Calixtus [St. Anselm]	"Not long ago" [1037-60]
19	Calixtus	[July 1064]
20	Calixtus	[1100-1110]
21	Calixtus	"In our time"
22	Calixtus	1100

*Information in brackets is supplied by context and analysis of the historical references.

whom they were performed or from those who had seen them performed. In the "Veneranda dies" sermon, he gives permission to future writers to record miracles if "two or three" witnesses attest to their veracity.

Calixtus is given credit for eighteen of the twenty-two miracles. In only six of them do we get any assurance of the truth of the narrative: he avers that he heard a miracle and "recognized [it] as true" (Miracle 1); he states that "it is reported" (Miracle 4). Miracle 5 opens "it is also worth remembering," an allusion, perhaps, to a previously recorded miracle. Miracle 19 opens with "It is known to everyone...in Compostela." Miracle 21 states "in our time" and Miracle 22 begins "it is told that." The remaining twelve miracles have no reference regarding source or how the compiler came upon them. Indeed, it would appear that the majority of the miracles in Book II are written for the first time by this compiler.

Only four of Book II's miracles are attributed to writers of ostensible authoritative repute. Two authors of the St. James miracles are indeed well-known: the Venerable Bede (Miracle 2) and St. Anselm (Miracles 16 and 17). Most scholars agree that, since Bede had died in the eighth century, it is unlikely that he was the author of this second miracle. On the other hand, Anselm certainly could have collected or written Miracles 16 and 17, and the fact is that Miracle 18, attributed to Calixtus, is found in the same miracle collection by Anselm for which the *Liber Sancti Jacobi* compiler had just retrieved Miracles 16 and 17.[80] There is only scant reference to a Humbertus of Besançon in the *Patrologia latina*,[81] who is given as author of Miracle 4. Thus the attributions given are faulty. It appears that the compiler was striving to impress his public with an appeal to authority. It apparently did not matter to the compiler whether the given source was the correct one, as it would later matter to readers in the twentieth century.

CHRONOLOGY

DATES OF THE MIRACLES

The twenty-two miracles in Book II appear to have occurred between the years 830 (Miracle 2) and 1135 (Miracle 13). The early date for the second miracle is based on two indications: that it was written by Bede (who died in 735) and that Bishop Teodomiro (d. 847) played a part in the miracle. Given the impossibility of the chronology here, most scholars believe that the ninth-century date was used to indicate a very ancient miracle. Unlike miracle collections connected to a geographic site, this compiler is not constrained to order the miracles by date. The first and

TABLE 2

CHRONOLOGY OF MIRACLES

DATE	No.
[Ancient]	2
1064	19
1080	4
1090	5
1093	1, 6, 22
1100-1110	20
1101	7
1102	8
1103	9
1104	10
1105	11
1106	12
1107	14
1108	3
1110	15
1123	3
1135	13
[11th century]	17
"Not long ago"	18
"In our time"	21

last miracles occurred in 1100, as did Miracle 6. Miracles 3, 4, 5, 16, 17, and 19 took place before the twelfth century. Although Miracle 19 is linked closely to an historic event, the taking of Coimbra in 1064, it may have actually been written later. Miracles 17, 18, 20,[82] and 21 carry no specific date (thus the formula-style introductory paragraph differs in these four miracles), although Miracle 18 does relate that it happened "a short time ago." While there is no perfect chronological order to the whole, one can perceive an order within sub-groupings: Miracles (1), 5, 6, 7, 8, 9, 10, 11, 12, 14, and 15 do contain a basic chronological order from 1100 to 1115, even though it is interrupted. What general chronology the miracles may follow in the middle of the collection is broken at the beginning (c. 1100, c. 830, 1108/1123) and at the end of the series of miracles (1093, no time, no time, 1064, 1100). The latest date, 1135, interrupts the collection almost exactly in the middle, at Miracle 13.

TIME WITHIN THE MIRACLES

Sense of time and passage of time in a miracle were important to the audience's understanding of a saint's powers to cure the afflicted. The audience needed to know how long a person had suffered prior to a cure and how long a supplicant prayed at a saint's tomb before being cured. In some cases, perhaps, overnight; in other cases three days and three nights, or in an extreme instance, three years might be spent at a saint's tomb. An audience would be especially gratified to hear that a sufferer was cured immediately after praying to a saint.[83] In this aspect, the thaumaturgic miracles of the *Liber Sancti Jacobi* conform to the other thaumaturgic saints' stories. In general the *Liber Sancti Jacobi* miracles show a great deal of attention to time. More than half the cases refer in some way to time of day or number of days passing between activities. Only seven miracles do not contain a reference of this nature to time. The author carefully arranges several to include the saint's feast days as he writes these miracles. The first miracle is so constructed that the pilgrim reaches Compostela for the December feast. The same construct is evident in Miracle 20. The second miracle's pilgrim reaches the apostle's tomb for the July 25 feast day. Thus the author opens his collection by referring immediately to both of the important feasts. Similarly, Miracle 17 cites the October feast day. Other kinds of references to the passage of time include a mention of the hour: the cock crowing, representing first light (Miracle 5); "at dawn" (Miracle 16) and "just as dawn was glowing" (Miracle 6); or "vespers" (Miracle 18). Others refer to the number of days or the amount of time a sick pilgrim suffered, or a pilgrim lay dead, a time period that varies from a day (Miracle 16) to three days (Miracle 17), to the thirty-six days the son was held alive on the gallows by Saint James (Miracle 5).

GEOGRAPHIC REFERENCES: MIRACLE LOCATION

As with chronology, the location of occurrence of miracles can often serve as a cohesive link in miracle collections. This is not the case with Book II. As we are told in the "Veneranda dies" sermon, Saint James "is always and everywhere at hand, without delay, for helping those at risk and those in tribulation calling to him whether on sea or on land." The miracles of Book II support this contention, for the miracles he works occur far and wide, on sea and on land. Only Miracle 14 does not identify the site of the occurrence. There is little evidence that the compiler followed a specific geographic structure in the collection. Although it opens and closes with miracles that occur on the Iberian Peninsula, the only other pattern is found in Miracles 7, 8, 9, and 10, which all occur on the Mediterranean Sea.

Nine miracles take place on the Iberian Peninsula, five occur in France, five in the Mediterranean Sea, and three in Italy. The first and last miracles occur on the peninsula, the first near Barcelona in northern Christian Spain, the last in Almería in southern Muslim lands. They occur to soldiers and a captive; in both instances the beneficiaries ultimately make a pilgrimage to Compostela. The last miracle ends with the freeing of the captive merchant in Almería, that is, in Moorish lands, but the story also serves as a reminder of the overwhelming ability of the apostle to work miracles anywhere, as he frees that same merchant from captivity in twelve other widely distant places throughout the Mediterranean area and beyond.

Beginning early, much of the importance of Saint James' cult was derived from the process of pilgrimage, rather than the actual place or relics themselves. The remaining seven miracles that occur on the peninsula happen to pilgrims who are either on route to or at the shrine. Three of the five miracles that occur to French pilgrims happen during a pilgrimage to Compostela, while the other two are performed for soldiers in battle and engender vows to make a pilgrimage to the saint. Of the three miracles that take place in Italy, two result in pilgrimages to Compostela. Those miracles that happen on sea have little to do directly with a pilgrimage to Compostela, but in the case of Miracles 9 and 10, the events do occur to aid pilgrims either to or from Jerusalem.

NATIONALITIES

In addition to references to locations where the miracles occurred one may also look for a pattern in the nationalities of the recipients of the saint's favors. Again, there is no controlled pattern. Saint James does not limit his work to his shrine, neither is he limited to any specific nation. In only two miracles are the recipients clearly residents or natives of the Iberian Peninsula: the twenty soldiers in the first miracle who are probably residents near Urgel (Lérida), and the Barcelona merchant of the last miracle. Twelve other miracle recipients are from places in France, another indication of the importance of France and French pilgrims to Compostela. There are four Italian recipients in the miracles. There are five other miracle recipients for whom nationality is not mentioned. Since four of these people are on the Mediterranean Sea when they receive the saint's help, and are pilgrims to or from the Holy Land, they could be from anywhere in Europe. Interestingly, no miracles take place in England, nor to English pilgrims, although we know that by the twelfth century pilgrims from the British Isles were not uncommon, and the "Veneranda dies" author had a certain familiarity with the geography of that area.[84]

PEOPLE

The miracles talk of men, women, and children. They are nobles, knights, merchants, and beggars. They are old and young. In general, however, the miracles' principal characters are males. There are some children, and, in fact, in the three miracle tales that include children (Miracles 3,

TABLE 3
ORIGIN OF MIRACLE RECIPIENTS
& MIRACLE SITES*

No.	Recipient	Origin	Miracle Site
1	20 soldiers	Urgel, Spain	Zaragoza, Spain
2	Male sinner	Italy	Compostela Cathedral
3	a] Father	France	Compostela Cathedral
	b] Son	France	Montes de Oca
4	Knight	Lorraine, France	St-Michel, France [near Cize]
5	Male son	Germany	Toulouse, France
6	Family: father & his 2 children	Poitiers, France	past Pamplona [in Navarra, Spain]
7	a] Frisonus (seaman)	none given	on sea [Mediterranean]
	b] All ship passengers	none given	on sea [Mediterranean] en route to Jerusalem
8	Bishop & others	none given	on sea [Mediterranean] returning from Jerusalem
9	a] Soldier	France	a] Tiberias [near Jerusalem]
	b] Same soldier		b] [Tiberias]
	c] Soldier & ship passengers		c] on sea [Mediterranean] returning from Jerusalem
10	Male	none given	on sea [Mediterranean] returning from Jerusalem
11	Bernard	Cosa, Italy	near Cosa, Italy
12	Soldier	Apulia, Italy	Apulia
13	a] Raimbert (serf)	Chavannes, France	France [Chavannes]
	b] Dalmatius (knight)	Chavannes, France	France [Chavannes]
14	Merchant	none given	none given
15	Knights	Italy	Italy
16	Knight	Lyon, France	Compostela
17	Gerald (tanner)	Lyon, France	France [7-10 days from Lyon]
18	Count Pontius & entourage	St-Gilles, France	Compostela Cathedral
19	a] Stephen (religious man)	Greece	Compostela Cathedral
	b] [Christians]		b] Coimbra, Portugal

No.	Recipient	Origin	Miracle Site
20	William (knight)	Forcalquier, France	a] Forcalquier Castle
			b] Prison
21	Guibert	Burgundy, France	Compostela Cathedral
22	Male (citizen)	Barcelona	Corociana [Corsica?]
			Zara, Slovenia
			Blasia
			Turkey
			Persia
			India
			Ethiopia
			Alexandria, Egypt
			Libya
			Barbary Coast
			Biskra, Algeria
			Bougie, Algeria
			Almería, Spain

*Places in brackets are supplied by context.

5, and 6), the children are the miracle beneficiaries: given life again (Miracle 3), transported on a donkey given by the saint (Miracle 6), and sustained by the saint on the gallows in Toulouse until his father's return from the pilgrimage (Miracle 5).

Women are mentioned only three times. In Miracle 3, the mother threatens to kill herself unless St. James restores her son to life. In Miracle 6 the wife dies in Pamplona, setting off the chain of events leading to the miracle. Finally, in Miracle 16, an old woman pilgrim (apparently traveling alone) gives her small sack to a knight-pilgrim on horseback. No woman is a direct beneficiary of a miracle from the saint.

Miracle recipients are both individuals and groups of people, but the former is more common. Only Miracle 1 (twenty Christians freed from the Saracen prison), Miracle 9 (ship passengers saved from a storm), and Miracle 18 (Count Pontius and his entourage who are able to enter the chapel late at night) have multiple miracle beneficiaries. Several of the miracles include groups of people who

TABLE 4
MIRACLES & PILGRIMAGE

No.	Pilgrim	Time of Miracle	Purpose of Pilgrimage	Size of Group
1	yes	Pre-pilgrimage	Give thanks	1
2	yes	Result of pilgrimage	Seek forgiveness	1
3	yes	a] Result of pilgrimage	Seek forgiveness	1
		b] During pilgrimage	Pay homage	> 3
4	yes	During pilgrimage	Pay homage	30
5	yes	During pilgrimage	Pay homage	Several
6	yes	During pilgrimage	Escape plague & pay homage	4; wife dies
7	yes	a] Pre-pilgrimage	Give thanks	1
		b] No mention of pilgrimage		
8	yes	Pre-pilgrimage	Give thanks	1
9	yes	a] Pre-pilgrimage	Ex-voto	1
		b] Pre-pilgrimage		
		c] During pilgrimage		
10	no	No mention of pilgrimage		
11	no	No mention of pilgrimage		
12	yes	Pre-pilgrimage	Give thanks	1
13	yes	Post-pilgrimage		
14	yes	Pre-pilgrimage	Ex-voto	1
15	yes	Pre-pilgrimage	Ex-voto	1
16	yes	Post-pilgrimage	Pray	3
17	yes	During pilgrimage	Customary	4
18	yes	End of pilgrimage	Pray	c. 200
19	yes	Post-pilgrimage	Pay homage	1
20	yes	Pre-pilgrimage	Give thanks	1
21	yes	Result of pilgrimage	Seek cure	2 + servants
22	yes	Pre-pilgrimage	a] Seek favor	1
		Post-pilgrimage	b] Give thanks	1

are pilgrims, but are not themselves the recipients of the miracle. There are large groups as in Miracle 19 (when Stephen, the Greek penitent, berates the group for calling Saint James "knight"), small groups in Miracle 2 (the Lorraine knights), Miracle 16 (three French knights), and

---

TABLE 5

TYPE OF MIRACLE

No.	Type of Miracle
1	Releases from prison
2	Forgives sin
3	a] Forgives sins; cures sterility
	b] Resucitates
4	a] Transports knight & dead companion by horse to Compostela
5	Preserves from death for 36 days
6	Gives donkey to pilgrims
7	a] Saves from drowning
	b] Saves from capture
8	Saves from drowning
9	a] Gives power in battle to defeat enemy
	b] Tells how to be cured of illness
	c] Saves from sea storm
10	Saves from drowning 3 days & nights
11	Releases from prison
12	Restores to health
13	a] Saves from beating
	b] Restores to health
14	Releases from prison
15	Saves from death in battle
16	Saves from demons; returns to consciousness; allows knights to die forgiven
17	Saves from demons; resuscitates
18	Opens Compostela Cathedral oratory gates
19	a] Foretells successful reconquest of Coimbra
	b] Conquers Saracens in Coimbra
20	a] Saves from execution twice
	b] Releases from prison
21	Cures paralysis
22	Releases from slavery 13 times

Miracle 17 (Gerald, his two friends and a beggar). Several of the groups are actually families: Miracle 5 (a German family) and Miracles 4 and 21 (French families).

The saint aids people in all professions and classes: religious persons (Miracles 8, 19); merchants (Miracles 14,

22), a serf (Miracle 13), and pilgrims to and from the Holy Land (Miracles 7, 8, 9, 10). Generally, however, the miracle recipients are traveling males, especially knights and soldiers, perhaps underscoring the other, militant, nature of Saint James.[85] The "Veneranda dies" sermon states that Saint James can even perform miracles for pagans, but there is no case of this occurring in this book's miracle tales.

In the "Veneranda dies" sermon the author also refers to thankful pilgrims who carry chains, the physical signs of their imprisonment, to the saint's tomb, and in the collection of miracles, thankful pilgrims do so: the Barcelonan carries his chains in Miracle 22, as does the freed merchant of Miracle 14.[86] There is no reference to a pilgrim going to the tomb barefoot, another description found in the sermon. Popular wisdom dictated traveling in groups in order to avoid the dangers of the route, like those listed in the sermon, but in at least a dozen of the miracles the pilgrims go alone to Compostela.

It is possible to discern that certain pilgrims made the journey on horseback or on mule, and that others went on foot. The miracles tell us that a mule or horse was used in Miracles 6, 16, and 21. One might guess that the knights in Miracles 1, 9, 15, 18, and 20 would have gone on horseback as well. The travel times listed in Book V, the Pilgrim's Guide, seem to be based on mounted travel, and the time that passes at various points in the Miracles is consistent with the Guide's travel indications.

SAINT JAMES IN THE MIRACLES

The saint works in many ways: he frees prisoners, he gives gifts (such as the mule to the family in Miracle 6). He acts an intercessor with the Virgin Mary and can resuscitate the dead. He forgives sins. The relic of Saint James' hand at Reading Abbey was primarily known for working thaumaturgic miracles. The Book II miracle collection, however, has the saint healing only three persons: two from illness and one from paralysis.

TABLE 6

APPEARANCE OF SAINT JAMES IN THE MIRACLES

No.	Appears in Miracle	Speaks in miracle
1	"brightness" made the sign of the cross	with "clarity of sound"
2	no	no
3	no	no; indirect discourse
4	"sitting on a horse like a soldier"	yes; foretells future events
5	no	no
6	a] as a man with a donkey "wearing decent clothing"	yes
	b] "wearing very bright clothing"	yes; foretells future events
7	yes	yes: to the group
8	"standing on the waves with his feet still dry"	yes
9	a] no	no
	b] yes: in a trance	indirect discourse to the shieldbearer
	c] "his face appeared... decent...elegant"	"in human form"
10	no	no
11	yes	yes
12	no	no
13	no	no
14	yes	no
15	yes	no
16	yes: in trance fights demons with weapons	yes: in trance foretells future
17	in trance, "young...handsome face, lean...brown"	yes: in trance
18	no	no
19	"adorned in the whitest clothing bearing military arms... transformed into a soldier"	yes: foretells taking of Coimbra
20	"most serene light...fragrance"	yes
21	yes	yes
22	yes	yes

James appears and/or speaks in a majority of the miracles. Most references to his appearance are brief; for example, in Miracle 1 he "appeared in brightness in the darkness" and spoke with a "clarity of this sound." Others offer more detailed descriptions. In Miracle 4 he is described for the first time as having a military appearance, "sitting on a horse like a soldier," and his direct speech is also quoted. He again appears in military garb in Miracle 19, "adorned in the whitest clothing, bearing military arms surpassing the rays of Titan...." Miracle 6 portrays the saint in two ways: the first time as a normal man who offers a donkey to the poor family; the second time "wearing very bright clothing" as he appears to the pilgrim again, this time inside the basilica. In Miracles 7, 8, 11, 14, 15, 20, 21, and 22 the narrations simply say he appears, adding no physical description, although in Miracle 8 it is explained that he stands on the water but does not even get his feet wet, and in Miracle 20 it is also added that the house is filled with a "serene light" and with a heavenly fragrance. In some, but not all, of these miracles the saint is quoted as he speaks. Miracles 9 and 17 offer some of the most detailed descriptions. In Miracle 9 his face is described as "decent...and elegant," while in Miracle 17 he is "young, with a handsome face, lean and...brown." Finally, in Miracle 16, the recipient describes Saint James' actions as he (the pilgrim) watches him attack the demons who were trying to steal the pilgrim's soul. These descriptions make the heavenly saint real, put what is ethereal into human language and form, and make the saint, whether soldier, life-restorer, or caring provider, more tangible to the audience.

THE PRESENT TRANSLATION

In the present translation we have attempted to render the twelfth-century text into clear modern English. Latin's often long and convoluted sentences, with many clauses strung together, do not correspond well to modern English style, and we have divided many of them, making shorter units when possible. We did not simplify for its own sake, but only to clarify. Our intention was always to keep as much of the medieval style as possible. By far the most difficult choices involved the occasional necessity of breaking ambiguities present in the Latin. The most frequent facet of this entailed providing subjects for Latin verbs, since expressed subjects, which are indispensable in English, are optional in Latin. Ironically, Latin, while not requiring a subject, has at its disposal a plethora of pronouns to be used when needed. A corresponding dearth of these in English often required the use of nouns in these places for the handily distinguishing Latin pronouns (*ipse, iste, ille, is, idem, hic, illic*) for clarity. In addition, the varied case endings in Latin allow for considerably more freedom of word order than is possible in English. This freedom of word order makes it possible to compress a great deal more information into a Latin sentence than one could hope to compress into an English sentence if one wishes to retain readability, if not intelligibility. Although the splitting of the Latin sentences often proved a necessity, there was a constant attempt to remain as close to the Latin as feasible, to respect the author's style, and to stray from the Latin only when English left no other choice.

For clarity we have utilized certain stylistic standards for modern readers. The obvious basics are the insertion of modern punctuation and paragraph style. The medieval author has cited many authorities (e.g., the Bible, Sedulius, Dioscorides). There are more than 100 biblical citations in the "Veneranda dies" sermon alone. We have employed the standard format of quotation marks for indicating citations within the text. If the passages are lengthy ones, they are set off from the text.

For a number of reasons, among them a desire to retain certain literary devices and to remain closer to the *Codex Calixtinus* text, we have translated all Latin citations as they are read in the text, including quotations from the Bible. In some cases, the Latin of the *Codex Calixtinus* differs from the standard text of the Vulgate. Thus in most cases, the translations here will not agree, word for word, with standard English translations. Our references to chapters and verses in the notes will guide the reader to the appropriate portion of text in any version of a Catholic Bible.

In itself, the Latin text is quite readable. With the help of four medieval dictionaries, we have positively identified most of the words. There are relatively few peculiarities in the language of the manuscript. The most salient of those found are a penchant for using the -*um* ending on *i*-stem words where one would normally expect -*ium*, for example *peregrinantum* rather than *peregrinantium*; the dropping of the -*ve*- of the perfect stem, for example *ministrarunt* for *ministraverunt*; and the rather capricious use of h, both adding the letter to words that do not have it and dropping it from words that do, resulting in slowing, but not impeding, the reading of the text.

Very few words presented difficulties. Some words are explicitly indicated in the text as coming from the language of the people, such as *sporta* and *ysquirpa* for "purse," *pacca* for "pay/money," and *cafhit* and *arroa* as particular units of measure. Other words exhibit peculiar shades of meaning: the verb *utor* often has the frequentative meaning of "to be in usage" or "to be accustomed" rather than just "to use"; *mica* means "white of the bread" rather than "crumb." We have not been able to verify in oustide sources a few words, such as *tunnella* for "barrel." One word is particularly revealing: *acum* has only one meaning in Latin, "needle," and yet it is obviously used as a type of money in this text. It appears to be a retrogressive Latin formation based on the French coin called the *écu*, which actually came from the Latin *scutum*. Finally, there are simply scribal errors, such as *ingecerunt* for *infecerunt*. Unusual words, whether found only in specialized medieval dictionaries or not found at all, are explained where they first occur, and they are also listed in the index for convenience in locating them.

It has been a temptation, especially in the case of the miracle tales, to compare the text to previous versions, possible sources, and certainly to later iterations with all of their emendations. The same is true for the references to the saint's *translatio,* as one reads it in the "Veneranda dies" sermon, compared with the two versions in Book III, or compared with what is found in Voragine's *Legenda aurea.* We have in most cases resisted this temptation, making reference to such works only when they were needed to clarify a particular passage, for example, when a hole in the manuscript required us to verify our interpretation with another source. We have limited ourselves to translating these three sections with explanatory material to make the works intelligible. An *explication de texte,* comparisons of versions, tracing folkloric motifs and religious symbolism, tracking down source materials for the miracles — are all activities awaiting further work.

The author had a wide-ranging knowledge of people, places, moneys, and daily objects connected with St. James' pilgrimage. A few items were impossible to identify, while others were difficult to explain to complete satisfaction. For example, it is not really possible to translate into modern terms the relative values of medieval moneys, such as solidi, farthings, deniers, and oboli. Likewise, comparisons to other popular saints and mentions of certain specific geographical locations are very important to these segments of the *Liber Sancti Jacobi.* For these, we have attempted specific identification and have included germane information in footnotes at that saint's or place's first mention. In general, the footnotes fall into four basic categories:

1. Manuscript "errors" and peculiarities, which are relatively infrequent, and emendations to the Whitehill transcription, since this is the most likely tool to which one would turn to read the Latin text.
2. Identification of Latin words that are not found in standard dictionaries, which tend to give classical Latin meanings only. In general, the sources for such information on

medieval meanings are from DuCange, Maigne d'Arnis, and Blaise. For place names, the standard source has been Graesse.

3. Identifications of the author's sources for quotes and of people and places mentioned in the text.

4. Identifications and explanations of the references used in the text: specific saints, such as Sts. Nicholas, William, Giles; places like Tours, Bari, Rome, Saint-Michel[87]; activities such as reading in a refectory.

In producing this book we have made pilgrimages to many libraries, and we have traveled the pilgrimage route itself to Compostela. We have used the modern miracles of internet and computers to compose and revise the text. Any errors that have worked into our translations are our own. As we have worked, we have found that the scenes have come alive for us, and we have suffered with those dying or those saddened by seeing their son hanging from the gallows. We have seen the calming effect that James places upon the waves, and the saint's power to rescue his faithful from dangerous battles and dark dungeons. The tales remain as vivid to us as they must have been when read eight centuries ago.

NOTES

1. Kemp, *Miracles.*
2. Huidobro y Serna (3:784-97), among others, lists several miraculous appearances of Santiago to aid the Spaniards in the conquest of the Americas.
3. Book II Miracle 5. See illustration, p. lxxx, for a seventeenth-century mural in Tafers, Switzerland of the hanged innocent pilgrim. Nineteenth-century British poet Robert Southey composed 95 verses, "The Pilgrim to Compostela," offering a comic rendition of the same miracle.
4. See Matthew 4:21, 17:1; Mark 1:19, 3:17, 5:37, 10:41; Acts 1:13, 12:2.
5. See, for example, Hitt 18-20.
6. See Van Herwaarden for a convincing discussion of the evolution of the importance of St. James in religious histories, beginning with a minor reference in a text by Clement of

Alexandria (c. 200) concerning the saint's conversion of companions in the Holy Land through the fifth- and sixth-century texts that elaborate on the saint's preaching in the Holy Land and his death there. López Alsina also clearly summarizes these historical documents.

7.   Whether or not Isidore himself used the phrase is not yet established. It is possible that it may be an eighth-century interpolation to his *De ortu et obitu Patrum.*

8.   Found in the *Martyrologium* of Usuard of St-Germain-des-Prés (PL 124:291). Several scholars of the Santiago tradition have written profusely about the Latin phrase and the succeeding references to James' relationship to Spain and Galicia. See Díaz y Díaz, "Literatura"; Fletcher, especially p. 55.

9.   There are two versions of the saint's *translatio* in LSJ Book III, and they differ in details. Chapter 1 refers to a *"matrona lupinariae,"* from which succeeding authors may have interpreted "Queen Lupa." In Iacobus de Voragine's version the local ruler is identified as Queen Lupa. Most of the miracles that have become a part of the popularized version of the saint's life are recounted in one or the other of the two *translatio* versions in Book III.

10.   Many historians now regard the battle as a later, spurious invention.

11.   For these etymological constructs, and others, see García Alvarez, especially Appendix A, and Portela Pazos. Also interesting are the reports by Piel and Bouza Brey (see Piel). See illustration, p. 162, for one view of a burial site found underneath the cathedral.

12.   See López Alsina.

13.   See Aznar for graphics of hypothetical constructions, and López Alsina for a good discussion of the urban development of Compostela.

14.   This sheds light onto yet another important segment in the complicated religio-political history of St. James. The miracle in which the Saint's tomb was left unharmed, but in which the church's bells were transported to Córdoba on the backs of Christian slaves, led to the need for the *invention* of Clavijo and compelled the creation of an official *voto,* the payment of support and moneys by the political body of the realm to the religious institution.

15.   See Rahtz and Watts, who use the term "modern material culture."

16.   See illustration, p. lxxvi.

17.   The confraternity or brotherhood of *cambiadores* (moneychangers) was already organized by the twelfth century, and was known by at least two names: the "Cofradía de San

Ildefonso" or the "Cofradía del cirial." One of their responsibilities was to empty the alms boxes within the cathedral on a weekly basis (Remuñán 117). Remuñán briefly discusses the organizations of artists, jet-carvers, shell-sellers, silversmiths, and innkeepers.

Commercialism has not eased in recent years. A single visit to a single shop in Compostela during the 1993 Holy Year netted six different styles of pins with the shell motif, seven with the figure of the apostle, plus the requisite bottle openers, key chains, pill boxes, and other paraphernalia — all small enough to put into a backpack.

18. This theme and the following, the Emmaus pilgrim, are picked up and expanded upon in the "Veneranda dies" sermon.

19. Many studies exist about the cult of saints, the importance of relics in the Middle Ages, and pilgrimages to holy sites to venerate, touch, and steal holy remains. See Davidson and Dunn-Wood for general discussion and bibliography; also Wilson, whose bibliography of more than 1,300 items is an excellent source and example of the fascination that this topic has for scholars.

20. According to doctrine, no relics could be gathered from the bodies of Christ or Mary after their deaths, because their bodies were *physically* in heaven. However, a few corporeal relics remained, those gathered and saved prior to their deaths, such as the relic of Christ's circumcision and the hairs of Mary. These hairs of the Virgin were popular in twelfth-century France, brought back from the East by the Crusaders. The Virgin's house was transported from Nazareth to the area near Loreto, Italy in the thirteenth century.

21. See Constable for a good summary of some of the views in the eleventh and twelfth centuries, especially the incongruity between pilgrimage and religious life. This ninth-century Irish proverb "To go to Rome, much labor, little profit..." (Constable 129) and the Spanish proverb "Ir romera, volver ramera" ("To go a pilgrim, to return a whore") are examples of the popular wisdom about pilgrimage.

22. Abundant bibliography exists on all of these motives. See Davidson and Dunn-Wood 21-23 as a bibliographical source. Especially important are Aronstam, Berlière, Maes, Van Cauwenbergh. In the early 1980s Belgian judicial officials began offering sentences of pilgrimage instead of jail to juvenile defenders. See Bell.

23. Melczer 74 n. 29. Melczer quotes the Latin text on page 13. The text can be found in PL 123:183.

24. See Mitchell, Stalley, and Storrs for various interpretations and for analyses of sea-travel records.

25.   This feast would have conflicted with and been overshadowed by a major feast — that of the Annunciation.

26.   Canto 34 of the Pérez de Villagrá's seventeenth-century poem details the Acoma battle. See the excellent compendium of toponyms, artistic representations and literary allusions to Santiago in the Americas in *Santiago e America,* a very detailed catalog from an exposition of the same name that took place in Compostela in 1993. Relatively few representations in the Americas portray St. James as pilgrim (see illustration, p. v). A rough estimate indicates that St. James' imagery in the Americas was as Matamoros by about a 95-to-1 ratio. Plötz also gives a nice overview of Santiago in the Americas.

27.   Died in 1582; canonized in 1622.

28.   This is not an exhaustive list of seventeenth-century tomes defending St. James. George Bull also wrote a defending tome in England in 1670. See Castro and Kendrick for summaries of the debate.

29.   Two good photos of this miniature are now available. One in *Santiago, Camino de Europa* (303; information on 315-16), and another on the cover of Caucci von Saucken, *Santiago.*

30.   See Gai, especially 313.

31.   One tells of the castrated pilgrim, two others deal with the dying (in this case, Genovese) pilgrim carried by a knight on horseback to Compostela. We know of five dramatic representations published in the sixteenth century and another dated 1613.

The Italian plays' titles generally begin *Rappresentazione d'uno miracolo di...*. Caucci von Saucken claims that many examples of these short plays were published between 1510 and 1621. He sees three types of plays: one set based on the hanged innocent pilgrim (Miracle 5); another based on Miracle 4; and the third set related to Miracle 17, all with variations and additions. See catalog item 156 in *Santiago, Camino de Europa* (476) and Caucci von Saucken, "La tematica."

32.   This *Esempio* is attributed to Francesco Minozzi Cieco. It is based on Miracle 4 of the LSJ (see Ulrich).

33.   See illustration, p. lxxx, for one scene. Evidence of the popularity of St. James and of the continued custom of pilgrimage to Compostela can easily be seen for Switzerland in *Chemins de Saint-Jacques en terre fribourgeoise.* This modern tourist bureau sixty-page publication contains more than 125 illustrations of artistic, architectural, historic productions relating to the pilgrimage, most of which date between the fifteenth and nineteenth centuries (see Boschung). In addition to many statues of the saint are pilgrimage mementos, including a *Compostela* dated 1783 for Jean-Jacques Bertschi. The booklet has a nice color photo of the entire panel of eight scenes of the hanged innocent miracle,

including the chickens (11). Henggeler also traces the saint's cult in Switzerland and his examples date predominantly from the fifteenth, sixteenth, and seventeenth centuries.

34.   See Lima for a detailed description and history of representations of this miracle and its relationship to Barcelos.

35.   See Sebold for an interesting study on this issue.

36.   "...toward the end of the year 1878 exploration works were begun in the basilica, with the laudable goal of finding the holy tomb of St. James the Apostle" ["...con el laudable objeto de dar con el santo sepulcro del Apóstol Santiago, emprendiéronse las obras de exploración en la basílica, a fines del año 1878" ("Sepulcro" 18; translation ours).

37.   Archeological work has continued intermittently since then. A tour under the cathedral taken in 1994 shows old excavations: several tombs, early church foundations, and footings of the original town walls. See illustration, p. 162.

The excavations have continued into the late twentieth century. There are several studies and descritopns of the excavations, but some, especially those about the 1878 excavations, are difficult to obtain. See Bartolini and Guerra Campos for information.

38.   Carro Otero 32.

39.   For the text of and references to this Bull, see Leo XIII in the bibliography.

40.   What Melczer terms the nascent interest in "Romanesque form-culture" (ix).

41.   The study made by Díaz y Díaz et al. is indispensable for information about the LSJ and the CC. Also useful are Herbers' *Der Jacobuskult* and the collection of articles based on the 1985 conference on the *Codex Calixtinus* at the University of Pittsburgh (see Williams and Stones).

Our purpose here is to offer a brief summary of materials about the manuscript and allude to the problems that surround our knowledge of its composition. This will allow the reader who is faced with texts that apparently contain certain, real facts (e.g., names of authors appended to certain passages) to appreciate how these seeming truths are part of a labyrinth of conflicting information.

42.   One also sees *Iacobi,* and some scholars prefer to call the work the *Iacobus,* taking that title from a statement in the manuscript itself. See Hohler, "Note"; Díaz y Díaz et al.; and Stones.

In earlier days, the Latin "I" was usually transcribed as "J" when it was used as a semi-vowel/semi-consonant. While this transcription is rare today, certain Jacobian usages of "Jacobus" and "Jacobi" may have already become ossified in the "J" form when the change in convention occurred.

43. Diego Gelmírez, bishop of Compostela (1096/1100?-1121) and later archbishop until his death (1121-1139/1140?). His see was raised to archdiocesan status in 1121 and subsequently to metropolitan status by Pope Calixtus II. The metropolitan status was contested and even lost on a number of occasions. There are several pieces of correspondence between Diego and Pope Calixtus in PL 163. For a detailed biography, see the books by Fletcher and Biggs.

44. A thorny identity problem as there are at least three people with the name William to whom this letter might have been directed in the Holy Land. Given the compilation date of the mid-twelfth century, the most likely candidates are the first patriarch who served 1128-1130 or William of Messina, who served from 1130 to 1145 (and died in 1185).

45. Pope Calixtus II (1119-24). Before his election as pope, Guy (or Guido) was archbishop of Vienne. A noble by birth and a reformer by inclination, he is probably best known for attempting reconciliation with the Holy Roman emperor and for his role in effecting the Concordat of Worms. His works are contained in PL 163:1073-1414 and consist primarily of the text, or indication of the location of the text, of 282 letters (columns 1093-1338), and of six letters sent to him (cols. 1338-60). Among the many letters of Calixtus, there are several sent to Cluny and several to Diego, bishop and later archbishop of Compostela; the present letter is not among them. There is also other biographical and bibliographical information as well as a discussion of Calixtus relative to the LSJ at cols. 1365-68. Among the dubious works at the end of the PL section, there are four sermons and the miracles as recorded by Vincent of Beauvais. For detailed information on Calixtus see Robert's *Bullaire* as well as his *Histoire*. The *Bullaire* edited by Robert contains over 500 letters of Calixtus. For the Introductory Letter, see Robert, *Bullaire* n. 84.

46. See Díaz y Díaz et al. (81-86) for succinct and clear information about these theories.

47. See Díaz y Díaz et al. (224-26, 321-25). He estimates that Book IV was extracted between 1610 and 1619.

48. All five books of the CC were re-bound together in 1966.

49. Díaz y Díaz et al. is the best source of information about the different manuscripts, and has a thorough listing and discussion of the various complete and partial copies of the LSJ, including a sixteenth-century copy of the LSJ on paper by Juan de Azcona. Appendix I (327-34) contains a succinct and clear chart showing the disposition of the folios of the LSJ as they are found in twelve manuscript copies.

50. It is now housed in Barcelona, with the designation Ripoll 99.

51. Page 136.

52. One copy, now in the British Library (Add. 12213) is thought to have been copied in the cathedral. In the United States, a photocopy is available at Harvard, but it is lacking several folios from Book I, including the "Veneranda dies" sermon. The other known fourteenth-century copy is now housed in the Vatican (Arch. S. Pietro C. 128). A photocopy of it is also in the Harvard collection.

53. There are extensive treatments about the multiple versions of the Turpin Chronicle in Mandach, David, and Hämel.

54. Vincent, bishop of Beauvais, lived 1090-1164. His works are collections of passages from previous authors' writings. Vincent carefully attributes all his material. Here due recognition was given to Calixtus and to the LSJ as his source.

Iacobus de Voragine, thirteenth-century author of the *Legenda aurea*, dedicates several pages to St. James the Greater and recounts a detailed biography for the saint.

55. Díaz y Díaz et al. recounts the story and some of the problems of Whitehill's work (126-28), as does Hämel (8-9).

56. In our translation of the three LSJ portions into English, we have come across a considerable number of deviations from the text of the manuscript. See the last section of this introduction for more information.

57. According to their introduction, the Spanish translation is of the Whitehill transcription. Only for the difficult passages or obvious errors did they try to consult the CC and use it as a basis (xv). They apparently try to indicate this in their footnotes, but it is not always clear where they have relied on other sources as the basis for their translation. The translation is also the first time that scholars have attempted to identify citations and sources, but there are enough errors to make one double check such supplemental information.

58. Several stories have surfaced about the publication of the facsimile already: about the difficulty in finding the right kind of paper, about the number of copies made. Most recent information indicates that there were 995 copies, 150 for the Compostela Cathedral. Perhaps another 75 copies were also produced destined for special collections, such as one copy to the king and queen of Spain, another to the pope. Although we have not seen any official notice to the effect, we have learned from several sources that scholars generally will be limited to the use of the facsimiles now housed in the Compostela Cathedral Archives, thus minimizing wear and tear on the actual manuscript.

59. We are concerned here only with editions that have portions of the segments of the LSJ that we have translated in this work. For general information, see Díaz y Díaz et al. For Book I,

see *Mass*; for Book IV, the Turpin Chronicle, see Mandach and Hämel; for Book V, the Pilgrim's Guide, see *Pilgrim's Guide.*

60.   Partial transcriptions can also been found in AASS July (6: 44-45) and Vincent of Beauvais' *Speculum historiale* 36.30 (col. 1065). Robert's *Bullaire* also contains a partial edition of the text of the Introductory Letter (257-58).

61.   See Werf and also the *Mass of St. James,* edited by Paul Helmer.

62.   The miracles are located on folios 13r-24r of MS 10252. The BN manuscript is not a complete copy, beginning at some point toward the end of an opening letter to the miracles. This letter is not the same letter that opens Book II of the CC. It is, instead, the letter that begins the entire LSJ manuscript and is the portion relating all of the miracles that happened to the author of the work. Ms. Connolly, because she did not have easy access to the LSJ transcription, was unaware of what the fourteenth-century author had done.

63.   King's summary is relegated to an appendix of her study (3:504-15).

64.   See Menaca. Her only stated reason for making the unannotated translation is that the miracle versions in Vincent of Beauvais and the *Legenda aurea* don't give all of the twenty-two miracles from the LSJ/CC.

There is an edition of the LSJ's miracles in AASS July 6:47-59, preceded by introductory commentary; a quite abbreviated version in Voragine (Graesse 425-29); and some are found in Vincent of Beauvais' *Speculum historiale* 36.31-41 (cols. 1065-68).

65.   The *Ars dictaminis* refers to a particular movement in letter writing that had its roots in the theories and examples of Alberic of Monte Cassino (1030-1106). His initial work was developed by Hugh of Bologna, Adalbertus Samaritanus, Henry Francigena, and others. While this art began as a helpful set of rules for letter writing, over time it developed into a set of complicated formulae to be slavishly attended to in correspondence. For an extensive treatment of this topic, see Murphy, especially chapter 5.

66.   The author's words are *"levi dictatu,"* and this comment is placed immediately after and in distinction to his appeal to the authority of Jerome, Ambrose, Augustine, and others.

67.   While it is virtually certain that this letter is counterfeit, it might prove interesting to analyze it further to see how various sections hold up in comparison to the letters of previous and succeeding popes. In doing this an analysis of how well the letter adheres to the *cursus,* which had been introduced into formal letters, along with the dictaminal style might also prove revealing. The *cursus* was a rhythmic pattern for syllables in the

final elements of clauses. There were three general rhythms: planus (' - - ' -), tardus (' - - ' - -), and velox (' - - - - ' -), where the (') represents accented syllables and (-) represents unaccented syllables. In addition, these patterns could be combined, and the caesura also played a role in the rhythm, making for a rather complicated system. For more information see Murphy 250-53.

68. "Familiares consolationes quae a praesulibus habebantur in aedibus sacris in quibus et interrogabant populum et interrogabantur a populo; ita enim *homilian* a *logo,* seu oratione, distingunt." We have transliterated the Greek for the words in italics.

69. For a succinct and helpful treatment of the art of preaching in the Middle Ages, see Murphy, especially chapter 6 on the *ars praedicandi.* The idea of "meta-rhetorical" is found in Murphy.

70. Page 102.

71. See illustration, p. lxxvii.

72. These miracles, collected in four books include sixty that Gregory collected from other sources. The other 127 took place between c. 571, the first year Gregory was bishop, and 592, and were narrated chronologically. See Van Dam for a study and translation. St. Martin proves himself to be a thaumaturgic saint in these narrations.

73. Ward 90.

74. See Kemp's translation of the miracles collected at Reading Abbey at the shrine of the relic of the hand of St. James ("Miracles"). There may be another collection at Pistoia also (see Gai).

75. Kemp, "Miracles" 4.

76. In the present translation we have omitted discussion of the later versions of these miracles. Although some were very popular in the Middle Ages and Renaissance, it would require another study to deal with this issue.

77. One of these miracles occurred in Navarre and another in Gascony, which was the scene of another, happier, miracle in Book II. Two other miracles happened in Besançon, where the author of Book II Miracle 4 apparently lived. The last miracle occurred in Montpellier.

These miracles were included in the AASS and in Vincent de Beauvais without indication of their location in the sources of the respective works.

78. Book V chapter 11. One miracle deals with fire, two with bread.

79. "One of the Becket registrars confessed that in some cases 'inasmuch as these have not produced witnesses, and the truth has not been perfectly sifted by us, we let their stories pass out of our ears as fast as we let them come in'" (Finucane 102, quoting *Materials for the History of Thomas Becket*).

80. Southern and Schmitt 208-9.

81. There is a copy of a letter sent by him, which forms chapter 90 of the *Probationes* appendix to the *De illustri genere Sancti Bernardi* (PL 185:1465). It begins "Humbertus, by the grace of God archbishop of Besançon,…set down at Besançon in the year 1155, in the second indiction."

82. Moralejo et al., 377n., dates this miracle between 1100 and 1110.

83. See, for example, the miracles performed by St. Martin of Tours in the collection written down by Gregory of Tours. One example, from among many, narrates that the sufferer endured his illness for four months, and after praying to the saint for four days, he was cured (*Life of Martin* 3.7; Van Dam 262).

84. See Storrs for a detailed, well-documented study about pilgrims from the British Isles.

85. Herbers believes that the writer wanted to attract the growing class of lesser nobility ("Miracles" 20).

86. In a conversation with cathedral personnel in November 1994 we learned that there is presently no known collection of chains or armor or handcuffs that thankful pilgrims might have left at the altar. The popular theory is that the army of Napoleon carried off everything. One North American pilgrim in Holy Year 1993 left his walking staff in the corner of the tomb room as a sign of thanks. The staff had disappeared by the next day and cathedral personnel could only say that such things were not kept.

87. We have regularized saints' names to their English forms (e.g. St. Giles), while using the specific country's spelling of names that refer to saints (e.g. Saint-Gilles).

Monster-devil eating humans, church doorway, Artaiz, Spain.

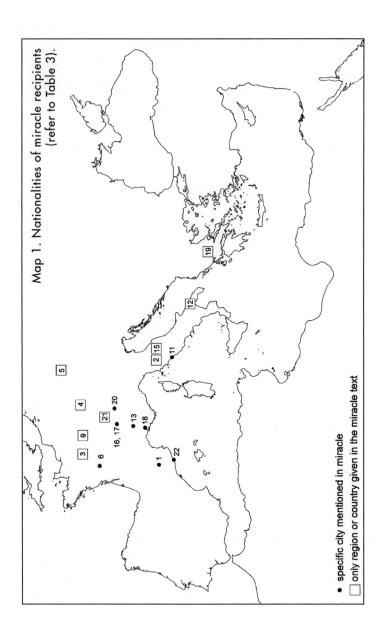

Map 1. Nationalities of miracle recipients (refer to Table 3).

● specific city mentioned in miracle

□ only region or country given in the miracle text

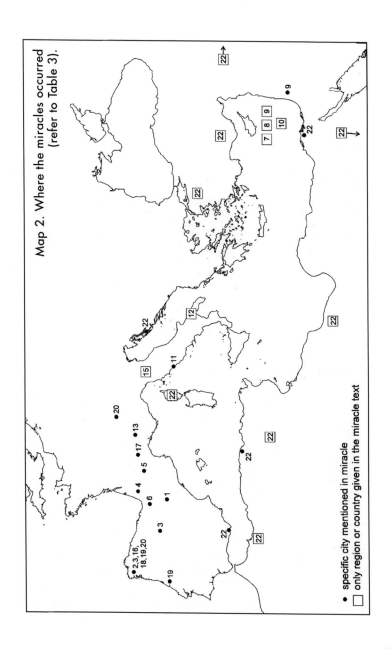

Map 2. Where the miracles occurred (refer to Table 3).

specific city mentioned in miracle

only region or country given in the miracle text

National groups visiting Lourdes, France, 1993.

Memento vendors, Lourdes, France, 1993.

Crutches and other mementos left at the Shrine of
Friar Pedro, Antigua, Guatemala.

Christ as pilgrim on the road to Emmaus, cloister sculpture, Monastery of Silos, Spain.

TRANSLATIONS FROM THE LIBER SANCTI JACOBI

St. James the Apostle as Santiago Matamoros. Twelfth-century portal, Cathedral of Santiago de Compostela.

St. James and the hanged youth, seventeenth century, Chapel of St. James, Tafers, Switzerland.

INTRODUCTORY LETTER OF POPE CALIXTUS

FROM THE MATERIAL COMES THE TITLE.
THIS BOOK IS CALLED[1] JAMES.
GLORY BE TO THE WRITER AS
WELL AS TO THE READER.

Here begins a letter of Blessed[2] Pope Calixtus.[3]

Calixtus, bishop and servant of the servants of God, to the most holy convent of the basilica of Cluny,[4] seat of his apostolic election,[5] to the very famous champions William, patriarch of Jerusalem,[6] and Diego, archbishop of Compostela,[7] and to all orthodox people, salutation and apostolic benediction in Christ.

Since in all the regions of the world[8] more excellent champions than you cannot be found either in dignity or honor, I[9] have sent this book about Blessed James unto your fatherly care, as preeminent authorities. To the extent that if you can find something in it to correct, you may carefully emend it out of love for the apostle.

In any case, I have suffered incalculable grief because of this book. For when I was a young scholar,[10] having loved the apostle from childhood on, and wandering through barbarian lands and provinces during the space of fourteen years, whatever I would find written about him, I would write down diligently,[11] even on a few vile and ragged sheets of parchment,[12] so that I might be able to compile them into a single volume, so that the devotees of Saint James might appropriately find all together the things necessary for reading on his feast days.[13] O wondrous fortune! I fell among thieves, and although all my goods were taken,[14] I still retained the book. I was pressed into workhouses and, although all my possessions were lost,[15] I still[16] retained the book. I fell repeatedly into the deep water of the seas[17] and was near death, yet on my escaping, the book, completely unharmed, came[18] with me. The house in which I was staying burned, and although all my belongings were consumed by flames,[19] the book escaped with me unburned.[20]

Because [f.1v] of these things, I began to ponder whether this book, which I was striving to complete with my own hands, would be acceptable to God. While I was pondering these things with great diligence, I was carried away one night in ecstasy: in a majestic and shining room,[21] I saw a young man, adorned in inestimable beauty, surrounded by a splendid light, dressed marvelously in majestic attire, crowned with a regal crown.[22] He entered the east door of this very room with several consorts, one of whom spoke in this way, "Behold the Son of the King."

And immediately the One sitting on the finest chair said to me, sitting at his feet, "Offer me the gloves[23] that you have in your hand." I willingly offered them to Him.[24]

When He had taken them from my hands and entered into the inner room, a certain member of His consort, as if he were His seneschal,[25] told me, "He is the Son of the Highest King." Then he added, "Just as He took the gloves from your hands, so also will He receive the apostolic book peacefully and willingly,[26] after you have completed it."

Another time, while I was thinking about the "Veneranda dies" sermon on the apostle's *translatio,*[27] and while I was holding the quarto with its writing in my hands, He appeared in an ecstasy, along with the Blessed James, saying, "Do not postpone writing these teachings, which are to be observed by all and which are pleasing to us. Write what you have begun, correcting the evils of the depraved innkeepers dwelling on the route of my apostle."[28]

Therefore, let no one think that I have written anything from my own mind in this book,[29] but rather from authoritative books, namely from both Testaments, and from the books of the holy doctors[30] Jerome,[31] Ambrose,[32] Augustine,[33] Gregory,[34] Bede,[35] Maximus,[36] and Leo,[37] and of other Catholic writers. Thus one should understand that it is obvious that I have excerpted[38] the things that are contained in the first book. The other things that are written down in an historical manner[39] in the following books, I either saw with my own eyes or found written or learned

from truthful reporting and wrote them down.[40] Therefore no one should belittle this book when one finds something written in a simple manner.[41]

For we have written our[42] sermons in a simple manner
in this book, so that these things might be accessible to
the unlearned as well as the learned. Many belittle what
they do not understand: the French belittle the Germans,
and the Romans belittle the Greeks, because they do not
understand the others' language. If I listen daily to a Greek
or German preaching and I do not understand, what use
is it for me?[43] For this reason the saints for ages have offered explanations on the four Gospels and on the proph-
ets, because they were not understood. If you should give
me unsliced bread at the table, I would happily accept it;
if you should give me sliced bread, I would take it up
more happily.[44] [f.2r] For the crust is of little worth until
the center of the bread[45] appears. A pure drink shows more
clearly what is contained[46] in it. A pure and open eye sees
more clearly than one covered or closed. A bright candle
that sheds light on all standing around is more useful than
one that offers light to some and denies it to others. In
this way, then, this work has been thrown open to all, so
that it might be profitable to those skilled in the art of
grammar,[47] as well as to those not understanding lofty
things.

But what part of this should we indicate for being read
in church? Whatever is written in the first two books up
to the sign that is similar to this[48]:
which denotes Jesus Christ, may be sung or read
in churches, according to ordinance, at matins
and masses, for it is authentic and declared with
great authority. Whatever is written in the books
following that sign may be read in refectories[49]
at meals,[50] for it is of great authority; but what
is contained in the first two books is quite sufficient for
reading at matins.[51] And if all the sermons and miracles
of Blessed James that are contained in this book[52] cannot
be read in church on his feast days because of their vol-

ume, they may at least be read afterwards throughout each week[53] in the refectory, and certainly at least on the day on which his feast occurred.

One should not hesitate to sing the responses and the canticles of the masses that we have compiled from the Gospels and written in this book.[54] There are some, however,[55] who say that the responses of the *Passion of Saint James* are apocryphal, such as "James the apostle of Christ walking through the synagogues,"[56] because not all the writings that are contained in the passions of the apostles are accepted on great authority in all areas. Some sing them; others do not sing them. Nonetheless, in the city in which they were[57] published, they are not sung in full. Other responses, once edited by a certain church leader of León,[58] are sung in a disorganized manner.[59] Some sing the response[60] appropriate for a single martyr or a single confessor for Saint James, "Saint James, apostle of Christ, hear your servants calling on you." Similarly, others sing the response of Saint John the Baptist, "Oh, special honor." Others inappropriately sing the response of Saint Nicholas[61] almost as if there were no responses proper to Saint James. A certain canon of Saint James, a cantor of this very basilica[62] by the name of Johannes Rudriz,[63] when it was his turn to work one week and he was filling his purse from the offerings of the altar, commemorated himself, which he did by singing a particular response of Saint Nicholas, "He knew how to offer fitting gifts to his servants." [f.2v] For this reason he used to sing this very response in the choir of Saint James on his feast day, but removing the name of the confessor [Saint Nicholas] and saying rather, "Blessed *James*, already having attained his triumph, knows how to offer fitting gifts to his servants." Therefore, as ecclesiastical usage is guaranteed when one does not sing the response of the apostles for a confessor, so also is this usage guaranteed when one does not sing the response of a single confessor or of a single martyr or of Saint John the Baptist or of whatever saint for an apostle. Some sing the introit "Let us all rejoice in the Lord" at the mass of Saint James, which the Church is accustomed to sing properly only for holy virgins, for example, for Agatha, the Virgin Mary, and Mary Magdalene.[64] Others sing the introit "Let all rejoice in the Lord"; others, "Excessively however for me"[65]; others, as I might say,[66] sing their own strophes according to the fancies of their own minds. For this reason we order that no one any longer presume to sing any responses about James according to his own fancy, unless they be authentic Gospel responses, which this book contains, such as "The Savior having gone forth a little,"[67] or the response "Behold I send you."[68] Similarly, no one should any longer sing any introit at his mass except "Jesus called James, son of Zebedee,"[69] with the canticles that follow it, or "Excessively however for me."[70] For whatever is sung for Saint James must be of great authority.

It is of utmost importance for his servants that it be observed that the clergy celebrate the matins of James with devotion, that there be a third reading with responses, that the hours not be omitted, and that the pilgrim people hear these things. We order this to be done by the clergy of Saint James in his basilica on all days except on the day of the Lord's birth and Holy Thursday and Good Friday[71] and the Saturday following and Easter and Pentecost.[72] Similarly, at the first mass on all days except the days mentioned above, the proper[73] of Saint James should be sung for the pilgrims.[74] Then after the first prayer of the mass, this prayer for the pilgrims should consistently follow: "May the ears of your mercy be opened, we beg, O Lord, to the prayers of the beseeching pilgrims of Saint James, so that for those entreating..."[75]; one may look up the rest in the first book.[76]

Therefore, anyone who presumes to speak against or spurn or render invalid the things that this book contains with inane arguments or with empty disputation be anathema with Arius and Sabellius.[77] Be well, all, in the Lord. Published at the Lateran on the Ides of January.[78]

THE "VENERANDA DIES" SERMON

THE SERMON[79] OF BLESSED POPE CALIXTUS FOR THE
SOLEMN FEAST OF THE CHOOSING AND TRANSLATION OF
SAINT JAMES THE APOSTLE, WHICH IS CELEBRATED ON THE
THIRD CALENDS OF JANUARY.[80]

A day to be honored, brethren, is the solemn feast of Saint
James the Apostle. It has dawned today on the world: let
us exult and rejoice in it. This is a day more celebrated
than many others, more renowned than many, more il-
lustrious than many, more worthy than the others, more
holy than the others — the day on which the great Apostle
James, patron of Galicia,[81] joyously adorned the heavens
with his spiritual arrival, looked toward the Spanish and
the Galicians for his bodily arrival, and enriched people
everywhere with his extensive miracles. He who has faithfully enhanced the lands has perennially enriched the
heavens on this day.[82] For this the court of angels delights
in heaven, and Mother Church rejoices here on earth.

A double solemn feast[83] is celebrated by the faithful
today: namely, the choosing of this very Saint James, or
how he was chosen by the Lord into the apostolic order
along with John, Peter, and Andrew near the shores of
Galilee; and his translation, [f.74v] that is to say, how his
most precious body was moved from[84] Jerusalem to the
city of Compostela.[85] These are, in fact, solemn, sacrosanct,
apostolic feasts to be honored, celebrated, and cultivated
by all peoples. These are the feasts on which heavenly
rewards are divinely given to the just and eternal salvation is promised to sinners.

The books of the Evangelists expound on how the venerable Apostle James was chosen. Of these Evangelists,
Matthew, among the others, says[86]: "Jesus, going forth
from there," namely near the Sea of Galilee, "saw two
brothers, James, son of Zebedee, and John, his brother,
repairing their nets in a boat with their father Zebedee;
and He called them. Having left their nets and their

father, they immediately followed Him."[87] Blessed Paul also mentions this choosing, saying:

> What stupid things of the world God has chosen, so that He may confound the wise; and God has chosen the weak things of the world so that He may confound the strong; and God has chosen the ignoble and contemptible things of the world and things which do not exist, so that He may destroy those which exist, lest any flesh be glorified in His sight.[88]

The splendid poet Sedulius, reflecting on the venerable choosing of Blessed James, also sang the praise of Christ with a faithful pen, saying:

> Furthermore, from fishermen He made men suitable
> For fishing human souls, which, rashly following the slippery
> Delights of the world like the azure waves of the Black Sea,
> Pass over the blindness and uncertainty of the deep.
> These He orders to be His disciples, and such as these He brings to
> Eternal life, whom a proud blood nourishes, not with a puffed-up
> Glory of speaking nor with a haughty nobility,
> But, being quiet with renown, shining with a humble
> Mind, that the brightness in heaven might make neighbors of the people.
> For God, the Powerful One, has chosen the foolish and lowly things
> Of the world, breaking the strong and destroying the wise.[89]

How the translation of this apostle occurred is declared from the mouths of many faithful people who say that after he was killed by Herod,[90] his whole body was carried across the sea with an angel of the Lord accompanying it in a boat from Jerusalem to Galicia, with his disciples as sailors,[91] and with various miracles experienced along the way. Galicia and Spain are regenerated by the grace of baptism, through his translation[92] and the preaching of the apostolic disciples, and the kingdom of heaven is enriched. It is right for this venerable translation to be spoken about, as[93] it was once written by a wise man: "A man

pleasing to God was made chosen and has been translated from living among sinners."[94] On this day honoring
the apostle, [f.75r] the delighted Church of the faithful is
accustomed to sing this verse three times[95]: "James has
pleased God and has been transported to paradise, that
he may give repentance to the people."[96]

But we should consider what there might be for us to
understand in his translation and in his being chosen. In
his being chosen, then, the setting aside of sins[97] and perseverance in good works are insinuated, and in his translation eternal rest is demonstrated.

Thus, in fact, the blessed apostle, on the day on which
he was chosen, not only set aside his boat, his father and
mother, and his own career, but also the faulty accumula-
tion of the old culture, because of divine love, and from
then on he persevered in good works. In this same way,
we must eradicate the whole collection of our faults and
persevere in good works. For this reason, in fact, the Lord
ordered that people set aside all possessions, because He
does not wish that those serving Him be preoccupied in
earthly things, but that they be focused only on the heavenly.[98] As the Apostle [Paul] says: "No one serving under
God's banner may implicate himself in worldly affairs, so
that he may be pleasing only to Him to Whom he has
proven himself."[99]

By the boat that Blessed James abandoned on the waves
of the sea when the Lord called, it is right to understand
the synagogue of the Jews, which was figuratively toss-
ing about on dangerous laws, just like a ship on the sea's
waves, and which[100] humankind abandoned, having heard
the evangelic word, just as James abandoned the little boat,
and then subjected itself to the Catholic Church. By the
nets it is right to understand the ancient law of circumcision and sacrifice by which the Jewish people were caught
and held captive like a multitude of fish in a net. Having
accepted the Church through the grace of the new baptism, they thus cast off the ancient law, just as James did
the nets. By Zebedee, the father of Blessed James, one can

interpret the devil, for as James abandoned his father like a fugitive, so the devil himself, leaving God, flees to hell[101]; the human race renounced the devil by taking on the precepts of Christ, just as James renounced his father, and ascended to the seat from which the devil had fallen.[102]

By the *translatio* of Blessed James, therefore, eternal rest is signified, since just as the apostle's venerable body is delivered from the place of his martyrdom to the place of his tomb and his soul is carried to eternal rest by the angels, so also are we to be raised from the harshness of our good[103] life to the eternal rest of paradise through perseverance in good works. The Lord makes it manifest that no one can move on to eternal rest except through the labor of this present harsh life, when He says: "Come to me, all who labor and are burdened...and you will find rest for your souls."[104] In the Book of Wisdom [f.75v] it is written: "God will return the price of the labors of his holy ones."[105] The Apostle also says: "It is necessary for us to enter into the kingdom of God through many tribulations."[106]

Thus the blessed apostle was chosen this day so that he may tear the world from the devils' jaws by his preaching.[107] He was translated so that he may strengthen with his patronage, bestow with his benefits, look down with his miracles and prepare seats in the heavenly realm[108] for those loving him with all their hearts, not only for the Galicians but also for those visiting his holy tomb.

At the time when ice is hard like crystal and snow is sowed over the world like flour and everyone is crushed under the pressure of the cold, the translation of Blessed James is celebrated. At the time when the fruit of the earth is collected and the storehouses are replenished with healthful grains, his passion is honored.[109] This is the meaning: it is a fitting time to honor the passion of Blessed James when the fruit of the earth is collected, just as the present age is a fitting time for doing good works. The time when his choosing is honored and his translation is paid reverence and every kind of mortal creature is crushed by the pressure of the cold indicates a future age in which no one will be allowed to work.[110] Whoever, therefore, should have performed no good works for their souls in this age, will beg in the future in an exceptional way.[111]

However, there should be no silence about apocryphal things. On the contrary, these things, which many irrational people, torpidly sliding toward heresy, are accustomed to say about James and his translation, should be announced so as to be corrected. What is worse,[112] people dare to write about these things with a false pen. Some, for example, think he is a son of the Lord's mother, because they have heard James called "brother of the Lord," both in the Gospel and in the Epistle to the Galatians; but this is not so.[113] Others say that he came from[114] Jerusalem to Galicia over the waves of the sea without a boat, sitting on a large stone[115] with the Lord instructing him, and that a certain part of this large stone has remained behind in Joppa.[116] Others say that this very stone arrived on the boat together with his lifeless body. However, I declare both stories to be false.[117] Truly when I once saw the great stone, I knew it was a stone created in Galicia.[118] There are, however, two reasons for which the great stone of Blessed James is to be worthily venerated: first because, as it is reported, the apostle's body at the time of its translation was placed upon it at the port of Iria Flavia; [f.76r] and second — and the greater reason — because the Eucharist was purposefully celebrated[119] on it.[120]

Some also say that the apostle of Galicia made a curse on the soil, so that it would not bring forth wine any more, because a certain matron by the name of Compostela, as they say, drunk on wine, weighted down by sleep, did not disclose to him a certain lord visiting the basilica, while he was dozing off in the lap of this very matron. In fact, as they say, the apostle had told her to tell him when the lord would arrive.[121]

Others, however, say that the Lord, appearing to her, stripped the bark[122] from a stick between his hands, and

He promised her that she would be cleansed just as that stick was stripped of its bark, and thus would people praying and seeking His threshold be cleansed from their sins. This is concluded to be an error in this way: if the sinner is cleansed like the stick, he is thus not well purified, since the stick cannot be purified on the inside but only on the outside, and since it would be necessary that the sinner be cleansed on the inside and the outside, namely in body and soul.

Some say that angels have spoken openly in James' basilica and that they once sang before everyone. Others dream that angels carried his body through the air from Jerusalem to Galicia without human help. Similarly, some babble that this same body was carried from Jerusalem to Galicia in a certain glass boat over the waves of the sea with men as sailors. We[123] judge dreams and tales of all of these types and others similar to them to be apocryphal. We reject them completely and we repudiate them entirely, even declaring anathema, so that no one may any longer dare to write anything about the saint except the authentic things that this codex called *Iacobus*[124] contains. This codex, in fact, relates those things that are necessary for reading or singing on the feast days of this very Saint James, and they are extracted from authentic codices, as are indicated in it. However, we grant permission to write down, for the edification of the faithful, those miracles that he is yet to have performed, as long as they have been testified to by two or three witnesses.[125] With us rejecting the aforementioned errors and asserting universally the truthful testimony about him and contemplating his most excellent deeds, there should be rejoicing on earth over him about whom the angels give thanks in the celestial domain.

The hearts of others echo with human praise, but let me have some time to commemorate just things. For the work of the victor is one of piety; for reason admonishes one to use one's talent to compose books. [f.76v] There

13

are two reasons for this: one reason is that it is fitting to relate great things about the great, for whoever conceals good things is the author of crime. The other reason is that one who has read his deeds is inflamed by love and desires better things.

"Praise the Lord," says the psalmist, "in His holy places."[126] If we are ordered to praise the Lord in his holy places, then how much more so through Blessed James, who looked upon the Son of God in human form transfigured by the will of the Father on Mount Tabor,[127] Whom Moses on Mount Sinai[128] and Abraham at the root of Mamre,[129] and Jacob on Mount Bethel,[130] and the other saints were never able to see fully. We must praise and commemorate him[131] with worthy veneration. He is, in fact, that "just one" who is kept alive in the eternal memory of angels and men, as the psalmist testifies, saying: "In eternal memory will the just one exist."[132] Eternal memory of the heavenly kingdom is said to be blessedness, in which the just one, working well, is praised by the angels without limit. By right, therefore, Blessed James is worthily kept alive in the memory of angels and men, since he has passed to the delight of the heavens, while he has settled in body alone in this earthly pilgrimage, and lives in thought and desire in the eternal land. Freed from the bonds of the flesh, he returned to the highest King double the talents given to him by the Lord.[133] To him the Lord will say most fittingly on the day of retribution: "Well done, good and faithful servant, since you have been faithful over a few things, I shall set you over many. Enter into the delight of your Lord."[134]

Thus it is right to understand about the praise of Blessed James what was said by a certain wise man: "The just one will germinate like the lily," and will flower for eternity before the Lord.[135] The lily's leaves die in winter, and it brings forth the finest white flowers with an aromatic shoot in the summer. By the lily, which dies in winter and sends forth white flowers with an aromatic shoot in the summer, Blessed James is represented, who in the winter is, as it were, crushed by the affliction of his passion in this world, and who in the summer richness, that is, in the pleasantness of paradise, flourishes eternally in the presence of God through the merits of his good works. The aromatic shoot brings forth the lily: Blessed James was, as Paul says, the good perfume of Christ in every place[136] — preaching, praying, working well, together with giving all kinds of good example to all. The lily's leaves die, but there is life in its roots, just as[137] [f.77r] Blessed James mortified his exterior person with many labors while he lived, growing and giving life to the virtues within him. Dioscorides, the teacher [138] of medicine, describes the powers of the lily, saying:

> The lily is known to physicians, and its powers can soften the hardness of sinews. Its leaves, when cooked and applied, are beneficial to burned areas, and they cure the damage of serpents. Its sap, when cooked and mixed with honey in a new vessel, mends old wounds. Its root, when roasted and rubbed with oil, is also suitable for burns from fire, and it even softens the womb and brings on a menstrual purging. Its seed, in fact, when given as a drink, provokes menstruation, brings on labor, and works for the bite of a serpent. The flowers of the lily are useful for any hardening of the womb.[139]

The powers of the lily are said to soften the hardness of bodily sinews, just as Blessed James, filled with the strength of the Holy Spirit, through the power of absolution, is allowed to release the sins from souls and the hard bonds of vices.[140] The leaves of the lily when cooked are beneficial to burned areas, just as the good works and eloquence of Blessed James, tested by the fire of the Holy Spirit, are beneficial to human kind, burned up until now with flames of corruption. The leaves of the lily cure the damage of serpents to people's bodies, just as Blessed James has cured the suggestions of the devil in the souls of sinners with his preaching and absolution. In fact, just as a serpent punctures the flesh with the venom of its bite, the devil injures one's mind with his depraved suggestion.[141] The sap of the lily mends old wounds, just as James mends the errors of the Old Law and the putrid wounds of sins through his mellifluous preaching and divine absolution. The root of the lily, when roasted and rubbed with oil, is fitting for burns from fire and brings on menstrual purging, just as the apostolic faith, mixed with the oil of piety and infused in his mind by the fire of the Holy Spirit, by means of divine preaching, gave a remedy for the flames of corruption to the burned human race, and through the washing of baptism brought it a purging of its sins. That the seed of the lily, when given as a drink, provokes menstruation and treats the bite of a serpent implies the same thing[142] as the root and even the flower. That it brings on labor shows that the virginal chastity of Blessed Mary Ever Virgin is to be believed by the faithful. A certain sage sang [f.77v] most splendidly about this in praise of this Virgin, saying: "The lily of chastity has flowered, as the Son of God has appeared."[143] Blessed James was, therefore, a lily and an honor for the world, since by living well, preaching, working divine miracles, and patiently tolerating various kinds of suffering, he sprouted on the earth and has flowered for all eternity before the Lord, crowned with a divine commission.

Again it is right to understand concerning him what the divine poet once sang: "The just shall flower like the palm, and shall be multiplied like the cedar of Lebanon."[144] The palm is a very good tree: it has a tough root in the earth, it expands greatly at the top, and it bears at its peak a round object like cheese, which is also sweet to eat and from which palms and spikes arise. Fittingly, those on pilgrimage returning from Jerusalem carry these in their hands, showing themselves to be victors over pagan vices and demons.[145] The palm tree with its tough root in the earth portrays Blessed James, who, while he was on earth, led a harsh life beset by many labors. Its rising from the earth and expanding greatly at the top portrays him, who has risen from "virtue to virtue,"[146] that is to say, from faith to certain hope, from hope to two-fold charity, from charity to perseverance in good works, from perseverance to the heights of paradise.[147] That it bears sweet food at its peak from which the palms arise implies the hope of future heavenly goods. For this hope, Blessed James, with the enemies of the faith overcome, delivered his venerable body to the various pains of martyrdom, and with the palm of victory he has not only passed through the heights of the air but has also penetrated the heights of the heavens, trusting in the swords[148] and spikes of heavenly virtues. Just as an army returning from the field of battle with its enemies conquered used to carry palms in hand through the city, praising the Creator who gave it victory, the assembly of saints, either through the shedding of blood or through the demonstration of good works, having overcome vices and the enemies of the faith, is accustomed to go toward the heavenly court with the palm of victory. With Herod conquered, Blessed James has arisen for these people, for he has penetrated heaven with the palm of victory.[149] The Hebrew children came to Jerusalem with palms to meet the Lord, just as the saints have passed from vices to heavenly virtues by living well and have met the Lord in the Heavenly Jerusalem after this present life.

The great James therefore now happily delights in perpetual glory. [f.78r] With the virtue of this great person, not only Spain but also Galicia now shine like the moon with the sun.[150] There is rejoicing in heaven, whose churches flourish in the world. He not only preached to Judea and Samaria but also graced Spain and Galicia and built that once impious people into the Church by the virtue of Christ. In fact, the Apostle's holy power, tranferred from the area of Jerusalem into the country of Galicia, shines anew with divine miracles. For at his basilica divine miracles are very often performed by the Lord through him.[151] The sick come and are cured, the blind are given sight, [152] the lame are lifted up,[153] the mute speak, the demoniacs are freed,[154] consolation is given to the mourning,[155] and, what is greater, the prayers of the faithful are heard,[156] and there the heavy burdens of transgressions are set aside,[157] and the bonds of sins are loosed.[158] O, with what holiness and grace Blessed James gleams in heaven, who by the power of God works such miracles on earth! Just as the height of heaven or the depth of the seas cannot be investigated or measured by anyone, the magnitude of his miracles and his powers cannot be counted by anyone. There, in fact, the choirs of angels frequently come down, accept the vows of the humble, and carry them back to the ears of the highest King in the heavens.

At this place the barbarous and civilized peoples of all the regions of the world arrive:[159] namely, French, Normans, Scots, Irish, Welsh, Germans, Iberians, Gascons,[160] Balearics,[161] impious Navarrese,[162] Basques, Goths, Provençals, *Garasqui*,[163] Lotharingians, *Gauti*,[164] English, Bretons,[165] Cornwallians, Flandrians, Frisians, Allobroges,[166] Italians, Apulians, Poitevins, Aquitainians, Greeks, Armenians, Dacians,[167] Norwegians,[168] Russians, Prussians,[169] Nubians,[170] Parthians, Romans, Galatians, Ephesians, Medes, Tuscans, Calabrians, Saxons, Sicilians, Asians, Pontics, Bithynians, Indians, Cretans, Jerusalemites, Antiochians, Galileans, Sardians,[171] Cyprians, Hungarians, Bulgarians, Slovenians,[172] Africans, Persians, Alexandrians, Egyptians, Syrians, Arabs, Colossians, Mauritanians,[173] Ethiopians, Philippians, Cappadocians, Corinthians, Elamites, Mesopotamians, Libyans, Cyrenes, Pamphylians, Cilicians, Jews, and the other countless peoples.

All languages, tribes, and nations go to him in troops and phalanxes, fulfilling their vows to God with thanksgiving and bearing tributes of praise. Whoever sees these choruses of pilgrims[174] keeping vigil around the venerable altar of Blessed James marvels with extreme delight: Germans remain in [f.78v] one area, French in another, Italians in a throng in another, holding burning candles in their hands, from which the whole church is lit up like the sun or the brightest of days. Each one sagaciously carries out his vigils by himself with his countrymen. Some sing with lutes, some with lyres, some with drums, some with flutes, some with pipes, some with trumpets, some with harps, some with violas, some with British or Gallic wheels, some with psalteries.[175] Some keep vigil by singing to the various kinds of music; some lament their sins; some read psalms; and some give alms to the blind. Various languages are heard there: various barbarian calls, the speeches and cantilenas of the Germans, English, Greeks, and the other tribes and various peoples of all the regions of the world. "There is no speech and no parlance with which their voices do not resound."[176] Assiduous[177] vigils of this type are held there: some come, some leave, and various people surrender various gifts. Thus someone approaches sad and leaves happy. A solemn feast is always being celebrated there without cease; a feast is performed zealously; a great gathering is cultivated day and night; praise and jubilation, joy and exultation are sung together. All days and nights are honored in an almost continuous solemn feast for the honor of the Lord and the apostle. The doors of this basilica are never closed day or night,[178] and it is never dark at night within it, as it gleams like noon from the splendid light of the tapers and candles.

To this place go the poor, the happy, the ferocious, the knights, the infantrymen, the satraps, the blind, the crippled, the aristocrats, the nobles, the heroes, the princes, the church leaders,[179] and the abbots. Some go with bare feet, some without their own goods, some bound in irons for the sake of penitence. Some bear the emblem of the cross in their hands like the Greeks, some give their things[180] to the poor, some bring iron or lead in their hands for work on the apostle's basilica, some, doing penance and bewailing their transgressions, bear in their arms iron bars and manacles from the workhouses of the impious from which they were liberated by the apostle.[181] This is a chosen race, a holy people, a people of God, the favored of peoples, the fruit of apostolic acquisition, the fruit of a new grace, the fruit of the penitents of the nourishing Church, the fruit offered by the apostle to God in His heavenly seat.[182] This fruit of the Lord's apostle may remain in the heavenly kingdom, as He promised when He said to him: "And your fruit may remain,"[183] as if He were saying to the apostles: [f.79r] "The fruit of your acquisition may remain in heaven."[184] It is believed, in fact, that whoever goes to the venerable altar of Blessed James in Galicia for the sake of pure and worthy prayer, if truly penitent, will obtain absolution from the apostle and pardon from the Lord for his transgressions. For the Lord did not take away from him after death that gift and that power that He had given him before His passion.[185] It was, in fact, granted to him by the Lord that whoever's sins he would forgive, would have their sins forgiven. The Lord, in fact, says to him and to the other apostles: "Whose sins you shall have forgiven, they shall be forgiven them."[186] It is therefore agreed that whoever's transgressions the renowned apostle shall forgive, will have them forgiven by the Lord.

O, how blessed are those who have such an intercessor and such a pardoner! Why, therefore, devotee of Blessed James,[187] do you delay in going to his place, where not only all the tribes and languages, but also the angelic hosts convene and where the sins of men are forgiven? For there is no one who can tell how many benefits the blessed apostle has bestowed on those seeking him with a sincere heart. Many poor people, in fact, have gone there who, with God's grace, afterwards were made happy, many weak were made healthy, many dissenters agreeable, many perverse pious, many lustful chaste, many worldly later monks, many misers generous, many usurers later bestowing their goods, many haughty later gentle, many deceitful later truthful, many taking the belongings of others later giving their own clothes to the poor, many perjurers later law-abiders, many declaring falsehood later[188] asserting the truth, many sterile later bearing children, and many dishonest later just. Behold that the city of Compostela, through the support[189] of Blessed James, has been made sacred and a salvation for the faithful and a help for those coming to it. O, with what reverence is that sacred place to be cultivated and feared in which many thousands of miracles are reported to have been performed, and in which the most sacred limbs of the apostle, which touched God when present in the flesh, are stored!

The great James is quick with divine miracles in Galicia, and he is also quick in other places if the faith of the petitioners requires.[190] Indeed, he also performs great and unutterable signs throughout the whole earth not only privately but publicly. For he gives back former health to the sick,[191] liberation to the bound,[192] fecundity[193] [f.79v] to those barren of offspring,[194] delivery to those bearing children,[195] a port of safety to those at risk on the sea,[196] guaranteed return to the homeland for pilgrims,[197] and food to the needy.[198] He often accords life to those placed in agony[199] and solace to all the poor[200]; he breaks bonds quickly[201]; he opens prisons rapidly[202]; he represses an overabundance of rain[203]; he brings serenity to the air[204]; he repels the winds of the storms[205]; he suppresses the conflagrations of evil fires with the prayers of men[206]; he restrains the thieves, robbers, and mischievous and treacherous people so that they may not harm the peoples of the faithful however much they may desire to do so[207]; he placates wrath and malice, and he grants tranquillity.[208] To everyone seeking he shows the desired help with the support of God, even to the pagan if he should faithfully call upon him.[209]

By right, therefore, this James, who has been accustomed to give great rewards to everyone everywhere, is called "Great." From this the question arises: Why does he perform miracles in places where he does not lie bodily, as he does in Galicia?[210] However, if a sense of discretion looks into it, it is quite quickly apparent. For he is always and everywhere at hand, without[211] delay, for helping those at risk and those in tribulation calling to him whether on sea or on land. Concerning the presence of the holy martyrs one may read thus:

Where the holy martyrs lie bodily, there is no doubt that they can show many signs and that they do so; and they manifest true miracles to those petitioning with a pure mind. However, since it is possible for weak minds to doubt whether they be present for listening, in places where a weak mind might doubt their presence it is necessary that these holy martyrs show even greater signs where it is agreed they are not present in body. However, those whose minds are fixed on God have so much greater merit in faith, in as much as they know the martyrs are there bodily and that they are still not out of earshot. From this Truth[212] also speaks about Itself, so as to increase the faith in the disciples: "If, in fact, I shall not have gone away, the Paraclete shall not come to you."[213] Since, in fact, it is agreed that the Paraclete, the Holy Spirit, proceeds eternally from the Father and the Son, why does the Son say that He will go away, so that He might come who never retreats from the Son? However, since the disciples viewing the Lord were thirsting to see Him physically with their eyes, it is rightly said to them: Unless I shall have gone away, the Paraclete will not come; as if He were saying: "If I do not take away my body, I shall not show what the love [f.80r] of the Spirit is. And if you shall not have stopped viewing me bodily, you will never learn to love spiritually."[214]

Therefore, Blessed James, who gladdens the eastern people through divine miracles, lies in corporeal presence among the western people.[215]

Who,[216] like the high lighthouse sends out[217] light toward the Indians,
Whom Spaniard and Moor, Persian and Briton love.
The Orient has him, the Occident has him, and Africa and the North have him,
Whom the world celebrates and whom every rain honors,[218]
And who also passes over waves of the ocean's boundary,
And so virtue proceeds, on the foot of which no one is certain.[219]

Therefore, Blessed James is to be honored by everyone everywhere, as he assists without delay everyone everywhere calling to him.

However, since we have dealt above with the various peoples going to him and with the remuneration given to them by the Lord, it remains for us now to treat the pilgrim route of these people.[220] The pilgrim route is the best way, but the most narrow. The road is, in fact, narrow that leads man to life, and the road is wide and spacious that leads to death. The pilgrim route is for the righteous: lack of vices, mortification of the body, restitution[221] of virtues, remission of sins, penitence of the penitent, journey of the just, love of the saints, faith in the resurrection and remuneration of the blessed, distancing of the infernal, propitiation of the heavens. It reduces fat foods, it checks gluttony of the stomach, it tames lust, it suppresses carnal desires, which militate against the soul. It purifies the spirit, it motivates man toward contemplation, it humbles the lofty, it beatifies the humble. It loves poverty; it hates the inventory[222] that avarice keeps but that generosity loves when one dispenses it to the needy. It rewards those abstaining and working well, it does not free those sinning and avaricious on it [the road].

Not without reasons do those heading for the thresholds[223] of the saints accept the staff and the blessed purse[224] in the church. When, in fact, we send them for the sake of penance to the seat of the saints, we give them the blessed purse with the ecclesiastical ceremony, saying:

> In the name of Our Lord Jesus Christ, accept the purse, this symbol of your pilgrimage, that you may be worthy[225] to arrive chastened and cleansed at the threshold of Saint James to whom you wish to go; and with your journey completed, may you return safe to us with delight, with Him as a guarantee, Who lives and reigns as God for ever and ever.[226] Amen.

Also when we give the staff to someone we say the following:

> Accept this staff as a support for the journey and for the labor [f.80v] on the route of your pilgrimage, so that you may be able to overcome all the throngs of the enemy and arrive secure at the threshold of Saint

James; and having completed your passage, may you return to us with delight, with the agreement of Him Who lives and reigns as God. World without end.[227]

The purse, which the Italians call *scarsella*,[228] and the Provençals call *sporta*,[229] and the French call *ysquirpa*,[230] signifies the generosity of alms and the mortification of the flesh. A purse is a narrow little bag, made from the hide of a dead animal, with its mouth always open and not bound with ties. That the purse is a narrow sack signifies that the pilgrim, trusting in the Lord, must carry along with him a small and moderate provision. That it is made from the skin of a dead animal signifies that the pilgrim himself must mortify his flesh with its vice and concupiscence, through hunger and thirst, through many fasts, through cold and nakedness, and through many insults and hardships. That it is not bound with ties but that the mouth is always open signifies that one must expend one's own things on the needy, and consequently one must be prepared for receiving and prepared for giving.

The staff, which the pilgrim prayerfully[231] accepts almost as a third foot for his support, implies faith in the Holy Trinity in which one must persevere. The staff is the defense for man against wolf and dog. The habit of the dog is to bark against man, and the wolf to devour sheep. The dog and wolf signify that waylayer of the human race, the devil. The demon barks against man when he incites men's minds toward sinning by the bark of his suggestions. He bites like the wolf when he drags men's limbs toward sinning and through the habit of guilt swallows the soul in his greedy jaws. For that reason we must admonish the pilgrim when we give him the staff that he remove his guilt through confession and frequently protect his breast and limbs with the banner of the Holy Trinity against diabolical illusions and apparitions.[232]

Similarly, it is not without reason that the pilgrims prayerfully coming back from Jerusalem carry palms, and that those returning from the threshold of Saint James bear small shells.[233] Notwithstanding, the palm signifies triumph and the small shell signifies a good work. For just as the victors returning from the battle once used to carry palms in their hands, showing that they have been triumphant, so also do the pilgrims returning from Jerusalem carry palms, showing that they have mortified [f.81r] all vices. Therefore drunks or fornicators or misers or covetors or the litigious or usurers or spendthrifts or adulterors or other corrupt people who are still warring with vices should not carry the palm, but rather those who have completely overcome their vices and who have adhered to virtues.

There are some fish in the sea of Blessed James, which the people call *veras*,[234] having two shields, one on either side, between which the fish is covered as if between two shells in the likeness of an oyster. These shells, of course, are shaped like the fingers of a hand, and the Provençals call them *nidulas*[235] and the French call them *crusillas,* and the pilgrims returning from the threshold of Blessed James sew them on their capes, and they wear them back to their own country with great exultation in honor of the apostle and in his memory and as a sign of such a great journey. Therefore, the two shields with which the fish is protected, one on either side, represent the two laws of charity with which the bearer must truly protect his life: that is, to love God[236] above all things and to love one's neighbor as oneself.[237] A person who loves God is one who keeps His commandments. A person who loves one's neighbor as one loves oneself is one who does not do to anyone else what he does not want done to himself and who does to others what he would justly want done for himself. The shields, however, which are modified in the shape of fingers, signify good works in which the bearer of this sign must persevere; and good works are beautifully signified by fingers, since[238] we work through them when we do something. Therefore, just as the pilgrim bears the shell[239] as long as he is in the course of this present life, he must also carry the yoke of the Lord, that is, submit to His commandments. And it is truly right and just that one who has sought such a great apostle and such a great man in such a remote region in toil and hardship persevere in good works, to the extent that he may receive with Saint James the crown in the heavenly land. If he has been a robber or thief, let him become a dispenser of alms; if he has been a spendthrift, let him become temperate; if he has been a miser, let him become generous; if he has been a fornicator or adulterer, let him become chaste; if he has been a drunkard, let him become sober. Similarly, may he restrain himself from now on from every guilt in which he was previously grasped.

O, pilgrim of Saint James, do not lie with that mouth with which you have[240] kissed his altar! Do not go toward depraved works with the feet with which you have taken so many steps for him! Do not work evil with the hands with which you have touched his venerable altar! If you have commended your whole body to him for [f.81v] safe-keeping, then preserve all your limbs for him. If as a faithful sheep you have[241] entrusted yourself to him, do not be a stray in the thorns of vices. Do not also give to the wolf what you have given to him. Do not serve the devil, when by right you must serve God and His apostle. If you wish to have a powerful patron, you have for yourself in Blessed James a protector, helper, and devotee. Many, in fact, give witness that they have experienced his help in many trials.

We must explain how the pilgrim road had its origins among the ancient fathers, and how it should be walked.[242] In fact, it takes its beginning from Adam, and it stems from Abraham and Jacob and the sons of Israel down to Christ, and through Christ and the apostles it is increased up to today. Adam is considered the first pilgrim, since because of his transgression of the commandment of God he was sent from paradise into the exile of this world, and he is saved by the blood of Christ and by His grace. Similarly, the pilgrim is sent by his priest on a pilgrimage into a type of exile from his own region because of his transgressions, and if he has confessed properly and has completed his life after taking onto himself proper penitence, he is saved through the grace of Christ.[243] Abraham the patriarch was a pilgrim, since he went forth from his country to another as he was told by the Lord: "Go out from your land and your people...and come into the land which I will show to you and I will make you grow into a great people."[244] And thus did it happen. He went out from his own land, and his holy offspring were increased in a foreign one. In a similar fashion, if the pilgrim leaves his own land, meaning his earthly business and his habitual depravities, and his own people, meaning those with knowledge of his guilt, and goes out and perseveres in good works, the Lord will without doubt cause him to grow into a great angelic people in blessed glory. Jacob the patriarch also arose as a pilgrim, since, having gone out from his country, he traveled to Egypt and stayed.[245] Just as Jacob stayed in Egypt, which is interpreted as mourning and darkness, so also must the pilgrim, having gone out from his own country and requesting the support of the saints, remain in grief of mind and eye and in the darkness of penance because of the memory of his sins. Thus the sons of Israel were pilgrims, while they traveled from Egypt into the Promised Land through their diverse experiences of hardships and vicious wars. Just as they entered the Promised Land through many hardships, the pilgrims also travel through the uncountable frauds of innkeepers, and the climbing of mountains, and the descent into valleys, and fears about plunderers, and worries about various hardships, while requesting the support of the saints, so that they might enter the heavenly [f.82r] country promised to the faithful.[246]

Our Lord Jesus Christ Himself, returning from Jerusalem, after He had risen from the dead, appeared first as a pilgrim, as the disciples meeting Him said: "You alone are a pilgrim in Jerusalem."[247] It is later written about these disciples that they recognized the Lord in the breaking of the bread. On the road the Lord is not recognized, but when someone is fed, he is recognized. Thus when the happy pilgrim feeds[248] the poor, he is recognized by the

27

Lord. For the Lord recognizes whoever feeds the poor, and He allows Himself to be recognized by him and makes him blessed, as the psalmist says: "Blessed is he who understands about the needy and the poor; on the evil day the Lord will liberate him."[249] He will be liberated "on the evil day," since on the day of judgment he will be liberated from the diabolical grasp, and he will be saved.

The apostles, therefore, whom the Lord sent out without money or footwear, were also pilgrims. Because of this it is in no way allowed for pilgrims to bring money, unless they expend this money on the needy. If He sent the apostles without money, what will become of those who now travel with gold and silver, eating and drinking to fulfillment and imparting nothing to the poor? Certainly they are not the true pilgrims, but the thieves and bandits of God. Those who take along their goods and give away nothing to the needy pilgrims are truly alienated from the apostolic company, and they appear to travel on another route. They may expect what the Lord Himself might say to His pilgrims on route: "Do not possess gold or silver or money in your girdles or a purse on the road or two tunics or footwear or a rod."[250] In the apostles' having been sent in this way it is given to be understood that it would not be permissible for a pilgrim to bring along his own things, unless he should strive to pay them out to the needy. He should either not bring along goods, or, if he brings them, he should strive to dispense them to the poor. If he should do otherwise, he may expect what the Lord Himself says[251] to a certain man questioning Him: "If you wish to be perfect, go and sell all that you have and give it to the poor and…follow me."[252] Therefore, it is not those who sell their goods and spend them on their pilgrimage who follow the Lord, but those who sell their goods and are generous to the needy. Just as the multitude of believers once had one heart and one soul and no one called something his own, but all held all in common, so must all things be held in common for all pilgrims: [f.82v] one heart and one soul. For it is very disgraceful and a great dishonor and a most grave sin when one of the pilgrims is thirsty and another is drunk. Every good brought forth for the common good shines more brightly. I also fear for the pilgrim who carries expensive goods on the journey beyond what is necessary for him, and does not spend them on the needy, but brings them back to his own home, lest he be damned[253] with Ananias and Sapphira who, in holding back on the price of a sold field, having received a curse from Saint Peter the apostle, suddenly fell dead.[254] If the Lord rode to Jerusalem not on a horse or a mule but on an ass, what will become of those who go there with large and plump horses and mules with saddle bags[255] of pleasant objects?[256] If Blessed Peter went to Rome without footwear or money and, being crucified, finally went to the Lord, why do many pilgrims go to him [St. Peter], riding with much money and a second set of vestments,[257] eating delicious[258] foods, drinking very strong wine, and sharing nothing with their needy brethren?[259] If Blessed James went through the world as a pilgrim without money and footwear and went finally beheaded to paradise, why do pilgrims go to him oversupplied with diverse riches and paying out nothing to the needy? If Peter and James walked through the world without money, and praying without interruption, what will become of those who go to their thresholds with money acquired from robbery or other harm or from usury or with corrupt extravagance or with false tales or with idle words or with contemptuous speech or with drunkenness or with chatter? If Blessed Giles[260] or Saint William[261] or the extraordinary Leonard,[262] confessors of Christ, had contempt for worldly happiness and, secluded from their relatives and friends and without any goods, sought remote, deserted places and led a celibate[263] life, sustained in it by raw herbs and water, intent upon frequent vigils and fasting, what will become of those who go to them with a great inventory, paying out nothing to the needy and eating and drinking to fulfillment? Furthermore, the one group appears to have taken a different route than the other has taken. For the

29

former group, paying out their goods to the poor, are made happy; the latter, not distributing theirs at all, are certainly in need of heavenly gifts. The former group will have abundance for ever; the latter will beg for eternity. What will become of those who keep and beg for their goods[264] — not, without doubt, their own but someone else's — and then die shamefully on the route itself with that money? [f.83r] The pilgrim who dies with money on the route of the saints is certainly dislodged from the kingdom of true pilgrims. Certainly one who gives sustenance to all those asking and who is made poor, if his goods have been relinquished for the sake of heavenly love, uses his inventory well on the route of the saints. The one who does not dispose of alms or resources received on the route from whatever pilgrim who has died, in the way the dead person ordered, but who keeps and spends them on himself is damned.

What does it profit someone, most beloved brethren, for a man to dash to[265] the pilgrimage route, unless one has gone legitimately?[266] Someone goes legitimately to Saint James' threshold if he forgives those who have injured him before he begins his journey; if he makes appeasement, if it is right for this to occur, of all prior acquisitions of which he is accused either by others or by his own conscience; and if he receives lawful leave from his priests or his subjects or his wife or any others to whom he is bound; if he gives back, if possible, what he has held unjustly; if he transforms dissent against his power into tranquillity; if he accepts penance from all; if he provides well for his house; if he arranges for his own things to be given, according to the advice of his associates and priests, as alms in the event of his death; if after he has begun the journey, he gives the necessities of body and soul, as far as is possible, to poor pilgrims as if to his brothers, as we have already said; if he speaks not idle words but saintly stories; if he flees[267] drunkenness, strife, and lust; if he hears the divine office, if not every day then at least on Sundays and feast[268] days; if he prays without interruption; if he

tolerates all adversities patiently; and if, after he has returned to his own region, he abstains from the illicit things
and perseveres in good works up until the end, so that he
may sing with the psalmist: "Your justifications were songs
to me, O Lord, in the place of my pilgrimage."[269] Whoever misses masses and matins because of the pilgrim
route, loses the better of two goods. If one is truly poor
and patiently endures both adversity and prosperity, he
may seek the necessary things for himself from those having them, and he may pray for the well-being of his bene-
factors and of all people.

It is to be carefully watched by all pilgrims on route,
that there be no split or strife among them. For, in fact, in
the venerable basilica of Blessed Giles, the most pious
confessor, I once saw on a certain night some people keeping vigil and arguing over his holy chair.[270] The French
were sitting on the seat, which is near the arch, and the
Gascons wishing to sit on it were fighting them. [f.83v]
Meanwhile, the fighting and striking with sticks and
stones and fists became so great among them that one of
them, being pierced through with a serious wound and
having fallen on the ground, died. Another one, struck on
the head, went down the road to Périgeux toward the new
castle and died there.[271] Because of situations like this, strife
is to be completely avoided by pilgrims — and drunkenness as well. In fact these are two vices that all the saints
and all the scriptures abhor. Concerning strife it was written by a certain sage: "The greatest strife sometimes grows
from the smallest words"[272]; and again: "Do not refer back
to the harsh words of past strife."[273] Concerning this
Blessed Paul says: "While among you there may be inten-
sity and contention, for are you not carnal...are you not
men?"[274] This is what the psalmist says: "Grow angry and
do not sin."[275] The wise man must patiently mitigate his
wrath, lest he sin. Again Blessed Paul says: "Let the sun
not set on your rage. Do not give a place to the devil."[276]
For whoever sins through wrath, without doubt gives a
place to the devil. Contention once increased so much that

it extended its foothold not only to the sons of Israel but also to the Lord's disciples. For dissension arose between Paul and Barnabas, such that they parted from each other. Contention also occurred among the disciples of Jesus, as to which of them appeared to be greater.[277] The Lord presented to them, with modest reason, the form of humility that they might follow: "Whoever might want to be first among you should be the servant of all."[278] And lest the mind of the one presiding be carried off to elation through love of his power, it is justly said by a sage: "They will ordain you as leader; do not be extolled but be among them as one of them."[279] Nevertheless one must be on guard lest one's teaching or judgment[280] as a superior be rigid or lest tolerance be abandoned.

Therefore, just as contention is tempered by humility, the vice of drunkenness should also be held in check by a modest drink of watered wine, as it is best said by a certain sage: "Drunkenness is a firebrand; drinking watered wine is peace."[281] The drunk provokes his comrade to battle, loves strife, hates peace, sows discord, breaks the heads of his comrades, even strikes his father and mother, offends God, loses his sense, serves lust, loses his force, and says shameful words. What more can there be? The poor drunk takes on horns. For this reason the wise once used to drink watered wine. For watered wine taken moderately renders a person healthy, happy, [f.84r] productive, sober, strong,[282] and loquacious. Wine imbibed immoderately, as we have said, renders a man drunk, oblivious, raging, idiotic, silly, insane, lustful, and given over to sleep. Concerning drunkenness it has been written: "Where wine rules, one keeps no secret."[283] Noah first planted the vine and, drunk from the wine, discovered his shame.[284] Of this Isaiah says: "Woe to those who are for drinking wine, and to men strong for mixing drunkenness."[285] And again he says:

> Woe to those who arise in the morning for seeking drunkenness and drinking until evening, that you

might burn with wine. The lute and the lyre and the drum and the flutes and wines are at your feasts, and you do not look on the work of the Lord, nor do you consider the works of His hands. Because of these things my people have been led captive, since they had no knowledge, says the Lord.[286]

Concerning the vice of drunkenness Joel the prophet says: "Arise, you drunk, and weep and cry out, all[287] you who drink wine in sweetness, since your soul has gone out of your mouth."[288] And since wine provokes venery in the body of the drinker, the wise one says properly: "Wine and women cause wise men to become apostates."[289] Of this Blessed Paul says: "Do not become drunk on wine, in which is found dissipation."[290] For dissipation does not come out of the wine, but lust is born from the one drinking wine. Therefore it is not the fault of the wine,[291] but the fault of the one drinking. Wine is a good and splendid thing, created, of course, by God; but since it is responsible for venery in drunks guzzling it without discretion, it should not be permitted for anyone to become drunk from it. That it should not be allowed for anyone to become drunk, Proverbs justly says: "May you not admire wine when it yellows in glass, and when its color will have brightened. For it begins blandly, but in its aged state it will bite like a snake, and it will spread its poisons like a basilisk."[292] The snake is accustomed to bite the sleeping man, and the basilisk not only to bite but also to diffuse deadly poisons in the wound. The snake that has bitten[293] the sleeping man, symbolically portrays the devil who excites and pierces with the fire of lust the one whom it finds sluggish from the vice of drunkenness. The basilisk, which diffuses poisons in the flesh of man, similarly represents the very enemy of the human race, who provides many vices to the hearts of the drunk, such as contention, envy, wrath, strife, dissension, jealously, hatred, fraud, venery, and an apostate mind — the vices born [f.84v] of drunkenness that Blessed Paul exhorts the followers of the Lord to avoid.[294] That these two vices, namely venery and drunkenness, should be prohibited for all Christians, Basil proclaims in pentameter verses in the *Book of the Twelve Wise Men*[295]:

> You should be held by love of neither venery nor wine,
>   For wine and venery injure in a single manner,
> As Venus[296] weakens one's forces, so also an abundance
>   of Bacchus;[297]
>   Both tempt one's steps and weaken one's feet.
> Blind love forces many to confess secrets,
>   Insane drunkenness uncovers mystery.
> Untamed Cupid[298] often stirs[299] up deadly war,
>   Bacchus himself often calls hands to arms,
> Insatiable Venus wasted Troy[300] with horrendous war,
>   And you, Iacchus,[301] lose the Lapitae,[302] in grave combat.
> In short, since both madden the minds of men,
>   And modesty and probity and fear are all absent,
> Restrain Venus with foot irons, and Lyaeus[303] with chains,
>   Lest either injure you with her or his feats.
> Let wines soothe thirst, let nourishing Venus serve those
>   To be created in birth; to have crossed this border is
>   injurious.

But what shall I say about evil innkeepers, who deceive pilgrims with so many frauds?[304] Just as Judas received the punishment for his guilt from the Lord Jesus Christ in His passion, and just as the thief received his reward for his confession, the evil innkeepers will also receive punishments in hell for their iniquities on the route of Saint James, and the truthful pilgrims are to receive the rewards of their good works and their hardships in heaven. Therefore the evil innkeepers on the route of Saint James are damned for violating pilgrims with countless frauds. Some, in fact, go out to meet them at the gateways of the villages, kissing them as if they were[305] their relatives coming from faraway regions. What more do they do? Leading them into their homes, they promise them all sorts of good things and do evil things. Whom shall I say they are like, except the traitor Judas who betrayed the Lord by kissing Him? For they show them ahead of time the best wine for sampling, and sell them inferior wine if they can. Some sell cider[306] for wine, and spoiled[307] wine for good. Some sell fish or meat cooked two[308] or three days before, from which the pilgrims grow sick. Some show them a large measuring device, but sell, if they can, with a small one. One has furtive measures for wine and oats, very large on the outside but narrow, scant, and not fully hollowed out on the inside, which the people call *marsicias*.[309] Isaiah makes reference to such a truly [f.85r] depraved innkeeper when he complains by saying: "They are the worst vessels for the fraudulent. For he produced thoughts for wasting the mild in the speech of falsehood."[310] Another, when he draws wine from the barrel,[311] fraudulently adds water in the vessel, if he can. Others promise them the best beds and give them bad ones. Some, when other guests come along, throw the first guests outside, having already got their pay.[312] The evil innkeeper does not give a good bed to the pilgrims, his guests, unless they have given him [the business from] a meal or a farthing.[313] If the pilgrim's farthing should be worth two farthings in the village where he seeks to eat, the evil innkeeper does not accept it except on a one-to-one par. If it is worth only one, he does not take it except for an obolus.[314] The evil innkeeper offers his guests the best wine so that he may inebriate them, and while they sleep steals their sack or bag[315] or something else. The evil innkeeper kills them with his mortal potions, so that he may be able to have their goods. To what[316] punishment will they go, who have in one and the same barrel a middle area, and place two wines in them, each standing apart from the other, of which they first offer the better for tasting and then later draw the inferior wine for the meal from the second area?[317] Some sell them a measure of barley or oats, which the Spanish call *cafhit*[318] or *arroa*,[319] for at least ten or twelve farthings when it could justly be had in the market of that village for perhaps six farthings. If, in fact, it is sold there for twelve, they take twenty farthings or two solidi[320] from them. Similarly, if a sesterce of wine in that village may be had for twelve farthings in that country's custom of sale, then they take from them either twenty farthings or two solidi for it.

And what shall I say about the wicked servant who, at the order of her mistress, pours out the water of the house when it is late, so that thirsty pilgrims might buy the innkeeper's wine when they find no water for drinking at night? And what about the one who steals oats or barley at night from the mangers,[321] with her innkeeper's consent? She is anathema. The innkeepers' servants on the route of Saint James who, for the sake of ravishing and of stealing money, are accustomed to go to the bed of any pilgrim at night at the instigation of the devil, are damned generally. The whores, who for this reason are accustomed to come between the Minean Bridge and Palas del Rey[322] in the wooded areas to meet the pilgrims, are not only to be excommunicated [f.85v] but also are to be held in shame by all and to have their noses cut off.[323] Usually a single one appears to a solitary traveler. I cannot write, brethren, in how many ways the demon can open his depraved nets and the cave of perdition to the pilgrims of Saint James.[324]

What shall I say about wicked innkeepers who out of cupidity keep for themselves the inventory of the pilgrim who has died in their house, and from which alms should be given to the clerics and the poor? Certainly they are damned. Wicked innkeepers of the city of Saint James give the first meal to guests without any charge, only to sell them tapers of wax. O violable charity! O false piety! O generosity filled with every fraud! If the pilgrims are caught in a deal to buy twelve candles, the harsh innkeeper gives them as a meal a first course of meat or fish, which can be had for a fair price of eight farthings in the market of the city, and he later sells them twelve tapers for six solidi, which he gets in the city market for four farthings, and at a price of six solidi he sells each one wrongfully by six farthings. Similarly, he sells them with this plate trick[325] four farthings worth of wax for six farthings, and likewise as many[326] solidi worth for six solidi. What more can there be? He gives them eight farthings worth of meat or fish to feast on, but he sells this fraudulently at a price of two solidi. O what an abominable market and detestable profit! Some even boil ram or goat fat or cooked and boiled broad beans[327] into the wax from which they make candles. Some tell the false or abominable tales, which we previously mentioned, to pilgrims asking about the true and venerable acts of Blessed James.[328] One accomplice, a herald from the city of Saint James, sent his representative all the way to the Portomarín to meet the pilgrims, and he spoke to them in this way: "My brothers and friends, I am a citizen of the city of Saint James, and I have not come here[329] for the sake of hospitality, but because I am watching the weak mule of a certain lord of mine in this village. Go therefore to his house and announce to him, I beg you, that his mule will soon be cured, and take up lodging there, since he will do all sorts of good things for you who are announcing these things, out of love for me." And going there they find all sorts of bad things. Another goes to meet them at Barbadello[330] or Triacastela,[331] and when he has found[332] and greeted[333] them and deceitfully talked to them about other matters, he then says to them: "My brothers who seek Saint James, I am a fortunate citizen of his city, [f.86r] and I have not come here for the sake of hospitality, but so that I might speak with a certain brother of mine, who is staying in this village, and if you wish to have good lodging in Saint James' city, stay as a guest in my house, and tell my wife and my family that they should provide well for you out of love for me, and I will give you a token, which you can show to them." And so with such words he will give a knife as a token to one group, a belt to another, a key to another, a bootlace to another, a ring to another, and a glove to another, sending them to his house. And when the pilgrims have traveled to his house and are lodged in it, and when they have been given the first course at the table of that inn, the lady sells them a taper worth four farthings for eight or ten. Thus are the pilgrims of Saint James deceived by the innkeepers.

And if any pilgrim should have a silver mark[334] to sell[335] which might be worth thirty solidi, his wicked innkeeper will lead him to a moneychanger, an accomplice of his, and the crafty innkeeper will give him underhanded advice that he should give the moneychanger that mark for twenty solidi, so long as that wicked innkeeper receives his unjust commission[336] from the seller, or twelve *passut*[337] more or less. They deceitfully call farthings *passut*, and *reva* is interpreted as "unjust commission." Similarly, if the pilgrim should have anything that might be of great value to sell, the innkeeper might suggest to him that he give it to him for a low price, so that the wicked innkeeper might get from the same seller or from someone else a large commission. And if he should have coins to be exchanged, the same innkeeper suggests to him for the sake of the commission that he wishes to have that he give twenty of his coins for twelve of that land in which he is passing through, while sixteen of them perhaps might be more their value. And thus the evil innkeepers deceive the pilgrims and are damned.

The guards who watch the altars of the basilicas along the route to Saint James,[338] namely those of Giles, Leonard, Martin of Tours,[339] Saint Mary of Le Puy,[340] and Peter the apostle at Rome[341] and the evil innkeepers are accomplices in fraud, when they lead the pilgrims to all the altars for the sake of cupidity and indicate to them that they should make offerings on them, so that the innkeepers might get from them a commission, and the guard fraudulently gets his portion. But what shall I say of the guard? After he has stolen the offerings from the top of the altar, he wishes to get his portion from what is left by the masters of that altar and of the church.

Pilgrims should be wary of the thieves, [f.86v] called by the people *cinnatores*,[342] who beset them on the road. Some, in fact, give them counterfeit money in an exchange; others, when they are making an exchange, steal the coins. Others sell either a bootlace or girdle or belt or glove or wax or anything, pretending that they are offering them at a low price. And while one of them shows these things to the pilgrim, and the pilgrim is giving him the coins, this thief places the good coins of this pilgrim in his sack and gives him counterfeit. One now and then throws copper ore on the road, when the pilgrims are passing by, and then, as if finding it, bends over, picking it up from the ground, with them watching. And then since these pilgrims are more or less finders of the ounce along with him, they want to have their share just like him. But this wicked thief, presenting himself as poor to them, sells them his share dearly either for four or five solidi or for the finest gold, when it may only be worth an *écu*.[343] Who is similar in this, except Datan and Abiron whom the earth has swallowed up?[344] Pilgrims should also be very wary of some evil innkeepers who fraudulently place a ring or silver cup[345] in the purses or bags of their guests by night while they are sleeping and follow them for about a mile beyond the village, when they are leaving the inn, then on this bald pretense, plunder them.[346] The Italians are above all damned,[347] as they allow thieves to kill pilgrims in secret places. If perchance the thieves should be captured, the Italians take the money from them and let the thieves go unharmed. Therefore they are damned with the thieves, since acting and consenting to it are punished with like pain in hell.

And what shall I say of false pardoners?[348] Hypocrites,[349] whether clerics or lay, filled with demons, dressed in religious habit, appearing as mild as sheep on the outside but rapacious wolves on the inside, who locate those traveling on the route to Vézeley or Santiago or Saint-Gilles or Jerusalem. If they locate careless pilgrims in remote places, they give them false penance. For sometimes going with them they offer the best words in the beginning, telling everyone all of the vices in order.[350] Then, speaking to each of them separately in secret, they ask the individuals about their consciences and the sins committed. As soon as the pilgrims have confessed to them, they impose thirty masses on one and thirteen on another [f.87r] for whatever sin. They tell the pilgrim: "As a sign of the thirty coins with which the Lord was sold, have thirty masses celebrated with thirty very good coins, which you have, by such priests as would never have anything to do with women or the flesh and who do not eat meat and who do not possess property." However, the one who does not know in what way he may find such priests offers[351] the thirty coins to the one who says he will find one. The taker does not care about the well-being of the sinner, but places the money in a sack and spends it lavishly, and, placing his soul under anathema, will be locked up in hell. One should be very wary of these who are like hungry wolves.

I am not sure what I should say about certain hypocrites who, although they are healthy, feign the appearance of sickness, sitting along the route of Saint James or some other saint, and show themselves to the passers-by. For some, out of cupidity, show the passers-by their legs and arms, dipped in rabbit blood or ashes, whipped with a quivering hide, in a most miserable appearance, so that they might extort alms from them. Some stain their lips or cheeks with dark coloring; some who have Jerusalem-type palms and capes, paint their faces and hands with exfoliated bulbs,[352] which the French call *lotuesses*,[353] so that they might have a sickly appearance. Similarly, others pretend that they are mute or deaf, although they are not. Some similarly stain their arm or foot, once cut off for robbery, with animal blood, as if they had lost it from some other illness, and show this to the passers-by. Some, blinded for thievery, sitting near the road, show themselves as if they had lost their eyes through some other illness. Some show their foot or hand as if it were twisted or dried up or rigid, although it is not. Some, inflated with an animal skin bag or a cow's stomach, show themselves to the passers-by for the sake of gaining money. Others, bandy-legged, who, to be sure, could walk upright with their staffs,[354] set aside the staffs[355] and appear on bended knees holding on to stools[356] with their hands, as if they were crippled,[357] crawl on the ground and in the solitude of the roads,[358] begging for alms.[359] They are so filled with pride that they do not want to accept bread or modest alms, but do take coins or cloth or wax.

Whoever shall give them alms out of love of God and of the apostle, will without doubt have a reward, however. These are not such as to be refused alms or repudiated, but are to be recalled from their perverse cupidity with the food of the divine word. "Do not choose," says Blessed Isidore, "on whom you should have mercy. Give to everyone seeking. You do not know through which one you may please God more."[360] Therefore, while you are going to the threshold of Blessed James or whatever saint, do not judge those to whom you should give alms, [f.87v] but correct them diligently when you return. For, as Blessed James says: "Whoever shall have caused a sinner to be converted from the error of his way, will save his soul from death, and will cover up a multitude of his own sins."[361]

And what shall I say of the women who make tapers to sell who place so little wick into the tapers and candles that they cannot burn for a mass or for readings? And what shall I say about those who sell to the multitudes of pilgrims coming to them in great numbers bread and wine and oats and fruit and cheese and meat and fowl too expensively? All iniquity and all fraud abounds on the routes of the saints.

And what shall I say about the false moneychangers who are called by the people *cambiatores*?[362] If twelve coins of the pilgrim are worth sixteen to the moneychanger who wants to have them, the moneychanger will not give them to him. Because of the prompting of the pilgrim's perverse innkeeper he will not get thirteen or fourteen for them. If they are worth twenty, the moneychanger will give only sixteen or less, if possible. If twelve coins of the moneychanger are worth sixteen of the pilgrim, he will not give them to him for less than twenty. If they should be worth thirteen, he will take sixteen from the pilgrim. If a mark of pure silver should be worth thirty solidi, the moneychanger will give him a maximum of twenty for them. The wicked moneychanger has various weights, large and small. He buys the mark and silver with the heavy and larger weight, and he sells them with the lighter and smaller weight. He praises his gold and silver and his happiness, he spurns that of others. He sells dearly, he buys cheaply. If he can, he deceives the other, he guards himself from this. He suspends the coins on a weight, which they call a *trebuchetum*,[363] with each one separately, and he would just as soon melt the one which is the most weighty in a fire in a furnace with other silver as sell it to others. He corruptly cuts and shaves larger[364] coins with pincers. Woe to him and again woe to whoever commits so many frauds! Again what does the crafty one do? He sells to the ignorant a ring or cup or candelabra or any bronze work if silverplated on the surface for pure silver, if he can. Similarly, if the work should be goldplated, he sells it corruptly for pure gold. He sells his silver mark and gold talent[365] dearly, if he can, for inspected silver and gold, although they have not been inspected, and he buys cheaply the inspected item of another for non-inspected, although [f.88r] it may have been inspected. If a mark or talent of a pilgrim should be evaluated at four farthings less than the true weight, he buys it for twelve less. If, however, it were the gold or silver of the same money-changer, in a ring or cup or candelabra or bit or in whatever work, he sells it for pure although it may not be pure, and he also sells it for an excessive price. And if the pilgrim should want to sell him the very same thing in the same type of work, he does not buy it except as non-inspected gold and silver. Similarly, he sells non-precious[366] stones, which resemble precious stones and which people call "counterfeit,"[367] to the ignorant as very precious ones.

He does these things, and things similar to them, such that the trap of hell may come to him who knows it not, and the snare which he hides may catch him, and he may fall in that very trap. Take warning, therefore, false moneychangers, of what the psalmist reports concerning you, saying: "Deceitful sons of men on the scales,[368] that from concern for the vain they may be captured in that very thing."[369] You are deceived in your works, for your works are leading you to the lower places. "With that same measure with which you will have measured, it will be measured back to you."[370] Measure upon measure, mark upon mark, pound upon pound are at your table. Await therefore what Proverbs says to you: "Weight and weight, measure and measure, either is abominable to God."[371] For the Lord once overturned your tables in the temple, as it is written in the Gospel: "The Lord upset the tables of the moneychangers and the chairs of those selling doves."[372]

But what shall I say about the crafty spice merchants?[373] For some keep types of plants up to the point where they putrefy and sell the putrefied for good. Others sell adulterated[374] types for the most costly. Some, so that pepper might weigh more on the scale, sprinkle water on it; others mix in the roasted grain of ginger[375] or dark sand similar to it; some add in a mineral[376] similar to alum, taking from it a light amount.[377] Some add the resin of pine or some other tree sap[378] to the frankincense. Some, when selling dye colors, sell other substances[379] similar to them; some sell to the unwitting green soil for Greek[380]; some put red[381] lead in the red tint. Others sprinkle water so that azure[382] might weigh more on the scales. Similarly, they adulterate the other colors and types with various foreign substances similar to them. [f.88v] Physicians do the same thing. They do not fear to adulterate wickedly electuaries[383] and confections and syrups[384] and other antidotes with foreign substances. They add the bad to the good and sell the bastard types for precious varieties.

And what shall I say about crafty merchants? Some buy cloth with a large measuring stick[385] and sell it [stretched out] thin; some keep cloth so long that it putrefies and[386] then sell from it as if it were good. Some sell the pilgrims bootlaces or skins from the forest animals or a girdle or gloves or whatever they have to sell more dearly than they sell to their neighbors. Others make false oaths frequently and for the least thing: for this they are damned. Some unjustly and malevolently stretch out in their hands the new cloth that they have for sale so that it might be made longer and wider. Some fraudulently sell sheep- or pig- or horse-skin for deerskin, either as girdles or purses or breeches,[387] or pig and sheep sheaths for those made of deerskin. O crafty cupidity, those who strive to make teachers of fraud out of their boys, sending them to Le Puy[388] or Saint-Gilles[389] or Tours[390] or Piacenza[391] or Lucca[392] or Rome[393] or Bari[394] or Barletta![395] For in these cities, above all, is a school of all fraud.[396]

O false innkeepers and crafty moneychangers and wicked merchants, convert to the Lord your God! Put off your wickedness! Set aside cupidity! Remove wicked frauds from yourselves! What will you say on the Day of Judgment when you will see all those whom you have defrauded accusing you before God? Know that God will look upon you in your uncountable iniquities! Truly, unless you shall be converted from your innumerable frauds, you will have the very saints,[397] namely James and Peter, Giles, Leonard, Mary of Le Puy herself, the mother of God, Mary Magdalene,[398] Martin of Tours, John the Baptist of Angély,[399] Michael on the Sea,[400] Bartholomew of Benevento,[401] and Nicholas of Bari,[402] as accusers before God, whose pilgrims you have defrauded. To convince God they will say about those of you coming to judgment: "These, O Lord, are the ones who deceived our pilgrims with so many and such great frauds, and perpetrated[403] so many iniquities on them." "Give unto them according to the works of their hands, give them their retribution, for they have not understood the works of the Lord, and so according to the works of their hands you will destroy them and shall not build them up."[404] "May death come over them and may they descend alive to hell, for there

are iniquities in their dwellings and in their midst."[405]
What will become of you? Where [f.89r] will you be able
to flee? Whose help will you seek, since on the Day of
Judgment you will have the greatest saints as accusers
whom you should have as supporters? You will have as
accusers those whom the whole world wants to have as
supporters, whom all the world venerates, to whose basilicas every people travels, whose tombs all embrace with
pious love, whose dust and ashes are kept diligently in a
vessel as if they were select gold or precious stones, and
by whose power and merit and prayer transgressions are
forgiven to sinners, the sick are cured, the blind see, the
lame are straightened up, the desolate consoled, the bound
freed, whose relics the vows of the pious honor. They stand
before God and pray night and day, so that sinners might
merit forgiveness for themselves. No one knows better
intercessors than these. For the things that these saints,
whom God chose and carried above in[to] the heavens,
wish to be done are soon done. And the things that are
sought through them from God, at the request of the
people, will all be granted as asked without limit with
God's consent. And unless you shall have come to your
senses in this world, not only these but also your iniquities will take away from you the kingdom of God in the
future. Those whom you have defrauded will rejoice in
heaven, but you will go to Tartarus in the fires of Gehenna.
They shall delight in heaven; you shall weep with Satan
in hell. They will be crowned in heaven; you will be
plunged into the eternal death of hell, as the Lord says
through Isaiah:

> Because I have called and you have not answered, I
> have spoken and you have not listened; and you were
> doing evil in my eyes, and you have done what I have
> not wanted. Because of this,[406] the Lord says these
> things: "Behold my servants shall eat and you shall
> hunger. Behold my servants shall drink and you shall
> thirst. Behold my servants shall rejoice and you shall
> be confounded. Behold my servants shall praise me

from exultation of heart and you shall call out from pain of heart and from sorrow, you shall make your breath howl, and you will give up your name."[407]

Know that you will give up in the future not only the riches that you have wickedly amassed[408] with innumerable frauds, but also your soul and your own name, and you will delight like the one who is captured by the enemy, is wounded, is plundered, is closed up in a work house, is racked with torture, and is truly tortured with hunger and cold and tedium to the ultimate[409] degree. You will no longer say: "I am the one who used to be a happy guest," but rather: "I am a wretch in pain." Whoever loses himself [f.89v] makes a poor profit and loses everything. Await what Ecclesiasticus says to you: "Whoever shall have shed blood and committed fraud, the hired servants are his brothers in reward."[410] Know that your profits, with which you fill your purses by ravishing pilgrims, are not profit but damnation. For a profit that blocks its master from the kingdom of God and sends him to hell is not a profit but a damnation. Your arts and your very sharp talents by which you deceive the pilgrims block you completely from the kingdom of God and introduce you into the depths of hell.

What does it profit you to amass money by wicked frauds and to lose your souls in hell? "What does it profit a man if he should gain the whole world, but lose himself and fashion his own defeat?"[411] You amass monstrous and illicit profits because of your cupidity, when you practice innumerable harmful vices. Of this Paul says: "Cupidity is the root of all evil."[412] Some seeking it have wandered from the faith and have come to see themselves[413] in great pains. Just as all good things are born of charity, so also all vices arise from cupidity. Through cupidity a man, having set aside faith, lies; he is made into a miser; he is held as a simoniac; Christ is sold; God is offended; the love of neighbor is abandoned; the poor person is forgotten; all charity is left behind; the kingdom of heaven is forgotten; human judgments are subverted in the court of

heroes; fornication and adultery are perpetrated; robbery
and sacrilege and false oaths are perpetrated; all kinds of
evils and vices are carried out deep within; even the cleri-
cal class, which is worse, is made vile; riches are amassed,
by which the true poverty that Christ orders the religious
to respect is violated; and all classes of vices are dis-
charged. If you did not have cupidity, you would not
hoard. If you did not have riches, you would not practice
vices. You would sometimes like to whore, to feast on
splendid things, to be dressed in precious clothes, to build
palaces, to be honored by all; but you lack the riches with
which these wishes can be fulfilled. Of this Isaiah says:

> Woe to you who join house to house and who couple
> field to field.... Woe to you who draw...sin like the
> chain of the plow.... Woe to you who call evil good
> and good evil, setting down darkness as light and light
> as darkness, [f.90r] placing the bitter in the sweet and
> the sweet in the bitter. Woe to you who are powerful at
> drinking wine, and who are men strong in mixing in
> drunkenness. Woe to you who are wise in your own
> eyes and who justify wickedness for tributes and take
> away the justice of the just man from him.[414]

Your insatiable cupidity, by definition, would violate all
if it had the chance. When you cannot violate someone,
then you are excessively grieved. You always have the will,
but the power is often lacking, whence guile is always at
hand for you. For that reason, it remains in that condition, because you are not able. If demons are damned because they wanted to have what God did not want to give
them, then you who want to have what God does not want
you to have are also damned by divine judgment. Your
avarice is asserted to be like the insatiable person with
dropsy. When one with dropsy drinks, he wants to drink
more. Similarly, when you acquire more riches from fraud,
you work to acquire even more. Your avarice is similar to
the bottomless abyss,[415] and to the deep well and to the
sea. Just as your cupidity is without measure, so also your
pains in the fires of Gehenna will be without limit. Await

what Isaiah says: "Because of these things hell has widened its soul and has opened its mouth without end; and its strong and its people and its high and glorious will go down into it."[416]

O monstrous grief! The glorious and mighty of the world descend into the lower regions. Remaining in your vices, you sometimes yearn for the kingdom of God, but your thought is frustrated. Thus does Isaiah speak to you, saying: "While he dreams, the hungry also eats...and the thirsty also drinks...when, however, he has awakened, his soul is still empty...thus will it be for the multitude of all the evil ones."[417] Here it is said openly by the people: "Whoever does badly and hopes well, works in vain." While other men take respite on feast days from the works of the flesh, many of you do not fear to violate your brothers in your business through your markets and shops. Because of this your transgressions transcend the infractions of others. The Lord scorns such manner of solemn feasts, saying Himself through the prophet:

> My soul hates your calends and your feasts; the deeds are affronts to me, I have worked sustaining it. And when you have extended your hands, I will turn my eyes from you; and when you have magnified your prayer, I shall [f.90v] not hear you; for your hands are full of blood.[418]

And elsewhere the Lord says: "Why do you call to me? Your grief is incurable."[419]

Therefore, whoever has not violated those traveling, whether in the market or in a shop or in a changing house or in an inn or in any of the previously mentioned frauds, but who has conducted himself most properly toward them, will without doubt have a reward here and in the future from the Lord. And whoever has violated them or taken anything from them by theft or by plundering or by any fraud, his share without doubt will be with Datan and Abiron[420] and the devil.

And what shall I say of those who charge tolls to the pilgrims of Saint James? The toll collectors at the gates[421] of Ostabat or Saint-Jean or Saint-Michel at the foot of the Pass of Cize,[422] who take unjust tolls from them are thoroughly damned. No tongue, in fact, can narrate how many evils they have brought upon pilgrims. Hardly anyone passes through there who is not robbed by them. By the authority of God the Omnipotent, Father and Son and Holy Spirit, and of all the saints they are excommunicated a hundred times and they are anathematized, and they are isolated from the threshold of paradise, through the mouths of the many holy bishops and priests and monks who are so frequently robbed there. For this reason it is better to be silent than to talk about them. And for this reason the aforementioned scoundrels, namely the innkeepers, the moneychangers, the merchants, and the gatekeepers, are to be admonished by all qualified people so that they may recover their senses.

If someone then would spurn me, speaking and writing on the previous vices of the perverse, let him hear the greatest instructor of all teachers, directing me in the following way: "Raise your voice and announce to my people their wickedness."[423] For if I should not announce to the wicked his wickedness, the Lord will seek the blood of his death on my hand, since I, by not correcting him, have become the murderer of his soul. Therefore, let those who have treated his pilgrims properly on his route in all their business dealings rejoice in the sacred solemn feasts of the most high Apostle James. Let the pilgrims exult who are seeking his threshold and who are about to receive the crown of glory[424] for their labors with his approval.

Let us celebrate happily in our lands his venerable feasts, most beloved brethren, in as much as on that immeasurable solemn apostolic feast we may deserve to have enjoyment in heaven. Let the people of Galicia, who have merited to take up such a great leader and shepherd, especially take delight. Let the Western peoples exult. Let all[425] the islands of the seas be illuminated [f.91r] by such a patron. Let Samaria, imbued with his example, rejoice. Let Jerusalem, reddened by his blood, be happy. Let all those celebrating his feasts, carrying proclamations of praise in heart and mouth and work, give thanks to the Lord.

O favored people of Spain and Galicia,[426] who are honored by the virtue of such a prince, not exalted by the praise of your goodness but elevated by the merits of the glorious apostle! He has enhanced you, he has adorned you, he has beatified you, he has honored you. Your night, which had no day, is turned into the light of the true faith whose splendor cannot be explained with speech. To you who once were without grace[427] is given great grace. You, once not knowing your Creator, now recognize your Maker through the apostle. You were once cast into error, but now you are called to apostolic faith. You, once given to vain laws and now founded on freed beginnings, have renounced what you were and have begun to be what you were not. You were the cultivator of unclean spirits[428] but now have become the caretaker of the true God. You, who once lay on the dung heap of infidelity, now shine in the apostolic faith. You, who were once like a widow, are now joined to the celestial man. You, once sterile, now bring forth children. You, once forsaken, are now reconciled to the Creator. You, once straying like a sheep without a shepherd, are now joined to the heavenly leader. You, once stupid without an instructor, are now joined to a faithful teacher. For just as the sun, having spread its light, dispels the darkness, he, having banished the darkness from you, has led you to the true light. And although some regions of the world may temporarily lose the rays of the sun, the ray of the true sun never ceases to shine for you with the splendors of its virtues. Although Titan[429] may not always shine on the world, the ray of the true apostolic sun, present in the divine miracles and support, shines on you always. For just as the mountains are illuminated first by the gleaming sun and then the valleys, so also you, the dark valley, once began to shine with the apostolic light. First the mountains are illuminated and then the valleys. First the apostles are illuminated and then the peoples. And as the brightness goes out from the East, gleaming up until the West, thus the apostolic ray shines through divine miracles, not only in your province but also through the whole world where its churches are built.[430] This marvelous light that rose in [f.91v] darkness shines like noon, for a light is born to the inhabitants in the region of the shadow of death. It is no wonder that you once lay in the darkness of infidelity, for you did not have the light of doctrine. For unless you should see the ray of the sun, you would not know the sun. You have known then the sun of justice, since you have looked on its[431] ray, the very sun, however, that illuminates every man coming into this world, the very sun of which the psalmist says: "He has placed his tabernacle in the sun."[432] Of this the prophet says: "On you who fear the Lord the sun of justice will shine,"[433] and elsewhere: "The sun has risen and the moon has stood in its place."[434] Then the sun set, when Christ died on the cross. Then it arose, when Christ arose from the dead. Then the sun sent out its rays, when Christ sent his apostles, filled with the Holy Spirit, throughout the world.

Therefore, live lawfully, people of Spain, for you have accepted one[435] of these rays. Keep the ray of the true sun with good customs, so that it may deign always to shine on you with its virtues. Guard the treasure, preserve the living rock, chosen by the Lord on the Sea of Galilee, honored among the apostolic rocks, built in the sanctuary of the Lord. Favored soil of Galicia who has merited holding such a treasure, you have found the celestial pearl; you have found the yearned-for treasure — a pearl shining with divine miracles — a treasure never lacking in divine service. The yearned-for treasure rests on your shores. Whoever has this treasure lacks nothing. For what can be lacking to the one who possesses the virtue of such a treasure? But why is it that you, the uncivilized people, should have such a treasure? It appears to have been fulfilled in you that proverb, which is spoken by the people: "To a fool on the street[436] a fortune is given." So tell me: Who has endowed you? Perhaps you will tell me that:

"The Orient has visited us from on high." You say the truth, for "the Orient visited you from on high,"[437] when it deigned to give you the virtue of its apostle. For when you were exiled at the end of the earth and, if I may say so, situated at the limits of the world, nevertheless, "the ray of the true sun arises for you, that it may shine on those who are in darkness and sit in the shadow of death, for directing the feet"[438] of the many seeking the apostle of the Lord in your country. For all the barbarian peoples of all regions of the world run to you in throngs [f.92r], bearing with happiness offerings of praise for the apostle of the Lord. For of you it is right to be understood what the Lord once said through Isaiah:

> Behold in my hands I have described you[439]; your walls are forever before my eyes.... I live, says the Lord, that you may be vested with all peoples as with an ornament, and you shall surround yourself with them as if a bride; for your deserts and your solitude and the land of your ruin will be narrow before the inhabitants, and they will be far put to flight who were absorbing you. Up until now the sons of your sterility shall speak in your ears: "The place is narrow for me, make space for me that I may live." And you shall say in your heart: "Who has begotten these for me? I, sterile and not bearing, exiled and captured, and who has nourished them? and I, destitute and alone, and they were yours?"[440] The Lord God says these things: "Behold I raise my hand to my people and I shall raise my sign to the peoples, and they shall bear your sons in their arms, and they will carry your daughters on their arms. And kings will be their nourishers and queens their governesses. With faces turned down to the earth they will adore you and will lick your dust. And you will know that I am Lord, over whom they will not be confounded who await him...I shall judge those who have judged you, and I shall save your sons. And I shall feed your enemies with their flesh and, as if with wine, they will be inebriated with their blood. And all flesh will know that I am the Lord who saves you."[441]

To whom shall I compare you except to a man finding a treasure hidden in a field, who, out of his joy, having sold all his things, buys that field.⁴⁴² Again I will compare you to a merchant, a man seeking good pearls, who, having found one precious one, gave away all of his things and settled on that one.⁴⁴³ What then have you given or what have you accepted? Certainly you gave yourself by believing, and you have accepted the pearl already singing in heaven. You have given yourself by erasing the idols, by building the church, and have accepted the apostolic virtue in preserving them. Your acquisition is better than any business of silver and the best and purest gold. The fruit of your acquisition is more precious than all opulence, and all the things that are yearned for and cannot be got. His routes are beautiful routes, and all⁴⁴⁴ his paths are peaceful. Concerning his most salubrious coming Blessed Fortunatus,⁴⁴⁵ [f.92v] that splendid poet, confessor, and leader, once advised you to take delight, in the book of his divine praises, saying:

Applaud, people of Galicia,⁴⁴⁶ new songs for Christ,⁴⁴⁷
At the coming of James give vows to God.⁴⁴⁸
Behold, the hope of the flock has come, father of the people
    and the patron of the city,
   Let the sheep be made happy by the gift of the shepherd.
With him feeding, the flocks are ruled⁴⁴⁹ in holy pasture,
   And they gather gifts from the seed of paradise.
May he keep pure the sheepfolds of the pious of Christ
   Lest they be exposed to quick wolves to be torn apart.
He governs⁴⁵⁰ the stable with the care of vigilance without
    stain
   Lest any plundering disturb the entrusted flock.
May he fortify the enclosed lambs with their precious pelt,
   And may this vigil protect those sleeping.⁴⁵¹
The flowering vine with divine cultivation grows fertile⁴⁵²
   That its grape may also be beautiful, when it is mature,
So that the storehouse of heaven be filled up with eternal
    fruits,
   Whence souls may drink at the live flowing fountain.
May thirst not torment, which a rich person with a moist
    finger
   Wanted to soothe when he was seeking opulence.⁴⁵³
But flourishing more in the lap of Abraham, may the shepherd

Lead his sheep toward the stars to be located in that peace-
ful bosom.
Whence with the talent committed to him well doubled
He may enter into the true delights of his Lord.
And crowned with the worthy reward of his labors, he may [454]
Obtain as a soldier of the king a place in the arch.

Therefore, ask with us, people of Galicia, the Lord's
apostle to intercede assiduously for our continuous fail-
ings by begging Christ the King, his venerable Teacher,
seated in heaven, that we may be able to reject the worldly
and love the heavenly, that we may have him as a sup-
porter on the last day who is to be seated over the twelfth[455]
seat and whom we believe will judge over the twelve tribes
of Israel, and that we may merit being placed together
with him, with the help of God.

O great and blessed James,[456] beloved of Christ, loving
offspring of Zebedee, brother of John the Evangelist, who
with the Lord reigns happily in the arch of heaven, whose
immense dwelling stands in Galicia,[457] conferring well-
being on his seekers, grant that those who seek you there
or anywhere may receive all useful things! And to the extent that they seek you and confide in you, may they experience you always as intercessor in all their needs
before God in heaven. Be a guardian of our souls on the
day of our death. O advocate of the pilgrims, Saint James,
most loving of all, who left not only what you possessed
but also all that you could have possessed, because of the
Lord's calling you near the bank of the Sea of Galilee,
[f.93r] grant us, we beg, that by your loving merits, all
things that displease God may be dismissed, and that
those that please Him may be carried out in all virtue,
and that we may deserve to be made sharers of perpetual
glory together with you. You, who have exercised great
powers before God by giving sight to the blind, correcting those straying, raising the dead,[458] illuminate by your
merits the fog over our hearts, breaking the bonds of our
depravity. For God exhibited such respect for you that when
He raised the daughter of the archpriest[459] he respectfully

allowed you in when he did not permit others to enter, so that He might make manifest to you the venerable miracle. And so we run to the freeing power of your holiness, that you might raise us from the death of the soul with your most glorious interventions and might obtain for us from God a spirit good for resisting vice and concupiscence, to the extent that the dispenser of forgiveness may agree to lament our committed transgressions that we no more return to them. You were worthy to climb with the Lord to Mount Tabor to see His Transfiguration,[460] and to hear the wonderful voice of God the Father, and to perceive the immense brilliance of His divinity. Because of these things, O renowned apostle, we implore your blessedness, that by your prayers you may allow us to climb from the valley of vices to the mountain of virtues, that we may deserve to enjoy perpetual brightness, together with you in the resurrection that you saw symbolically on Mount Tabor. You, who arrived by the sword of Herod at the starry inner chamber, consort of holy angels, obtain for us solace in tribulation, strength in every time of temptation, that we may merit overcoming the adversary. You, honor of the Spanish, refuge of the poor, strength of the weak, consoler of those in tribulation, vigor of the pilgrims, fisher of souls, eye for the blind, foot for the lame, hand for the destitute, protector of those sailing and calling on you, intercessor of peoples, father of all, destroyer of vice, builder of virtue, we beg you with humble heart that with your pious intercession you extinguish the fires of our vices and that you kindle in us the fervor of chastity and love and the other virtues. We all believe in your prayers, from whatever necessity we have called on you for help, for we know that whatever you petition from God is most easily obtained.

For God has offered a gift to you that all barbarian peoples [f.93v] of all the regions of the world run with offerings, singing the praise of the Lord. Indeed the route from Dacia and Ethiopia to Galicia[461] turns worthily into a route of penitence and into salvation from sin because of you. For thus the prophet once prophesied[462] by describing and saying: "Nations from afar shall come to you, and bearing offerings they shall adore the Lord in you, and they shall hold your land in holiness. They will call a great name in you."[463] And after a bit he says: "You, however, shall rejoice in your children, for all shall be blessed and shall be gathered to[464] you. Blessed are all who love you and who delight over your peace."[465] For the Lord speaks thus through Isaiah:

> The work of Egypt and the business of Ethiopia and the Sabaeans,[466] high men shall pass over to you and will be yours. They shall walk after you, they shall go bound in manacles, and they shall adore the Lord in you and shall beseech you. God is so much in you.[467]

James, precious brother of the virgin John, who piously called Hermogenes,[468] who was ferocious of heart, from the vices of the world to the honor of the Omnipotent,[469] pray for us all with continual prayer. James, hope of slaves and medicine for your own, take up in mercy the pious vows of your slaves. Restore life, desired for so long a time, to yours so that we may deserve to be joined above on the fields in the stars.[470] Remember, therefore, most splendid father, your children throughout the ages, and you should never cease for it is[471] yours to pray for the pilgrims asking you, so that we, removed from all the narrow places, may all deserve to possess together with you the perpetual kingdom of heaven. May Jesus Christ our Lord deign to guarantee this who lives with the Father and Son and reigns[472] as God. World without end. Amen.

THE MIRACLES OF SAINT JAMES

HERE BEGINS THE SECOND BOOK
OF SAINT JAMES OF ZEBEDEE,
THE PATRON OF GALICIA,
ABOUT HIS TWENTY-TWO MIRACLES.

The Attestation[473] of Pope Calixtus: [f.140r] Above all, it is worthwhile to commit to writing and to consign eternally to memory the miracles of Saint James for the glory of our Lord Jesus Christ. For when the stories of the saints are told by experts, the hearts of listeners are moved piously toward the sweetness and love of the heavenly realm.

Turning my attention to this while wandering through barbarous lands, I[474] found various writings in various places: some of these miracles in Galicia, others in France, others in Germany, others in Italy, others in Hungary, others in Dacia,[475] others beyond the three seas,[476] and yet others on barbarian shores.[477] I learned some from those for whom the blessed apostle deigned to work them, hearing them from those who had seen or heard them. I saw others with my own eyes, and I have diligently committed them to writing for the glory of God and the apostle.[478] The more beautiful they are, the more dear they are.

Let no one think that I have written down all the miracles and stories that I have heard about him, but only those that I have judged to be true, based on the truest assertions of the most truthful people.[479] For if I had written down all the miracles that I had heard about him in the many places and in the accounts of many people, strength and parchment[480] would have run out and hand would have worn out, before the stories had run out. Because of this we have ordered that this manuscript be considered among the true and authentic manuscripts, and that it be read diligently both in churches and refectories on the feast days of this apostle and on other days if it be pleasing. Here ends the attestation.[481]

HERE BEGIN THE TITLES
OF THE SECOND BOOK OF SAINT JAMES
ABOUT HIS TWENTY-TWO MIRACLES.

Chapter 13. About Dalmatius, the soldier, whom the apostle brought to justice for the sake of Raimbert, his pilgrim.

Chapter 14. About the merchant whom the apostle freed from prison.

Chapter 15. About the soldier whom the blessed apostle rescued in a war, after his comrades had already been killed or captured.

Chapter 16. About the soldier who, in the agony of death, was oppressed by demons, and whom the apostle freed with the staff of a beggar and the little sack of a little woman.

Chapter 17. About the pilgrim who, for love of the apostle and at the instigation of the devil, killed himself and whom Blessed James led from death back to life with the help of Mary, the Mother of God.

Chapter 18. About the count of Saint-Gilles for whom the apostle [f.141r] opened the iron gates of his oratory.

Chapter 19. About Stephen, the Greek bishop, to whom the blessed apostle appeared and to whom he revealed unknown things to come.

Chapter 20. About William, the captured soldier, whom a count struck on his bared neck with a sword, but whom he could not wound.[482]

Chapter 21. About the crippled man to whom the blessed apostle appeared in his basilica and whom he caringly restored to health.

Chapter 22. About the man who was sold thirteen times and who was freed by the apostle the same number of times.[483]

1 A MIRACLE OF SAINT JAMES WRITTEN DOWN BY HIS EXCELLENCY POPE CALIXTUS[484]

Saint James the apostle, who in the fervor of obedience was the first of the apostles to suffer the pain of martyrdom,[485] undertook, through countless signs of his powers, to remove the peoples' roughness, which he saturated with the doctrine of his holy preaching.[486] Saint James, who arose by divine influence as the worker of such power, after he has wiped away the sweat of his labor with the cloth of reward, now pours a display of his powers abundantly over those who tirelessly and unceasingly petition him. Therefore we will tell straightforwardly a certain miracle that we heard and recognized as true, in its proper order in the series[487] of those following it.

At the time of Alfonso, king over the regions of Spain,[488] the fury of the Saracens increased quite sharply. A certain count named Ermengotus[489] saw the Christian religion oppressed by an attack of the Moabites.[490] Girded[491] with the support of his army for the purpose of overcoming their ferocity, and based on indications of certain victory[492] he attacked. However, despite the merits of our side, with his stronghold overcome, he ran into the contrary of triumph.[493]

As a result, the savagery of the enemy, filled with a pride of elation bordering on arrogance, led the twenty men encouraged by a wave of faith — and among whom there was a priest — into captivity in the city [f.141] of Zaragoza as a sign of victory.[494] Here, in the semblance of the perpetual blindness of hell, in the intolerable darkness of prison, the prisoners, bound with restraints of various types, chained together, with divine inspiration and with the priest's advice,[495] began to call upon Saint James in this way, "James, precious apostle of God, you who piously come out of mercy in aid to those in the snares of their oppressors, and who offer your hand of consolation toward the wailing from unspeakable[496] captivity, hasten to free those of us who are crushed so inhumanely."

Saint James, hearing their voices of inconsolable pain, appeared in brightness in the darkness of the prison, saying, "Behold, here am I, whom you have called."

The prisoners, whose heads were bent over onto their knees because of the magnitude of their pain, were encouraged[497] by the clarity of this sound, and they threw themselves at the feet of the saint. Saint James, feeling their pain deeply[498] and pouring the salve of his power on them, broke through their chains. Then with his potent right hand joined to the hands of the captives, the saint, with divine approbation, released them from this perilous prison and took them to the city's gates, with him in the lead. When the saint had made the sign of the cross with apostolic reverence, the gates willingly granted exit,[499] and once the prisoners had exited, the gates returned to their former closed state. Saint James the apostle, quite some time after the cock's crow and with the first ray of light almost shining on them, led them to a certain castle held in safety by the Christians. Then after telling them that he could be called on by them, he rose toward heaven. Then, calling on him with a loud voice, as he had just told them to do, the gates opened, and the former captives were taken inside.[500]

On the next day they left the castle and started toward their homes. After some time one of them, seeking the threshold of Saint James,[501] told everyone on the feast day of the saint's *translatio,* which in our time is celebrated annually on the third calends of January,[502] that all these things had happened in the way in which we have written down here.

This was accomplished by the Lord and it is miraculous in our eyes. Therefore, let there be honor and glory to the supreme King for ever and ever. Amen.[503]

2 A STORY OF SAINT JAMES WRITTEN DOWN BY VENERABLE BEDE, THE PRIEST AND DOCTOR [504]

[f.142r] During the time of blessed Teodomiro, bishop of Compostela,[505] there was a certain Italian man who scarcely dared to confess to his priest or bishop a great sin that he had once iniquitously committed. When finally the sin was heard, his bishop, who was horrified by such a great offense, did not dare to give the sinner a penance. Instead, moved by piety, the bishop directed the sinner to write down this sin in a note[506] and to go to the threshold of Saint James for the sake of penance. He also ordered the man to implore the blessed apostle's help with all his heart and to submit to the judgment of the bishop of the apostle's basilica.

The man went without delay to Saint James in Galicia and, repenting of having committed such a crime, and begging forgiveness from God and the apostle with tearful sobs, he placed the note with his crime on it upon[507] the saint's venerable altar at the first hour[508] of the saint's feast day, which is on the eighth calends of August.[509]

When blessed Teodomiro, the bishop of Compostela, had dressed in his episcopal garments[510] and went up to[511] the altar on that day at the third hour[512] in order to sing mass, he found the sinner's note[513] under the altar cloth, and he wondered why and by whom it might have been placed there. The penitent ran up to the bishop on the spot and tearfully and on bended knees told him, not without tears and with everyone listening, about his sin and about the command of his own bishop to whom he had gone. However, when the holy bishop opened the note, he found nothing written on it, as if no letters had ever been written down at all.[514]

This is a miraculous occurrence and a great joy. May great praise and glory to be sung for God and the apostle forever. It was accomplished by the Lord and it is miraculous in our eyes.[515]

This holy bishop, believing that the sinner was obtaining forgiveness from God through the merits of the apostle, did not wish to give him any penance for the already-forgiven crime. He merely prescribed that the sinner fast on the sixth day after that[516] and sent him, absolved from all sins, back to his own country.

It is to be understood from this that whosoever is truly penitent, and is from faraway shores, and has sought to request with all his heart forgiveness from the Lord and help from Saint James in Galicia, without doubt will have the slate of his sins wiped clean in eternity. May Jesus Christ Our Lord deign to guarantee this, Who lives with the Father and the Holy Spirit [f.142v] and Who reigns as God. World without end. Amen.

3 A MIRACLE OF SAINT JAMES WRITTEN DOWN BY HIS EXCELLENCY POPE CALIXTUS

In the year of Our Lord[517] one thousand one hundred eight, on the shores of France, a certain man, desiring to have progeny, as is the custom, married a woman in legitimate fashion. Although he remained with her for a long time, he was frustrated in his hope for children because his sins weighed down upon him. Suffering painfully from this since he lacked an heir, he decided that he would go to Saint James and that he would appeal to the saint for a son. What more can one do? There was no delay: he went to the saint's threshold. Standing there in the saint's presence, weeping and crying and begging him with all of his heart, he managed to deservedly obtain what he begged[518] from the apostle of God. According to the normal custom, when his prayer was ended, he returned safely to his country, after having sought the permission from Blessed James. After resting for three days, and after having said a prayer, he went to his wife. From that union, his wife became pregnant, and after the requisite number of months had passed, she bore a son, to whom they, out of joy, gave the name "James" after the Apostle James.

When the son had nearly reached his fifteenth year, he undertook the pilgrimage to the blessed apostle together with his father and mother and some other relatives. While he arrived at the Montes de Oca[519] in good health, he was struck by a serious disease and breathed his last.[520] His parents lamented his death, filling the whole grove and houses with screams and wailing in the manner of those who are delirious.[521]

His mother, almost beside herself with grief ,and crying out in great pain, spoke with these[522] words to the Blessed James, "Blessed James, to whom such great power was given by God as to grant me a son, give him back to me now. Give him back, I beg, because you are able to do so. For if you do not do this for me, I will kill myself at once."[523] While everyone was assisting, both those attending to the funeral service and those heading toward the tomb, through the mercy of God and the prayer of Saint James, the son awoke almost as if from a deep sleep.

All those nearby rejoiced and praised God for such a great miracle. Then the boy who was restored to life began to tell all those standing there how Saint James had received his soul, which had left his body [f.143r] from the third hour of the sixth day until the ninth hour of the Sabbath,[524] in eternal sleep in his bosom, and how at the Lord's command he restored it back to his body, raised him by the right hand from death, and commanded him to walk the path[525] of the Saint James' pilgrims with his parents without delay. The young man also said that being in that heavenly life then was sweeter[526] for him than being in this present miserable life. Then he went forth with his parents to the threshold of Saint James. What more can one say?[527] He was offered up at the venerable altar of the saint at whose prayers he was created.

This was accomplished by the Lord and it is miraculous in our eyes.[528]

It is a new[529] and thus far unheard-of event for a dead person to bring a dead person back to life. Saint Martin, while still living, did so[530]; and Our Lord, Jesus Christ, raised three dead people.[531] However, Saint James, while dead, brought a dead person back to life. Now, someone may say in objection: "If Our Lord and Saint Martin are said[532] to have brought back to life exactly three dead people before their own deaths and no one after their own deaths, then it is asserted that a dead person is not able to bring a dead person back to life but that a living person can do so." Saying these things, it can be concluded that if a dead person is not able to bring another dead person back[533] to life, but a living person is able to do so, then Saint James, who has brought a dead person back to life, is truly living with God. Thus it is agreed that both before and after death any saint can bring a dead person back to life with God's help. The Lord says, "Whosoever believes in me, will do the works which I myself do and will do the greater of these things."[534] "All things are possible for the believer,"[535] says the Lord elsewhere, Who lives with the Father and the Holy Spirit and Who reigns as God. World without end. Amen.

4 A STORY OF SAINT JAMES WRITTEN DOWN BY MASTER HUBERT, A MOST PIOUS CANON OF THE CHURCH OF MARY MAGDALENE AT BESANÇON.[536] MAY HIS SOUL REST IN PEACE. AMEN.

In this present miracle of Saint James of Zebedee, the apostle of Galicia,[537] it is affirmed that what Scripture attests to is true: "It is better not to vow than to go back on it after having vowed."[538]

It is reported that in the year one thousand eighty, thirty heroes from the area of Lorraine[539] proposed to visit the threshold of Saint James in Galicia out of a devotion to piety. [f.143v] However, since the human mind sometimes is changed for many reasons, they undertook to make a pact, promising each other the assurance of mutual service and the common charge of keeping their resolution. However, one member of the group did not wish to involve himself in this oath.

All of the men then set out on the planned journey and came safely to the city in Gascony called Porta Clusa.[540] There one of the men was afflicted with an illness and could not continue on. Because of the pact of keeping their resolution, his companions carried him by means of their horses and by hand, and with great toil, up to the Cize Pass[541] in fifteen days, a journey that normally was covered by footsoldiers in five days.

Then, finally, burdened and afflicted with excessive fatigue and disregarding their oath, they abandoned the sick man. However, the one who alone had not made a promise to him, offering the sick man a work[542] of faith and piety, did not abandon him. During the following night he kept vigil over him in the town of Saint-Michel[543] at the foot of the previously-mentioned mountain. When the next day had dawned, the sick man said to his comrade that he would try to climb the mountain, if the healthy man would give help to him according to his strength. The healthy man answered that he would[544] not desert him until death. As they ascended the slope of the mountain together, and as day was coming to an end, the most blessed soul of the ailing man went out of this worthless world and settled into the sleep of paradise in a worthy manner because of his merits, with Saint James leading the way. When the surviving man saw this, he was greatly terrified, first by the loneliness of the site, then by the darkness of the night, then by the presence of the dead man's body, and, finally, by the horror of that barbarous people — the impious Basques[545] — who were lingering around the pass. He was afraid beyond measure.

Since he could find no help either from within himself or from anyone else, setting his thoughts on the Lord, he asked help from Saint James with a supplicant heart. The Lord, as the font of piety Who does not desert those who believe in Him, deigned to call on this desolate man through His apostle. Saint James, sitting on a horse like a soldier, came to this man who was placed in such difficulty.[546] He said to him, "What are you doing here, my brother?"

"Lord," the man answered, "I need very much to bury my companion here, but I do not have the wherewithal [f.144r] to bury him in this wasteland."

The saint responded, "Hand me this dead man, and sit behind me on this horse until we come to the burial place."

Thus it was done. The apostle held the dead man, facing him, carefully in his arms, and he had the living man sit behind him on the horse.[547] Blessed power of God! Blessed clemency of Christ! Blessed help of Saint James! During that night they crossed the distance of a twelve days' journey.[548] Before sunrise the next morning, the apostle set down from his horse those whom he had carried, about a mile on this side of the monastery of the aforementioned apostle, on the Monte de Gozo.[549] He indicated to the living man that he should request the canons of the basilica of the aforementioned saint[550] to bury this pilgrim of St. James.

Then he went on to say, "After you have seen the burial ceremonies completed for your dead friend, and after you have kept vigil in prayer for the accustomed length of time, you should start the return journey. You should meet up with your friends in the city named León.[551] Say to them, 'Since you acted unfaithfully toward your companion by deserting him, the blessed apostle is telling you through me that your prayers and your pilgrimage are displeasing to him until you have sincerely done fitting penance.'"

Having heard all these things, and realizing that the speaker was the apostle of Christ, the man wanted to fall down at his feet, but the soldier of God no longer was visible to him.

With all of this done, on his way back he found his friends in the town mentioned above and he told them, in order, the things that had happened to him after they had abandoned him and how many were the threats [of the apostle] for not keeping their word to their companion in

its entirety. Having heard these things, they were indescribably[552] surprised. They received penance from the
bishop of León on the spot, and they finished their pilgrimage journey.

This was accomplished by the Lord, and it is miraculous in our eyes. These are, in fact, things that the Lord
has done. Let us exalt and rejoice in them. If there is something to be established by this miracle, it is that whatever
is vowed to God must be fulfilled with joy, inasmuch as
someone fulfilling worthy vows obtains forgiveness from
the Lord. May Jesus Christ our Lord Himself deign to be
our guarantor of this, Who lives with the Father and the
Holy Spirit and reigns as God. World without end. Amen.

5 A STORY OF SAINT JAMES WRITTEN DOWN BY HIS EXCELLENCY POPE CALIXTUS[553]

[f.144v] It is also worth remembering that in the year of
Our Lord one thousand ninety, certain Germans, traveling as pilgrims to the threshold of Saint James, reached
the city of Toulouse with an abundance of their riches[554]
and they took lodging there with a certain rich man, who
was evil, but as if hiding under a sheepskin, feigned the
gentleness of a sheep. He received them properly, but compelled them under the guise of hospitality to become in-
ebriated[555] with various drinks. O blind avarice! O
worthless mind of man prone toward evil! Finally, with
the pilgrims weighed down by more than their usual tired-
ness and by their drunkenness, the cunning host, driven
by a spirit of avarice, secretly concealed[556] a silver cup in
one of the sleeping pilgrim's knapsacks, so that he could
have them convicted of theft and, once they were convicted,[557] get their money for himself.[558]

After the cock crowed the next morning, the evil host,
with an armed band, pursued them, shouting, "Give back,
give back the money stolen from me!"

The pilgrims said to him, "You may condemn at your will the one on whom you might find it."

When the search was carried out, the host brought the two — a father and a son — in whose knapsack he found the cup, to court,[559] and unjustly took away their goods. The judge, however, moved by pity, ordered that one of them be let go and the other condemned to capital punishment. O depths of mercy! The father, wanting the son to be set free, indicated himself for the punishment.

The son, on the other hand, said, "It is not just that a father be handed over to the peril of death instead of his son; it is the son that should receive the infliction of the announced[560] penalty." O venerable contest of clemency! The son, at his own wish, was hanged for the freedom of his beloved father; and the father, weeping and mourning, went on to Saint James. After he had visited the venerable apostolic[561] altar, and after thirty-six days had passed, the father returned from Compostela and made a side-trip to the body of his son, still hanging.[562] He cried out amidst tearful sighs and pitiable exclamations, "Woe to me, my son, that I begot thee! Woe to me that I have lived to see you hanged!"

How magnificent are your works, O Lord! The hanged son, consoling his father, said, "Do not grieve, most loving father, about my pain, but [f.145r] rather rejoice. For it is sweeter for me now than it had ever been before in all my former life. For the Most Blessed James, holding me up with his hands, revived me with all manner of sweetness." The father, hearing this, ran to the city, calling the people [to witness] such a great miracle of God. The people, coming and seeing that the one whom they had hanged long ago was still alive, understood that he had been accused by the insatiable avarice of the host but that he had been saved by the mercy of God.

This was accomplished by the Lord and it is miraculous in our eyes. Therefore, they took the son from the gallows with great honor, but they hanged the host then and there as he had deserved to be for his evil, after he had been condemned to death by common judgment.[563] Therefore, those who are designated by the name "Christian" must watch with great care, lest they contrive to perpetrate against guests or any other acquaintances[564] any fraud of this type or any similar to it. They should, rather, strive to impart mercy and benign piety toward the pilgrims, since it is thus that they may deserve to receive the rewards of eternal glory from Him who lives and reigns as God. World without end. Amen.

6 A STORY OF SAINT JAMES WRITTEN DOWN BY HIS EXCELLENCY POPE CALIXTUS

In the beginning of the year of Our Lord one thousand one hundred, during the time of William, count of Poitiers,[565] when Louis, king of the French, was a prince,[566] and a deadly plague grievously assaulted the people of Poitiers, so much so that sometimes the father of a family went to the grave with all of his relations, a certain hero of the time, frightened by such devastation and wishing to avoid this scourge, decided to go through the region of Spain to Saint James.

With his wife and two small children seated on a horse, this pilgrim arrived at the city of Pamplona.[567] However, when his wife died there, an evil innkeeper nefariously took the goods that the man and wife had brought with them. The pilgrim, deprived of his wife and completely fleeced of his money and the horse on which he was transporting his children, began his journey again, bearing his children in his arms with great suffering.

Another man, wearing decent clothing and with a very strong donkey, met this pilgrim who was fettered by anxiety and in great distress. When this compassionate stranger had grasped [f.145v] the type and extent of the adverse things that had happened to this poor man from this man's own recounting, he said to him, "Since I consider your anguish[568] to be very great, I will supply you with my best donkey for transporting your children to the city of Compostela, of which I am a citizen, provided that you return it to me there."[569]

Thus the pilgrim accepted the donkey and placed his children on it and arrived at the threshold of Saint James. When at last he was devoutly spending the night in a secluded corner of the venerable basilica,[570] the most glorious[571] apostle, wearing very bright clothing, appeared to him, saying simply, "Don't you know me, brother?"

The pilgrim responded, "Not at all, my lord."

To this the other responded, "I am the apostle of Christ who in the region of Pamplona supplied you with my donkey when you were in such grief. Now, however, I am supplying you with the donkey from now until you have returned[572] to your own area, and I am announcing to you that your wicked innkeeper in Pamplona is about to fall headfirst from his seat and die from this serious fall, because he took your goods unjustly. I also declare to you that all evil innkeepers dwelling on my road who unjustly take the inventory from their guests, whether living or dead, which should be given to the church and to the poor for the redemption of souls, will be condemned for all eternity."[573]

As soon as the prostrate pilgrim tried to embrace the feet of the one speaking to him, the most reverend apostle disappeared from his worldly eyes.

Afterwards, however, the pilgrim, who was gladdened by the apostolic vision and so much consolation, started back from the city of Compostela together with the donkey and his children as dawn was just glowing. Arriving in Pamplona, he found the innkeeper quite dead, having fallen from his seat in his house and having fractured his neck, just as the apostle had predicted. When he had arrived safely in his own country and had taken his children off of the donkey at the entrance to his house, the donkey disappeared from sight. Many people marveled at this in an indescribable way upon hearing it from the pilgrim, and they have said that it was either a real donkey or an angel that appeared in the form of a donkey such as the Lord often sends into the midst of those fearing Him so that it might rescue them.

This was accomplished by the Lord and it is miraculous in our eyes. Therefore, it is plainly shown in this miracle that all crafty innkeepers are condemned[574] to eternal death [f.146r] if they unjustly take the inventory of a guest, whether living or dead, which should be given to the churches and the poor of Christ as alms for the redemption of souls. Through the merits of Saint James the apostle, may Jesus Christ Our Lord deign to avert completely from all believers any crime or fraud, as He lives with the Father and the Holy Spirit and reigns as God. World without end. Amen.

7 A MIRACLE OF SAINT JAMES WRITTEN DOWN BY HIS EXCELLENCY POPE CALIXTUS

In the year of Our Lord one thousand one hundred one, a certain sailor named Frisonus[575] piloted a ship traveling over the sea and filled with pilgrims wishing to go to the Lord's sepulcher in the area of Jerusalem in order to pray there.[576] At a certain point a Saracen named Avitus Maimon,[577] wishing to take all the pilgrims away with him into the land of the Moabites,[578] approached Frisonus' ship for the purpose of doing combat. When the two boats — that of the Saracens and that of the Christians — came together and fought fiercely, Frisonus, outfitted with his metal breastplate and his helmet and his shield, fell between the two ships into the depths of the sea. When, through the mercy of God, he regained some strength, he began to call on Saint James within his heart, saying these words, "Great and most glorious James, the indescribably pious apostle, whose altar I once kissed with my unworthy mouth, deign to free me together with all these Christians who are committed to you."

Thereupon the blessed apostle appeared to him in the depths of the sea, and, taking him by the hand, brought him back safely to the ship. Immediately, with everyone listening, the apostle said to the Saracen, "Unless you let this boat of Christians go free, I will hand you and your galleon[579] over to their power."[580]

Avitus responded to him, "Why, if you please, glorious hero, do you strive to take away my booty?[581] Would you, who would resist our people on the sea, be god[582] of the sea?"

The apostle said to him on the spot, "I am not the god of the sea, but I am the servant of the God of the sea, who comes in aid to those who are in danger and who cry out to me whether they be on land or sea, inasmuch as God wills it."

Through the power of God and [f.146v] the help of Saint James, the ship of the Saracens immediately began to be put to a dangerous test by a great storm. The Christians' vessel, with Saint James leading with divine approval, arrived at its desired site; and Frisonus, after having visited the Lord's tomb, went to Saint James in Galicia that same year.

This was accomplished by the Lord and it is miraculous in our eyes. May honor and glory be to Jesus Christ Our Lord, the King of Kings, for ever and ever. Amen.

8 A MIRACLE OF SAINT JAMES WRITTEN OUT BY HIS EXCELLENCY POPE CALIXTUS

In the year of Our Lord one thousand one hundred two, as a certain bishop, who was returning from Jerusalem, was sitting at the edge[583] of the ship and singing from his open psalter,[584] a strong wave surged up and swept him, along with several others, into the sea. When they were floating away on the wave and already at a distance of sixty cubits, they called in a loud voice to Saint James, who was there for them immediately. Standing on the waves of Thetis[585] with the soles of his feet still dry, he said to those in danger and calling on him, "Do not fear, my little children." Then he immediately ordered Thetis[586] to return to the ship those whom she had taken from it; and he called out from afar and advised the sailors to halt the boat.[587]

Thus it occurred. The sailors halted the ship, and the wave of Thetis, with the saint's help, returned all those whom it had swept off of the ship — including the bishop with the book from which he was reading still open — safely and completely unharmed. Then the apostle immediately disappeared.

This was accomplished by the Lord and it is miraculous in our eyes.

Afterwards, this venerable bishop of the Lord, who had been rescued from the dangers of the sea through the help of Saint James, went to the most glorious[588] apostle in the region of Galicia and composed the following responsory in the saint's honor in the first tone of the musical art.[589] He intoned it joyously singing in this way: "O help for all ages, O honor of the apostles, O bright light of the Galicians, O advocate of the pilgrims, James, supplanter of vices, release the chains of our sins, and lead us to the port of safety." Afterwards he composed a versicle in this form: "You who help those at sea or on land calling out to you in their peril, help us now and in the trial of our death." Then he repeated "Lead us [f.147r] to the port of safety."[590]

May Jesus Christ Our Lord Himself deign to be our guarantor, Who, with the Father and the Holy Spirit, lives and reigns as God. World without end. Amen.[591]

9 A MIRACLE OF SAINT JAMES WRITTEN DOWN BY HIS EXCELLENCY POPE CALIXTUS

In the year of Our Lord one thousand one hundred three, a certain glorious and very noble soldier from the nation of France, near Tiberias[592] in the region of Jerusalem, vowed that if the Apostle James would give him the power of conquering and destroying the Turks[593] in war, he would go to James' threshold. With the help of God, the apostle conferred on him such power that he overcame all of the Saracens who did battle with him. However, just as every man is said to be untrustworthy,[594] this soldier consigned his vow to the apostle to oblivion; and because of this, he deservedly became weak to the point of dying. When he became unable to speak because of his excessive weakness, Saint James appeared to his shieldbearer in a trance and told him that if his master would do what he had promised to the apostle, then he would be immediately cured.[595] When the shieldbearer informed his lord of this, the soldier understood. Then he indicated to the priests who were there that they should give him the pilgrim's staff and blessed purse.[596] When he had accepted these accouterments and had packed the necessary provisions, he recovered from the sickness by which he was plagued. He immediately began to travel toward Saint James.

While he was aboard ship, the boat began to be threatened by a savage storm, so great that, with the waves sweeping[597] across the ship's deck, all the passengers who were within the ship might be drowned. Immediately, all of the pilgrims[598] exclaimed in unison, "Saint James, help us!" Some promised to make a pilgrimage to Saint James' threshold, others pledged various sums for the work of his basilica there.

This soldier collected these sums of money on the spot, and immediately the blessed apostle appeared in human form to these people in difficulty on the ship, saying, "Do not be afraid, my children, because, behold, I on whom you have called am here with you. Be confident in Christ and well-being shall come to you here and in the future." He immediately loosened the cords of the sail,[599] cast the anchor, stabilized the vessel, and controlled the storm. Then, after having brought about great tranquillity on the sea, the apostle disappeared.

His face appeared in this way: decent, if you will, [f.147v] and elegant, and of such a type as none of them had occasion[600] to see either before or after.[601]

This was accomplished by the Lord and it is miraculous in our eyes. After this, the ship and its passengers came to the desired port in Apulia with smooth passage.[602] Then this soldier happily went to the basilica in the region of Galicia with the other pilgrims, and he placed the sum of money that he had collected in the coffer of Saint James for the work on the church. May glory and honor be to the King of Kings forever and ever. Amen.

10 A MIRACLE OF SAINT JAMES WRITTEN DOWN BY HIS EXCELLENCY POPE CALIXTUS

In the year of Our Lord one thousand one hundred four, while a certain pilgrim was returning from Jerusalem and was sitting on the edge of the ship for the sake of digestion,[603] he fell from the ship into the open sea. While he was appealing to Saint James, one of his companions threw down his shield[604] from the ship to him in the sea, saying, "May the most glorious Apostle James, whose help you invoke, assist you."

The drowning man grasped the shield and for three days and three nights, with St. James leading with divine approbation, swam through the sea's waves, following the wake of the ship, until he came unharmed to the desired port. He then told everyone how Blessed James had guided him from the moment when he had called to him by holding his head with his hand.

This was accomplished by the Lord and it is miraculous in our eyes. May glory and honor be to the King of Kings for ever and ever. Amen.

11 A MIRACLE OF SAINT JAMES WRITTEN DOWN BY HIS EXCELLENCY POPE CALIXTUS

In the year of Our Lord one thousand one hundred five, there lived a man named Bernard who was captured near the town of Cosa[605] in Italy, in the diocese of Modena, who was then bound[606] in chains and thrown into the depths of a tower by his enemies.

As he implored the help of Blessed James night and day with a continual cry, the most glorious apostle of Christ appeared to him, saying, "Come, follow me to Galicia."[607] When this man's chains were broken, James disappeared.

Immediately the pilgrim, with his shackle around his neck, climbed to the top of the tower, supported by the help of Saint [f.148r] James but without the help of any human. What more can one say?[608] He made a single jump from the top of the tower to the ground outside without incurring any harm. The height of the tower was sixty cubits; thus it was a great wonder that someone who fell from such a height avoided death, let alone be unharmed.

This was accomplished by the Lord and it is miraculous in our eyes. May glory and honor be to the King of Kings for ever and ever. Amen. Amen.[609]

12 A MIRACLE OF SAINT JAMES WRITTEN DOWN BY HIS EXCELLENCY POPE CALIXTUS

At the beginning of the year of Our Lord one thousand one hundred six, a certain soldier in Apulia[610] became as swollen in the throat region as a sack[611] full of air. Since he could find no recovery of his health from any physician, he entrusted himself to Saint James and said that if he could find a shell,[612] which pilgrims are accustomed to bring back with them on their return from Saint James, and if he could touch his ailing throat with it, he would immediately be cured. When he had found one on a certain pilgrim who happened to be his neighbor, he touched his throat with it and he was cured. Then he set out toward the threshold of Blessed James in Galicia.

This was accomplished by the Lord and it is miraculous in our eyes. May glory and honor be to the Lord Himself, Father and Son and Holy Ghost, for ever and ever. Amen.

13 A MIRACLE OF SAINT JAMES WRITTEN DOWN BY HIS EXCELLENCY POPE CALIXTUS

In the year of Our Lord one thousand one hundred thirty-five, a certain Allobrogian soldier named Dalmatius from Chavannes,[613] unjustly[614] struck Raimbert, who was one of his serfs and a pilgrim to Saint James, on the cheek[615] with his fist, when he quarreled with him. While Raimbert was being struck by the solder, he said, "God and Saint James, help!" Immediately, with divine wrath at work, the soldier was felled to the ground as if unconscious, with his arm twisted and broken.

After having been absolved by priests,[616] he asked forgiveness from his serf. "O Raimbert," he said, "pilgrim of Saint James, pray to the apostle, in whom you confide, for my well-being."

After being asked by Raimbert to do this, Blessed James restored the soldier to his original condition [f.148v] through divine mercy.

This was accomplished by the Lord and it is miraculous in our eyes. May glory and honor be to the King of Kings for ever and ever. Amen. Amen.[617]

14 A STORY OF SAINT JAMES WRITTEN DOWN BY HIS EXCELLENCY POPE CALIXTUS

In the year of Our Lord one thousand one hundred seven, a certain merchant, wishing to go to a market fair with his goods, approached the lord of that land to which he wished to go. This lord had, by chance, come to the city in which the merchant was staying. The merchant asked and implored the lord to conduct him safely to the fair and then to conduct him back to his home. The lord agreed to his request, promised that he would do so, and gave the merchant his guarantee.

The merchant, believing the words of such a great man, set out with his goods toward the region in which the fair was taking place. Afterwards, however, the lord, who had given his guarantee that he would protect the merchant and his goods and conduct him to and from his destination, was moved by the instigation[618] of the devil. He went to see the merchant, took his goods, threw him into jail, and held him fast.

The merchant, however, recalling to his memory the countless miracles of Blessed James that he had heard from many people, called on the saint to come to him in aid, saying, "Saint James, free me from this jail and I promise to give myself and my belongings to you."

Saint James indeed heard the merchant's sighs and prayers, and one night, with the guards still on watch, he appeared to the merchant in the jail, and[619] he ordered the merchant to get up, and he led him to the top of the tower, which bent itself so much that it appeared to place its top on the ground. The merchant stepped off of the tower without jumping; without lesions[620] and freed from his chains, he walked away. The guards went after him and came up next to him and, finding nothing, went back from there blinded.

The merchant took the chains by which he had been held along with him to the basilica of the blessed apostle in Galicia, and they hang there today in front of the altar of the most glorious James in testimony of this deed.[621]

This was accomplished by the Lord and it is miraculous in our eyes. For this may honor and glory be to the Supreme King for ever and ever. Amen. Amen.[622]

15 A STORY OF SAINT JAMES WRITTEN DOWN BY HIS EXCELLENCY POPE CALIXTUS

[f.149r] Toward the beginning of the year of Our Lord one thousand one hundred ten, soldiers from two cities in Italy, which were feuding with each other, gathered for battle. One group of them, overcome by the other group, turned their backs and began to flee in confusion.

Within this group was a certain soldier who was accustomed to seek the threshold of Saint James. While he was fleeing, he saw one group of his fleeing comrades already captured and another group killed, and he despaired of his life. He began to call out to Blessed James to provide aid to him with hardly any voice left but still loudly with a sigh. Finally he said with a loud voice, "Saint James, if you will deign to free me from this imminent danger, I shall dispatch myself and my horse to your court without delay. I hold nothing more precious. I shall hasten to your presence."

When this prayer was completed, Most Blessed James, who does not deny himself to those asking with a proper heart, but who is, on the contrary, ready to help, hastened to appear between the soldier and the enemies who were savagely pursuing him and were anxious to capture him and who had already imposed death by the sword or captivity on all the others who were fleeing. And James freed the soldier from his enemies by protecting him with his shield for a distance of six leagues.[623]

Lest this miracle be attributed to the power of the soldier's horse instead of to the glory of Saint James, as is customarily done by those who assail the Church and are envious of its goods, and so that any question of these envious people be answered, it was evident that this horse was not worth twenty solidi in terms of money.[624]

Lest his vow remain unfulfilled, the soldier offered himself and his horse in the presence of the blessed apostle, and, so that he might complete what he had vowed, he hastened to the gates of the altar, over the protests of the guards. Because of their joy over this miracle, both clerics and lay persons, as is the custom, ran to the church and gave thanks to God with hymns and psalms.

This was accomplished[625] by the Lord and it is miraculous in our eyes. May honor and glory be to the Lord Himself for ever and ever. Amen.

16 A MIRACLE OF SAINT JAMES WRITTEN DOWN BY SAINT ANSELM, ARCHBISHOP OF CANTERBURY[626]

Three soldiers from the diocese of Lyon and from the church in the town of Donzy[627] agreed that they would go to the region of Galicia for the sake of praying to Saint James the apostle; [f.149v] and so they set out.

While they were en route on this pilgrimage, they encountered a small woman who was carrying the things she needed in a little sack.[628] When she saw the horsemen, she asked them to have mercy on her and carry her little sack on their[629] horses out of love for Saint James and thus relieve her from the toil of such a great journey. One of them agreed to this pilgrim's request and took her bag and carried it. As evening was drawing near, the woman, who had followed the horsemen, took what she needed for herself from the little sack, and at the first crowing of the cock, when pilgrims on foot typically set out, she gave the little sack back to the horseman. Thus unimpeded, she made the journey a happier person. In this way, the soldier was helping the woman out of love for the apostle as he was hastening toward the desired place of prayer.

When they were twelve days[630] away from the city of Blessed James, this soldier came across a poor sick person on the road who began to beg him to give him his animal to ride on until he could arrive at Saint James. Otherwise, the sick man would die on the road, since he was unable to walk any further. The soldier agreed, dismounted, placed the beggar on the horse, and took the beggar's staff[631] in his hand, still carrying around his neck the little bag that he had accepted from the woman.

As he traveled along in this way, and as he was afflicted by the heat of the sun and by the weariness from such a long journey, he began to grow sick. When he noticed this, he took into account that he had often offended a great deal in many ways, and he endured his discomfort calmly out of the love for the apostle, going all the way to the threshold on foot. There, after he had prayed to the apostle and found lodging, he lay down[632] in a small bed and remained there for several days with increasing weariness from the malady that had begun on the road. When the other soldiers, who had been his friends, saw this, they went to him and counseled him to[633] confess his sins, to seek[634] the other things that are appropriate for Christians, and to prepare for his impending death.

When he heard this, the sick pilgrim turned his face away and could not answer. He lay in this way for three days without uttering a single word. Because of this, his friends were afflicted with a heavy grief: partly because they were distressed about his health, but especially because [f.150r] he could not ensure the health of his soul. One day, however, when those sitting around him and awaiting his death thought that he would soon breathe his last breath, he said to them with a great sigh, "I give[635] thanks to God and to Saint James, my lord, because I have been freed."

When those present asked what this might have meant, he said, "From the moment I felt myself growing worse from my weakness, I silently began thinking to myself that I might want to confess my sins, to be anointed with holy oil, and to be fortified by receiving the body of the Lord. But while I dealt with these thoughts in silence, a band of dark spirits[636] suddenly came toward me, which oppressed me to such a degree that from that hour forth I could not[637] indicate either with word or sign anything that might pertain to my well-being. I understood well what you were saying, but I could not respond with any speech. For the demons flocked together, some plucking at my tongue, others closing my eyes, still others turning my head and body first this way and then that, according to their desires and against my will.

"However, just a little while before I began to speak to you, Saint James entered here, holding in his left hand the woman's little sack, which I had borne on the road. In his right hand he was holding the beggar's staff, which I had carried while he had ridden my horse on the day when I took sick. He held the staff as a lance and the little sack as a weapon. He immediately came toward me in a kind of indignant fury, raised the staff and tried to strike the demons who had held me. Terrified, they fled immediately and he followed them, forcing them to leave here through that corner. Behold, after being liberated from those who were harassing and tormenting me, I am able to speak through the grace of God and Saint James. Send quickly and[638] get a priest who can give me the viaticum of Holy Communion.[639] For in fact I do not have permission to remain in this life any longer."

After they had sent for the priest and while he delayed in coming, the dying man admonished one of his companions publicly, saying, "Friend, do not fight for your former lord, Girinus the Bald,[640] to whom you have until now owed allegiance. For he truly has been damned and is about to die an evil death in the near future."

The matter proved true in just this way. [f.150v] For afterwards the pilgrim came to rest with a good conclusion to his life and he was given burial. When his companions had returned home and had told what had occurred, Girinus, surnamed "the Bald," who had been a rich man, considered their story a dream, and he did not correct his depravity in the least. For this reason, not many days later, it happened that while he was killing a soldier in an armed invasion, he also died, run through with the soldier's lance.

Therefore, may honor and glory be to the King of Kings, Our Lord Jesus Christ, for ever and ever. Amen.[641]

17 A GREAT MIRACLE OF SAINT JAMES WRITTEN DOWN BY SAINT ANSELM, ARCHBISHOP OF CANTERBURY[642]

Near the city of Lyon is a village in which a certain young man named Gerald dwelled. He was instructed in the art of tanning[643] and lived from the just labor of his hands, supporting his mother, as his father had died. He ardently loved Saint James and was accustomed to travel to the saint's threshold every year to make an offering. He had no wife but lived a chaste life alone with his old mother. While he could contain himself for a fairly long time, finally on one occasion, he was overcome by the voluptuousness of the flesh and fornicated with a certain maiden.

When the next morning arrived, since he had previously arranged it, he set out on his pilgrimage to Saint James in Galicia with two of his neighbors and brought a donkey with him. While they were on the road, they met up with a beggar going to Saint James and took up with him for the sake of company and even more so out of love for the apostle, sharing with him the necessities of life.

Continuing their travel, they spent several days together happily. The devil, however, who envied their peaceful and charitable[644] company, approached in charming human guise the young man who had secretly fornicated back home and said to him, "Do you know who I am?"[645]

The young man answered, "Not at all."

The demon said, "I am James the apostle, whom you have been accustomed to visit every year for a long time now and to honor with your offering. May you know that I took great joy from you and that I had hope that great good would come from you. However, just before you left your[646] home you fornicated with [f.151r] a woman, and between then and now you have done no penance, nor have you wanted to confess this act. Thus you have set out to a foreign land with your sin, as if your pilgrimage would be acceptable to God and to me. It must not occur in this way. For whoever wishes to make a pilgrimage out of love for me, must first disclose his sins through a humble confession, and afterwards wipe out those acts through making a pilgrimage. Whoever does otherwise will have his pilgrimage go unheeded."[647]

Having said this, the devil vanished from the young man's sight. After having heard these things, the man began to grow sad, thinking in his mind that he should return home to confess to his priest and then return to the journey that he had started.

While he was running this course of action through his mind, the demon came to him in the same form in which he had previously appeared and said to him, "What is this that you are thinking in your heart about wanting to go back home to do penance, so that you might be able to return to me more worthily afterwards? Do you think you can erase such a great crime with your fasting or tears? You are acting very foolishly. Believe my advice and you will be saved. Otherwise you will not be saved. Although you may have sinned, I still love you, and because of this, I have come to you, so that I might give you counsel by which you can be saved, if you should wish to believe me."

The pilgrim said to him, "I was just thinking along the same lines as you are saying, but now that you assert that this course of action is not beneficial for my salvation, tell me what action is pleasing to you by which I may be saved and I will willingly carry it out."

The devil then said, "If you wish to be completely[648] cleansed from sin, cut off very quickly the manly parts with which you have sinned."

After having heard this advice, the terrified man said, "If I do to myself what you are advising, I will not be able to live,[649] and I will be my own murderer, which I have often heard is damnable in the eyes of God."

The demon, laughing, said, "O, you fool, how little you understand the things that could be a benefit for your salvation. If you should die in this way, you will, without doubt, come to me, since, in effacing your sin, you will be a martyr. O, if you were so prudent that you would not hesitate to kill yourself, I would certainly come to you immediately with a multitude of my followers and would gladly accept your soul to remain with me. I," he said, "am James the apostle who advise you. Do as I have said if you wish to come into my company and find [f.151v] a remedy for your sin."

After having said these things, the simple pilgrim turned his mind toward his crime, and while his companions were sleeping at night, he took out a knife and cut off his manly parts. Then, turning his hand, he raised the knife, thrust its sharp point into his stomach and pierced himself through.

As the blood flowed freely and as the man was causing a commotion by thrashing about, his companions were awakened and they called to him, asking what was the matter. When he did not give them any answer, as he was anxiously drawing his last breath, they became alarmed, got up, lit their lamps, and found their half-dead companion unable to respond to them. They were stupefied and stricken with great terror, lest his death be blamed on them if they should be found in that place in the morning. They took flight and left him, rolling in his blood, and the mule and the beggar as well.

The next morning, when the family of the house arose, they found the slain man. As they did not know[650] to whom they might ascribe this murder, they called[651] their neighbors and carried the dead man to church for burial. There they placed him in front of the doors because of the flow of blood, while the grave was being prepared. After a short delay, the man who had been dead came to and sat upright on the funeral bier. When those who were present saw this, they fled and cried out in terror. Alarmed by their cry, people ran up, and asked what had happened, and heard that a dead man had returned to life.

When they came closer and began to speak to him, he told all of them freely what had happened to him. He said, "I, whom you see raised from the dead, have loved Saint James since childhood and I have been accustomed to serve him as much as I could. However, a short while ago, I decided to make a pilgrimage to his tomb, and as I was approaching this village, the devil deceived me, saying that *he* was Saint James...." Then he told the whole series of events, just as it is set forth above, and added, "After I took my life and after my soul was taken from my body, that same malignant spirit who had deceived me came to me, leading a great hoard of demons. [f.152r] Without mercy, they immediately grabbed me and took me, weeping and uttering miserable cries, to their torments.

"They directed their course toward Rome. When we had to come to the forest that is situated between the city [of Rome] and the town that is called Labicum,[652] Saint James, who had followed[653] behind us, flew up to us and said to the whole group of demons, 'From whence do you come and whither do you go?' They said, 'O James, certainly this is none of your business. For this man believed us to such an extent that he killed himself. We persuaded him; we deceived him; we must have him.' The saint said to them, 'You give no answer concerning what I ask, but you rejoice by boasting that you have deceived a Christian. For this may you receive ill thanks. This is my pilgrim, whom you boast of possessing. You will not bear him off with impunity.' Saint James appeared to me to be young with a handsome face, lean and of that moderate color that people call 'brown.'[654]

"With him coercing us, we turned toward Rome. Near the church of Blessed Peter the apostle, there was a green and spacious place on an airy plain, to which an immeasurable crowd had come for a council, over which Our Lady Mary, the Venerable Mother of God and Perpetual Virgin, presided, with many admirable nobles sitting at her right and left. I began to contemplate her with a great affection in my heart, for never in my life have I seen such a beautiful creature. She was not of a large, but rather moderate, stature, and pleasing in appearance with a most beautiful face. The blessed apostle, my most pious advocate,[655] sat in front of her and before all of the others, and he publicly made complaint concerning the treachery of Satan with which he had deceived me. She immediately turned to the demons and said, 'O you miserable creatures! What were you seeking in a pilgrim of my Lord and Son, and of James, His faithful one? Your pain should be enough for you. There should be no need for you to increase your pain through this depraved act of yours.'

"After this most Blessed Lady spoke, she compassionately turned her gaze[656] on[657] me. The demons, however, were beset by great fear, as all those sitting in council were saying that the demons had acted unjustly against the apostle by deceiving me, and the Lady ordered that I be returned to my body. Saint James immediately picked me up [f.152v] and brought me back to this place. That is how I died and was restored to life."

Upon hearing this, the inhabitants of the place rejoiced enthusiastically and took him[658] directly to their house. They kept him with them for three days, telling everyone about him and exhibiting him, as the one on whom God through Saint James had worked such an unusual and miraculous thing. For his lesions were healed without delay with scars alone remaining in the place of his wounds. In place of his genitals there grew a sort of wart through which he could discharge urine.

When the days during which the residents of the place had kept him[659] with them out of joy came to an end, he prepared his donkey and set out on his journey along with his beggar friend who had joined him on the road. As he was approaching the threshold of the blessed apostle,[660] lo and behold, he met up with his friends who had abandoned him and who were making the return journey. While they were still at a distance, and when they saw the two men goading[661] the donkey, they said to each other, "These men are similar to our companions whom we left behind, the one dead, the other alive, and the animal that they are goading is not much different, as far as can be seen, from the one that we left behind with them." Then, as they were approaching the two men, and as each group began to recognize the other, they learned what had occurred, and they exulted fervently. When they returned home, they told everything just as it had happened.

Furthermore, the man who had been raised from the dead confirmed[662] in substance what his friends had earlier said, when he returned from Saint James. As the story spread far and wide, he retold the story, showed his scars and even showed what had been in his most private place to the many people wanting to see it. Saint Hugh, the most reverend abbot of Cluny,[663] along with many others saw this man and all the signs of his death; and it is said that he was accustomed to assert rather often, out of admiration, that he had seen it.

We have also consigned this miracle to writing out of love for the apostle, lest it be dropped from memory. And we give the order to all that every year[664] on the fifth day of the nones of October[665] a feast should be celebrated in all churches with worthy ceremony for this miracle and for the other miracles of Saint James.[666]

Therefore, may honor and glory be to the King of Kings, Who has deigned to work so many and such great miracles for His beloved James, for ever and ever.[667] Amen.

18 A MIRACLE OF SAINT JAMES WRITTEN DOWN BY HIS EXCELLENCY POPE CALIXTUS[668]

Not long ago a count of Saint-Gilles[669] named Pontius[670] came to Saint James with his brother in order to pray to the saint. [f.153r] When they had entered the church and were unable to enter the oratory in which the apostle's body lay,[671] as they wished[672] to do, they asked the guard to open the oratory for them so that they could spend the night keeping vigil in front of the saint's body. When they saw that their request had no effect,[673] since it was the custom that the gates of this oratory remain closed from the sun's setting until it shone again the next day, they departed sadly toward their lodging. When they arrived there, they ordered all the pilgrims of their group[674] to come together. The count said to all those present that he wanted to go to Saint James, with those of a similar mind accompanying him, if, by chance, the place should deign to open for them all by[675] itself.

Since they all accepted this idea harmoniously and freely, they prepared lamps, which they held in their hands, while keeping watch. With the evening thus spent, they lit their lamps and went to the church with about two hundred in their number. As they approached the front of the apostle's oratory, they prayed in a loud voice and said, "Most Blessed James, apostle of God,[676] if it please you that we might come to you, open your oratory for us so that we may keep vigil[677] before you."[678]

What a miraculous event! Hardly had they finished these words when lo and behold, the oratory's gates made such a noise that all who were there thought that the gates would break into small pieces. The bolt, bars, and chains with which the gates were locked[679] were unfastened and shattered. Thus the gates were opened by an invisible power and not by human hands and offered entry to the pilgrims.

They rejoiced[680] enthusiastically and entered, and they exulted all the more over this miracle in as much as they saw that they had demonstrated that this blessed apostle, who is a soldier of the Invincible Emperor, most truly lives, whom[681] they saw attend to their petition so quickly. In this event, one can examine how attentive the saint is to a pious petition, since he was so gracious in attending to this petition from his servants.

May your clemency, most gracious James, apostle of God, come to our aid, so that we might thus avoid the deceits of Satan in the course of this present life and inherit the heavenly kingdom through our good efforts, [f. 153v] and be able to arrive in this kingdom with your help, through Christ Our Lord, Who lives and reigns as God. World without end. Amen.[682]

19 A MIRACLE OF SAINT JAMES WRITTEN DOWN BY HIS EXCELLENCY POPE CALIXTUS[683]

It is known to everyone, both cleric and lay, dwelling in Compostela, that a certain man named Stephen, who was endowed with divine powers, set aside the episcopal dignity[684] and the pontifical office out of love for Saint James, and set out from a region of Greece for the threshold of the apostle. He renounced the enticements of this world so that he might adhere to the divine dictates. Therefore, he refused to return to his own region, and he approached the guards of the building in which the most precious treasure and honor of Spain, namely, the body of Blessed James,[685] is located. He cast himself at their feet and begged them to grant him an out-of-the-way place in the church where he might be permitted to devote himself to continuous prayer. He asked this out of love for the most precious apostle, out of love for whom he had rejected worldly delights and earthly pleasures. Although he was wearing poor clothing and conducting himself not as a bishop but as a poor pilgrim, they did not hold him in contempt, but agreed to his just request. They prepared a sort of dwelling for him. This was constructed out of rushes in the manner of a cell and located inside the basilica of the blessed apostle, and from its right front he could look at the altar. In this place Stephen spent his celibate and most blessed life in fasts, vigils, and prayers both day and night.

One day, however, while he was engaged in his customary prayer, a crowd of peasants who were gathering for a special feast for the most precious James and were sitting next to this most holy man's cell near the altar, began to appeal to the apostle of God with these words, "Blessed James, good soldier, remove us from current and future evils."

This most holy man of God reacted indignantly to this word, and because the peasants had called[686] James a "soldier" he said to them angrily, "You stupid peasants, you foolish people. It is not proper to call Saint James a 'soldier,' but rather a 'fisherman,' in remembrance of the time when,[687] at the Lord's calling, he left the fishing profession, followed the Lord and after that was made a fisher of men."

On the night following the very day [f.154r] during which the most holy man had said this about Blessed James, Blessed James appeared, adorned in the whitest clothing, bearing military arms surpassing the rays of Titan,[688] transformed into a soldier, and holding two keys in his hand. After calling to him three times, James spoke in this way, "Stephen, servant of God, you who ordered me to be called not a soldier but a fisherman, I am appearing to you in this fashion, so that you no longer doubt that I am a fighter for God and his champion,[689] that I precede the Christians in the fight against the Saracens, and that I arise as victor for them.

"I have sought something, in fact,[690] from the Lord, as I am[691] a protector for those loving me and calling on me with a proper heart, and as I am a support against all dangers. So that you might believe this, I will open the gates of the city of Coimbra[692] with these keys that I am holding in my hand. At the third hour tomorrow I will hand over the city, which has been held under siege for seven years by King Ferdinand, to the power of the Christians who will then have entered there." After saying this James disappeared from sight.

On the following day, when matins were finished, Stephen called on a great number of clerics and lay people and told them exactly what he had seen with his eyes and heard with his ears. Afterwards, this was shown to be true for a number of reasons. They had written down the day and hour that Stephen had told them; on these points, messengers sent by the king after the city's capture offered a confirmation of accuracy, as they asserted that the city had been captured on just that day and at just that hour. When the truth of this was recognized by him, Stephen, the servant of God, asserted that Saint James was stronger than others for those calling out to him in battle, and he preached that he should be called upon by those fighting for truth.[693] So that he himself might merit the saint's protection, he increased his penance, kept vigil[694] more efficaciously with prayers, spent the rest of his life there in the service of God, and finally received[695] burial in the basilica of the blessed apostle.

This was accomplished by the Lord and it is miraculous in our eyes. Therefore, may honor and glory be to the King of Kings for ever and ever. Amen.

20 A MIRACLE OF SAINT JAMES WRITTEN DOWN BY HIS EXCELLENCY POPE CALIXTUS

As, over the course of much time passing by and still in our own times, Most Blessed James the apostle[696] has enriched the whole [f.154v] world both far and wide with many signs of miracles, it happened that a very great war arose between the count of Forcalquier[697] and one of his soldiers by the name of William. As the soldier resolutely rode into battle against the count, they both came together in battle along with their soldiers. However, since the soldier's army was weak and turned tail, the soldier was captured in the war and brought into the count's presence.

As the count himself ordered him to be beheaded the soldier called out in a loud voice, "James, apostle of God, whom Herod killed with a sword in Jerusalem, help me and free me from the sword of the executioner."[698] With his hands raised toward heaven, he withstood the blow on his lowered neck three times, and no trace of injury appeared on it.

When the executioner saw that he could not harm the soldier with the sword's blade, he directed its point at his stomach, so that he might run him through. However, Saint James dulled the sword so that the soldier did not even feel the blow. When the count as well as all the others who were there marveled at these events, the count ordered the soldier to be bound and locked up in his castle.

As the next morning was just dawning, and as the soldier[699] was calling on Saint James between his sobs, lo and behold, the apostle himself was standing before him, saying,[700] "Behold, I whom you have called am here." Then, the whole house was filled with a most serene light and with such a fragrance that all the soldiers and all the others who were there thought that they had been transported to the delight of paradise.[701] In this gleam, with Saint James leading and holding his hand, the soldier arrived at the outermost castle gate in full view of everyone, but with the guards almost blinded. After the gates had opened both went together for a mile beyond the walls.

Because of this, it happened that the soldier, who was burning with love for Saint James, reached the saint's body and church on the feast of his[702] *translatio* and recounted[703] all these things in the same order as we related them here.

This was accomplished by the Lord and it is miraculous in our eyes. Therefore,[704] may honor and glory be to the highest King for ever and ever. Amen.

21 A MIRACLE OF SAINT JAMES WRITTEN DOWN BY HIS EXCELLENCY POPE CALIXTUS

In our time[705] a certain famous man named Guibert from Burgundy had been suffering for fourteen years a loss of the use of his legs, such that he could not take a step. The man set out for Saint James, together with his wife and his servants, mounted on two [f.155r] horses.

While he was in the hospital of the apostle, near the church,[706] not wanting to be lodged anywhere else, he was admonished to devote himself to continuous prayer in the saint's church until the saint extended his constricted legs. After he had kept vigil in this way in the apostolic basilica for two nights and while he was keeping vigil with prayer on the third night, Blessed James came and took his hand and raised him up. When the man asked who he was, he said, "I am James, the apostle of God."

The man, who was restored to health, kept vigil for thirteen days in the saint's church[707] and revealed these things to everyone with his own tongue.[708]

This was accomplished by the Lord and it is miraculous in our eyes. Therefore may honor and glory be to the Supreme King for ever and ever. Amen.

22 A MIRACLE OF SAINT JAMES WRITTEN DOWN BY HIS EXCELLENCY POPE CALIXTUS

It is said that in the year of Our Lord one thousand one hundred a certain citizen of Barcelona[709] came on pilgrimage to the basilica of Saint James in the area of Galicia. However, he had asked only that the saint might free him from captivity by his enemies, if perchance he should fall into this predicament. Thus, after he had returned to his affairs and had set out for Sicily,[710] he was captured at sea by the Saracens. What more can one say?[711] He was bought and sold thirteen times at markets and fairs. However, those who bought him could not hold him, because each time Saint James released[712] the bonds and chains. The first time he was sold in Corociana,[713] the second in the city of Zara in Slovenia,[714] the third in Blasia,[715] the fourth in Turkey,[716] the fifth in Persia,[717] the sixth in India,[718] the seventh in Ethiopia,[719] the eighth in Alexandria,[720] the ninth in Libya,[721] the tenth in Berber Africa,[722] the eleventh in Biskra,[723] the twelfth in Bougie,[724] and the thirteenth[725] time in Almería,[726] where he was firmly tied by a Saracen with double bonds around his thighs.

As the captive implored Saint James on high, the apostle himself appeared and said, "Because, when you were in my basilica, you asked me only for deliverance of your body and not the salvation of your soul, you have fallen into these dangers. However, since the Lord has had mercy on you,[727] He sent me to you so that I might remove you from this slavery."

The blessed one immediately broke his chains through the middle and then disappeared from sight. [f.155v] The man, thus freed[728] from his bonds, began to go back openly to the land of the Christians, through the cities and the strongholds of the Saracens with the Saracens looking on, and he carried a section of the chain as witness to the miracle. When a pagan happened on him and tried to capture him, the man showed him the section of chain and his adversary immediately fled. Hoards of lions, bears, leopards, and dragons attacked him in order to devour him as he walked through the wild places, but once they saw the chain that the apostle had touched,[729] they retreated far from him.

I met this man myself between Estella and Logroño, as he was walking back toward the threshold of Blessed James[730] with the chain in his hands, both feet bare and lacerated, and he told me all of these things.

This was accomplished by the Lord and it is miraculous in our eyes.[731]

In this story[732] those people are to be rebuked who seek from the Lord or from the saints a wife or earthly happiness or honors or wealth[733] or the death of their enemies or other things similar to these, which pertain only to the benefit[734] of the body and not to the salvation of the soul. If the necessities of the body are to be sought, then the necessities[735] of the soul are to be more sought, namely good virtues, such as faith, hope, charity, chastity, patience, temperance, hospitality, generosity, humility, obedience, peace, perseverance, and others similar[736] to these, through which the soul may be crowned on thrones amongst the stars. May He deign to guarantee this, Whose kingdom and empire remains without end for ever and ever. Amen. Amen.[737]

END OF THE SECOND BOOK.
MAY GLORY BE TO THE ONE WRITING
AND TO THE ONE READING THIS.

NOTES TO TRANSLATIONS

1.   The structure *vocat ipsum*, "it calls itself," is a somewhat rare precursor of the reflexive structure that had all but replaced the usual passive (*vocatur*, "it is called") of classical Latin. These reflexive forms, such as the Spanish *se llama* and the French *s'appelle*, ultimately won out over the passive voice in the vernacular. Whitehill 1 erroneously transcribes the word as *vocatur*.

2.   The word *beatus*, "blessed," is used frequently but not necessarily as an indication of a formal state prior to canonization, as is the case today. It appears in this work both as a synonym for "saint" and with a more generic meaning. We consistently render it "blessed."

3.   See the introduction, xxxv, xxxix-xl, lxix n. 44, for information about Pope Calixtus II and his relationship to the *Liber Sancti Jacobi.*

4.   Cluny, the powerful seat of a reform movement within the Benedictine order, is located near Mâcon in southern France. It was the site at which Guido of Vienne was elected Pope Calixtus II in February 1119. Cluny's efforts to be a part of the pilgrimage movement bore fruit when the mother house began taking control of various monasteries and attendant churches along the route to Santiago.

5.   This is the most probable meaning in view of his having been elected there; however, the Latin word endings also permit "apostolic seat of his election."

6.   This could refer to either of two patriarchs named William, the first serving as patriarch from 1128 to 1130 and the second, William of Messina (d. 1185), from 1130 to 1145. Neither suggestion is completely satisfactory, and this is one indication of the spurious nature of this letter. Díaz y Díaz et al. discusses the several possibilities, including an association with the more famous William, archbishop of Tyre, 1130-90 (51-52). To this William is attributed a song for the services for July 26, Book I chapter 27, in which both Galicia and Spain are mentioned and in which the saint is invoked to give liberty to those who are in captivity and to guard those pilgrims on his roads.

7.   See the introduction, xxxv, lxix n. 43, for information about Diego Gelmírez.

8.   The word *cosmus* from the Greek *kosmos* meaning "world" is found in DuCange.

9.   The use of the first person singular by a pope is most unusual and is one indication that this letter is counterfeit. The author alternates between "I" and "we" various times in this

letter and throughout the CC. It is virtually the rule for popes to use the "we" form at all times, but "we" does not appear until nearly halfway through this letter.

10. The word *scholaris* is found in DuCange and Maigne d'Arnis, as a feminine to indicate "student" and as a masculine to indicate "teacher." Both of these deviate from the classical meaning of "pertaining to school." To avoid potential problems, we translate "young scholar."

11. This passage seems to imply that the author saw other manuscripts relative to St. James. Concern for veracity is a recurring theme for this author. Twice more in this Introductory Letter the author stresses that the material of Book I came from authoritative holy writers, while the other books are based on known historical events as well as on oral reporting. In the miracles of Book II, for example, the author suggests that both written and oral sources were consulted and included.

12. The Latin *schedulis* is clearly chosen for its disparaging connotation, such as the paper that one might use for making a schedule and then throw out when its function was served. This idea is reinforced by the word *hirsutis* to indicate using the "hairy" side of parchment, the idea being "ragged."

13. The focus on the importance of St. James' feast days is set out early in the codex. Later it becomes clear that the author is referring to the material of Book I. This paragraph is a good example of the clear but convoluted Latin in which the author wrote.

14. The miraculous events that occur to the author are echoed in events that occur to others in several miracles in Book II. See Miracles 5, 6, and 14.

15. See Miracle 22.

16. The Latin *tantum m°*, was transcribed by Whitehill 1 as *tantum meo*, "only to my," rather than *tantum modo*, "only." To retain a parallel structure with the preceding sentence and to avoid the notion of "all was lost, only the book remains" which does not carry over well into English, we render it as "still" in this sentence.

17. See Miracles 7, 8, 9, and 10.

18. The Latin is *evasit*, but the *e* appears almost to be a *c* in the manuscript — an obvious scribal slip.

19. Whitehill 1 transcribes the Latin *cremat* as *crematur.*

20. Surviving a fire as a sign of divine blessing is also found in the life of St. Martin of Tours. Gregory of Tours tells that everything but a book containing the *Life of St. Martin* was destroyed by fire in a monastery in Marmoutier, France (*Miracles of St. Martin* 3.42; Van Dam 275-76; PL 71:983-84). The theme of fire appears as a punishment elsewhere in the CC. In Book I chapter 2 and the last chapter of Book V fire punishes those who do not venerate St. James or his pilgrims properly.

It is also worth noting that the author is explicitly tested by two of the four elements — fire and water — with a third — earth — implicit in the wandering through barbarian "lands." Similar themes surface in several of the miracles of Book II, such as captivity in barbarian lands (Miracles 1 and 22) and drowning (Miracles 7 and 8).

21.　The manuscript exhibits a word resembling an *a* followed by three minims and another *a. Aula* seems to be a reasonable transcription, but this conclusion is based on context and process of elimination rather than a clear text. The problem is compounded by its repetition a few lines later with the same lack of scribal clarity.

22.　Compare this description of Christ with the descriptions of St. James in Miracles 9, 19, and 20, especially the last two, which refer to light.

23.　The Latin is *chirotecas* for which Maigne d'Arnis gives "gloves," as does DuCange with a good number of examples.

24.　Whitehill 1 gives *qui,* "Who," for the manuscript's *cui,* "to Him."

25.　Maigne d'Arnis gives this meaning for the Latin *dapifer.*

26.　These mollifying words help avoid an intimation of the medieval custom of "casting down the gauntlet" to provoke a confrontation.

27.　See n. 80 for the use and meaning of *translatio* and "choosing."

28.　This reference to situations encountered by pilgrims on their way to Compostela is an important element, since it links this letter to the collection of materials in Book I and Book II, Miracles 5 and 6.

29.　Whitehill 2 gives *meo,* an intensifier for the idea of "my" already expressed with *proprio,* rather than *in eo,* "in it," meaning "in the book."

30.　These references are a part of the author's desire to underscore the veracity and authority of his own manuscript. The first four are the Latin Fathers of the Catholic Church. The author-compiler of Book I attributes the sermon in chapter 1 and the homily in chapter 8 to Bede; the expositions of chapters 10, 11, and 13 (among others) to St. Jerome; the homily in chapters 14 and 18 to St. Gregory; the sermon in chapter 15 to Sts. Maximus and Leo; part of the material in chapter 20 to Augustine and Gregory. In other words, the author is careful to cite authors whom his knowledgeable public would expect. These attributions are not at all certain. According to Hämel (46), this reference to authorities in the CC is a near copy of the letter of the *Homilary* of Paul the Deacon. The Venerable Bede is the only addition to the list. See the introduction, xxxiv-xxxv and xlvii-lix, for more discussion.

31.   St. Jerome was responsible for the translation of the Bible into Latin (the Vulgate). He died 420; his feast is September 30. See BHL 3866-78 and his works in PL 22-30.

32.   St. Ambrose, bishop of Milan, is famed for his many theological writings. He died in 397; his feast days are April 4 and December 7. See BHL 377-81 and his works in PL 14-17.

33.   St. Augustine, bishop of Hippo, was a voluminous writer and spiritual leader. He died in 430; his feast is August 28. See BHL 785-801 and his works in PL 32-47.

34.   St. Gregory I, the Great, was pope 590-604 and was considered the father of medieval papacy. A portion from his *Dialogues* is quoted in the "Veneranda dies" sermon. His feast date is March 12. See BHL 3636-51 and his works in PL 75-79.

35.   St. Bede the Venerable was an English monk who died 735. See biography and more information in n. 504 below.

36.   St. Maximus was bishop of Turin and wrote many homilies and sermons, none of which is apparently the sermon cited here. He died in 408 (or 423) and his feast day is June 25. See BHL 5858 and his works in PL 57.

37.   St. Leo I, the Great, was pope from 440 to 461. His feast date is April 11. See BHL 4817 and his works in PL 54-56.

38.   The word *excerp[s]isse* lacks the indicated *s* in the manuscript.

39.   DuCange gives this meaning for the unusual Latin *historialiter*, while Maigne d'Arnis gives "in an historical style."

40.   Whitehill 2 transcribes *meis* for *in eis*.

41.   See the introduction, xl, for a discussion of the author's style.

42.   The first use in this letter of the "we" form of self-address, which is standard for popes.

43.   It is interesting that the languages of France and of Rome are understood in this passage. This could be a hint of French authorship, since a French monk might well understand French and Latin, but not German or Greek.

44.   The actual Latin made a contrast between *incisum* and *abscisum*, "cut into" and "cut off," respectively. There may also be a contamination of meaning in the writer's mind through analogy with *ustus* and *inustus* where the first is definitely "burned" while the second is either "burned up" or "not burned." A similar situation exists in English with the words "flammable" and "inflammable." The meaning is that the more easily accessible bread is more readily appreciated.

45.   The Latin *mica* really means "crumb." Here, however, the context is clearly that which it eventually took on in French, "the white or center of the bread." Latin seems never to have quite reached this meaning, although one can find *mica* used

for "white bread" in DuCange and "small bread" in Maigne d'Arnis. This expression offers another clue to French provenance.

46. The Latin *latet* literally means "hidden," but "contained" serves the context better, since the idea of being "hidden" in a "clear" liquid fails to carry over into English.

47. One of the seven liberal arts, which was part of the lower division of the trivium of grammar, logic, and rhetoric. The upper division, or quadrivium, was comprised of arithmetic, geometry, astronomy, and music.

48. A sort of expanded *crismon* is drawn here. It is a rather elaborate version of the chi-rho sign found today. Here, upon close inspection, one can find the forms for all the Greek letters for Christ's name, XRISTOS, in the symbol. The mark reappears after Book II, thus dividing the material of Books I and II from that of Books III, IV, and V. This closely resembles the design of a monogram proposed by Alberic of Monte Cassino, teacher of the preceding pope, Gelasius II, and found in MS 19411, f.62v, of the Bavarian State Library in Munich. The only appreciable difference is the location of the "S" attached at the top rather than at the bottom of the monogram. Alberic uses both the term "crismon" and "monogram" in describing this figure.

49. While *refectorium* was originally used only adjectivally, Maigne d'Arnis gives the word as a noun as well.

50. This refers to the monastic custom of having someone read to the monks while they were eating. Most monastic refectories had an elevated podium where a lector would stand to read to them.

51. Matins was the earliest of the monastic prayer services held each day and was followed later by one or more masses. Concerning the use of music and liturgy of the current collection in Santiago de Compostela at the time, see *Mass*.

52. Whitehill 3 gives *in hoc codex* for *in hoc codice* of the manuscript, thus placing it incorrectly in the nominative case rather than the correct ablative of the text.

53. The Latin *hebdomada* is given as "week" by Maigne d'Arnis; in former times it meant "seven in number."

54. The point of this entire passage is that one must use the correct proper of the mass for the saint whose feast is being celebrated. "Proper" means the prayers such as the introit, gradual, offertory, secret, communion, post-communion and others.

The story about the canon who uses the wrong prayer to celebrate his own pilfering shows to what extremes one may stray if one does not pay attention to official instructions about appropriate prayers.

55.   Whitehill 3 transcribes the *sed*, "however," of the manuscript as *sunt*, "they are."

56.   Cf. the opening of the *Passion* of James found in Book I chapter 9.

57.   Whitehill 3 gives the non-existent *fueret* for the manuscript's *fuer&*, where *fuerunt* or *fuere* would be required by the context.

58.   León is referred to in Miracle 3 also.

59.   This is probably a reference to an antiphonary originally composed in Evora in the mid-tenth century, later copied by Totimundo or Teodemundo of León in the eleventh century. For a fuller discussion of this antiphonary, its antecedents and transmission, see Pérez de Urbel.

60.   Although *responsorium* was originally used this way only in the plural, Maigne d'Arnis gives both the singular and plural for it.

61.   St. Nicholas was a fourth-century bishop of Myra. For more information, see n. 402 below.

62.   Probably the cathedral of Santiago de Compostela.

63.   John of Rudriz "Arcediano" at the end of the eleventh century-beginning of the twelfth (Moralejo et al. 5 and López Ferreiro, *Historia* 1:413, n.1).

64.   Agatha was a virgin martyr of Sicily in the third century; her feast day is February 5. Her legend was a popular one in the Middle Ages, but is probably without much historical foundation. She was a noble Christian courted by a Roman consul. When she rejected him, he punished her as a Christian, including having her breasts cut off. As such she is represented in art, carrying her breasts on a plate. For information on Mary Magdalene and the Virgin Mary, see the introduction, n. 20, and nn. 340 and 398 below.

65.   This is found in Book I chapter 24. The words *mihi autem* are omitted. The source is Psalms 138:17. Biblical references are to the Latin Vulgate. Translations are our own. See introduction, lxi-lxii.

66.   This is a perfect example of the use of the rhetorical figure of *moderatio*, which was carried out by using such expressions as *quasi*, "as if," *quodammodo*, "in some way," *ne dicam*, "lest I say," *ut ita dixerim*, "as I might have said," or here *ut ita dicam*, "as I might say." It is an powerful and clever rhetorical figure, recommended by Alberic of Monte Cassino, father of the dictaminal style, which flourished in the twelfth century. This figure allows the speaker to make a strong statement and then back away from taking full responsibility for actually saying it.

67.   This is found in Book I chapter 23: "Salvator progressus pusillum...."

68.   We have not found the "Ecce ego mitto vos" among the suggested responses in Book I.

69.   This introit is suggested in Book I chapter 26: "Iesus vocavit Iacobum Zebedaei...."

70.   See n. 65.

71.   Maigne d'Arnis gives this translation for the word *Parascheve*.

72.   This appears to be special permission to celebrate in honor of St. James on days other than his feasts, with the caveat that such celebration not take precedence over the major feasts of Christmas, Easter, and the others explicitly set out here. Maigne d'Arnis gives the word *Pentecostes* with the meaning "Pentecost."

73.   The special prayers "proper" to the feast of St. James. See n. 54.

74.   This is the first reference to the attendance of pilgrims at services dedicated to St. James. What follows here clearly deals with pilgrims to the cathedral in Compostela.

75.   The manuscript reads *supplicantum* while we would expect a participle to have the i-stem *-ium* ending.

76.   "Pateant aures misericordiae tuae" is found as a suggested prayer in Book I chapter 27.

77.   Arius was the fourth-century author of the Arian heresy, after whom it was named. He was condemned by several councils with the approbation of Pope Sylvester I (314-35) among others. Sabellius was a third-century heretic, condemned by Pope Calixtus I (217-22).

78.   January 13.

79.   See the introduction, xl-xli, for a consideration of the style and length of this "sermon." The sermon begins on f.74r in the manuscript.

80.   The word "choosing" refers to Jesus' asking James the fisherman to join Him as an apostle (cf. Matthew 4:21-2). The word "*translatio*" is here used in the special sense of the movement of a holy body from one place to another, in this instance from the Holy Land to Galicia. The feast was celebrated on December 30. See the introduction, xxx, for information about the saint's various feast days and dating.

81.   This the not the first sermon in Book I to mention Galicia and Spain or the pilgrimage. For example, the sermon in chapter 2 for July 24, also attributed to Calixtus II, begins with a reference to St. James as the "apostle of Galicia." It also speaks about bad practices along pilgrimage roads, including the route to Compostela.

82.   Note the all-encompassing geographical references beginning with the largest and ending with the most specific: heaven, earth and especially the Iberian Peninsula.

83.   Whitehill 141 transcribes *sollemnitas* as *sollemnitatis*.

84.   Whitehill 141 transcribes *a* as *in*, changing the direction of the movement by 180 degrees.

85.   This is one of many examples of the Latin ablative used after the preposition *in*, when the context would require the accusative. It is a characteristic of this text not to observe carefully the distinction between ablative for "place where" and accusative for "place to which" after the prepositions that normally make this differentiation.

The author of this sermon will speak both literally and figuratively about these two aspects of the saint's legend as he continues the sermon. Book III, the shortest book of the manuscript, contains four chapters, three of which concern the *translatio,* giving two slightly different versions. The information in this sermon is much dryer and more succinct.

86.   Whitehill 142 omits the line *venerandus Apostolus Iacobus electus sit: sonant evan-*. It should be the first line.

87.   Matthew 4:21-22. Biblical references are to the Latin Vulgate.

88.   1 Corinthians 1:27-9. This passage does not refer to Christ's choosing of James. However, our sermon writer uses it as support and amplifies the idea of a lowly fisherman being raised to the rank of apostle, expanding the activity to a figurative and moral commentary.

89.   Sedulius was a fifth-century Christian poet, about whom we know fairly little. He is most famous for his *Carmen Paschale,* a retelling of the Bible in five books, book one devoted to the Old Testament and the other four books concerning the New Testament. This quote is from *Carmen Paschale* 2:220-30 (see PL 19:621-22). Again the CC author presents the theme of unlikely people being chosen as God's servants.

90.   Herod Agrippa I (10 BC to 44 AD) ruled from 41-44. James' martyrdom is recounted in Acts 12:1-3. Commentary on the saint's martyrdom forms a larger part of the sermon for July 25 in Book I chapter 7.

91.   Part of the St. James legend includes a small coterie of disciples. Book III's prologue mentions twelve disciples: three chosen in Jerusalem, the other nine in Galicia. Of those nine, seven returned to Jerusalem with St. James; after his martyrdom they were responsible for conveying his body back to Galicia. In a slightly different version of the *translatio* legend, seven disciples are named in Book III chapter 1, two other names are given in chapter 2. But the story does not detail exactly how the disciples came to the Holy Land so that, ultimately, they were responsible for the transportation of the saint's body back to Galicia.

92.   Whitehill 142 transcribes *translationem* (accusative case) as *translatione* (ablative case).

93. The Latin word *quod* was mis-set in Whitehill 142 as *ponb*. The word was probably composed correctly and then set upside down.

94. Wisdom 4:10.

95. At this point the manuscript contains the interlinear notation *iii~* for "three times." This is not noted in Whitehill 142.

96. Cf. Ecclesiasticus (Sirach) 44:16. Here Enoch has been replaced by James. This is the verse that opens the Calixtine sermon, Book I chapter 19, and also the verse of a vespers reading in Book I chapter 29.

97. Whitehill 143 omits the line: *intellegi, nobis est considerandum. Porro in eius electione de-*. It should be the first line.

98. Perhaps an oblique reference to the biblical story of the man who asked what he should do to enter the kingdom of heaven and whom Jesus told to sell his goods and to follow Him (Mark 10:17-23 and Matthew 19:16-23). The author quotes this story later in the sermon. See p. 28.

99. Paul in 2 Timothy 2:4. The reference directly concerns soldiers of Christ, and as such St. James identifies himself in Miracle 19. The reference to James as "soldier of Christ" is also clearly stated in Book I chapter 7, the sermon for July 25.

100. The manuscript reads *qa* with a barred descender on the *q*, not an expected abbreviation for *quam*, but the context calls for such an accusative ending.

101. The Latin here uses *Orcus*; it is one of several words used for hell in the text, and as such we have translated it. "Orcus" appears seven times as a synonym for hell.

102. In these two paragraphs a number of light/dark and water and shell images are mixed. The devil, named Lucifer or "morning star," fell from heaven, thus falling from light to darkness. In Latin mythology we also find Venus, born of water, arising on the shell, as a name for morning star. The sea, water, and shells are blended in this story line are is Baptism, the *translatio* over water, and the shell as a badge of the pilgrim of St. James.

103. Here "good" is used in the sense of "a good life" as opposed to "an evil" or "a sinful" life. "Harshness" refers to the suffering related to the human condition.

104. Matthew 11:28-29.

105. Wisdom 10:17.

106. Acts 14:21. Here Paul is preaching to his disciples after his having been stoned in Lystra.

107. See the illustration, p. lxxiii, of the Romanesque sculpture on a church portal of a huge monster eating a human. For a description of the visual representations of the devil's jaws as the mouth of hell, see Mâle, 355-89.

108. Whitehill omits the line *ditet, miraculis perlustret, sedesque in caelesti patria*. It should be the first line of his page 144.

109. This refers to the saint's feast on July 25.

110. The reference is to the time when people will be in heaven.

111. The Latin is *peculialiter* for *peculiariter* — a probable scribal slip of the pen.

112. The manuscript reads *pereius* with the barred descender indicating the *per* prefix. Whitehill 144 corrects it to *peius*.

113. Passages open to such interpretation can be found in Matthew 13:55, Mark 6:3, and Galatians 1:19. The Latin *quod abest*, probably does not mean "which is not there," the literal translation, but that "it is not so" in the sense that such an interpretation is not there.

114. Whitehill transcribes *a* as *in* before the word Jerusalem. Neither the manuscript nor the context indicates this reading.

115. The Latin *petronus* is found only with the meaning "pile of rock" (cf. Maigne d'Arnis and DuCange). Here the context would point to a contamination with the vulgar usage of the *on* suffix/infix to indicate "large stone."

116. The Latin is *Iopen*. The modern English for this is Joffa or Joppa. It was at the location of the modern Tel Aviv.

117. Note the change from the "we" discourse to "I."

118. For a discussion of these stones, the development of the Santiago cult from an ancient stone cult, and the megalithic heritage of the Galician region, see Peake.

119. The manuscript originally read *celebratam* but was corrected by dotting under the final *-m*; Whitehill 144 transcribes the word with the *-m*.

120. This could be a reference to the stone now housed under the altar of the parochial church in Padrón, a village only a few kilometers up river from Iria. See illustration, p. vi.

121. This scene is illustrated in the twelfth-century sculpture of the lady holding a skull from the Compostela Cathedral Platerías Portal.

An infortuitous combination of factors leads to an ambiguity in this and the next paragraph's passages in Latin: e.g., lack of capitalization to indicate lord/Lord; a lack of the need for pronouns in Latin; *dormienti* has third declension endings, which do not indicate gender. The Moralejo et al. translation interprets "lord" as a reference to Jesus Christ's coming to the cathedral (193). Neither this legend nor the following one about cleansing and the use of the stick as an example have been found in other St. James' lore.

122. There is no Latin word *scortice*. In all likelihood this is a prothetic *s*- attached to *cortice*. In the context of the story of a "woman who deserves punishment," it is difficult to avoid

mentioning possible confusion with and thus influence of such words as *scortum*, "harlot," and *scortari*, "to whore."

123. The author resumes the "we" discourse. The sermon will move between "I" and "we" several more times.

124. See the introduction, pp. xxxiv-xxxvi and lxviii, n. 42, about the naming of the manuscript.

125. The miracles' author-compiler repeats this concern in the preface of Book II. See p. 57 and n. 479.

126. Psalms 150:1.

127. Cf. Matthew 17:1-8, Mark 9:1-7, and Luke 9:28-36. Although the name of the mountain is not given in the Gospels, it was held in the Middle Ages to be Mount Tabor.

128. Cf. Exodus 19:20.

129. Cf. Genesis 18:1.

130. Cf. Genesis 28:19.

131. The Latin is slightly ambiguous. Close reading of the text leads us to believe that the "he" and "him" in this passage refer to St. James.

132. Psalms 111:7.

133. Cf. Matthew 25:14-30. This is a reference to the parable of the talents, in which one servant brought back to his master double the amount of money that had been allotted him while another servant returned with only the talent itself. The Latin reads literally "the talent doubled."

134. Matthew 25:23.

135. Cf. Osee 14:6. Here *Israel* has been replace by *Iustus*. The second clause is of unknown origin.

136. Cf. 2 Corinthians 2:14-15. Paul is not referring specifically to St. James.

137. The Latin *quia* actually implies a more causal relationship than the "just as" might indicate.

138. DuCange gives "teacher" as a possibility for the Latin *didasculus*, while Maigne d'Arnis gives only *doctissimus* or "most learned." Both of these differ from the standard meaning of "pertaining to instruction."

139. Dioscorides, *Herbal*, 3:116. Dioscorides' first-century Greek herbal was popular throughout the Middle Ages. It was translated and produced in many languages and in many places. For example, the manuscript was translated into Arabic directly from a Greek manuscript in 948 in Córdoba. Another manuscript drafted c. 1100 is now in Rome (Vatican GR 284). A modern English edition is available of Goodyear's seventeenth-century translation.

Goodyear's version indicates that the sap should be mixed with *"acetum,"* which is a sour or vinegar-based substance; and that the root should be mixed with *"rosaceum,"* which we interpret to be a member of the rose family.

140. See, for example, Miracle 2.

141. See Miracle 17.

142. Whitehill 147 transcribes *idem,* "the same thing," as *id est,* "that is to say."

143. The source of this quote is unknown.

144. Psalms 91:13.

145. See Dante's *La vita nuova* 40: "If they [pilgrims] cross the sea they are called 'palmers,' because they frequently bring back palm leaves. Those who go to the church in Galicia are called 'pilgrims,' for James' tomb is farther from his native land than that of any other apostle. 'Romers' designates those who go to Rome...." [Translated by David M. Gitlitz.]

146. Psalms 83:8.

147. Constructed with the rhetorical device of *gradatio, climax,* or "verbal staircase," with the last word of one element becoming the first word of the next. It is especially well done here where the destination of the "climax" is paradise.

148. The Latin *spatulis* normally would be either a spatula or an instrument for stirring. DuCange however gives "sword" as a possible meaning.

149. Since the palm is often a symbol for martyrdom in religious iconography, this is clearly a reference to the saint's martyrdom by orders of Herod Agrippa, but Herod serves also as a metaphor for the non-believers.

150. The sermon writer now begins to turn his thoughts toward the pilgrimage and its virtues. Note the differentiation between Spain and Galicia. This is another instance of light imagery, which is found elsewhere, such as in Miracle 20.

151. Only six of the twenty-two miracles in Book II occur within the cathedral at Santiago. This is the first of this sermon's several lists of miracles that the saint performs.

152. No miracles of this nature occur in the cathedral in Book II.

153. Cf. Miracle 21.

154. No miracles of this nature occur in the cathedral in Book II.

155. Cf. Miracle 3.

156. This category encompasses all of the miracles that take place in the cathedral.

157. Cf. Miracle 2.

158. Cf. Miracle 16.

159. This list of seventy-four peoples contains a mixture of Christians and non-Christians, of peoples in Europe, Africa, and Asia. A general order of west to east apparently governs the list overall. But a lack of geographical pattern prevails within the list: the author skips among sites in Asia, Asia Minor, east and

west Africa, northern and southern Europe. The author mentions places as far north as Norway, as far south as Ethiopia, east to India, and west in Europe to Ireland and in Africa to Mauritania.

When mentioning sites in modern Italy, the author names six different regional groups; for France, nine groups; for Germany, three; for the British Isles, four. However, for the Iberian Peninsula he names only "Iberians," "Basques," and "Navarrese," apparently unfamiliar with the Christian kingdoms such as Aragón and Castile. Similarly, the author enumerates several African sites and Moslem groups, but does not mention any of the *taifas,* or Saracen groups, of al-Andalus. Some of the eastern groups mentioned are peoples to whom St. Paul preached: Ephesians, Sardians, Galatians, Philippians.

Chapter 7 of Book I (for July 25) also refers specifically to large numbers of people rushing to the saint's tomb in Galicia. They go, having heard about the "innumerable" miracles that the saint has performed and they travel repenting their sins. There is no enumeration of individual peoples or nations, however. Even today it is quite normal to see large national groups of pilgrims visiting Lourdes, France, displaying banners that tell their origin. See illustration, p. lxxvi.

160. The Latin *Vasconi* would normally indicate the Basques; however, they are mentioned below with the word *Bascli.* This may refer to the Gascons living to the north of the Pyrenees.

161. The Latin *Baioari* was transcribed by Whitehill 148 as *Baleari.* Following the pattern of the groupings found here, this might make sense, since the other likely solution would be "Bavarians." Inhabitants of Bayonne or Bayeux are other possibilities.

162. The Navarrese are the only people to be singled out with an adjective. The author of this sermon had a similar opinion about the Navarrese as did the author of Book V, the Pilgrim's Guide, who describes them as liars and thieves (Melczer 88-89).

The division into chapters of the Pilgrim's Guide were those of the twelfth-century author. Melczer's translation of the Pilgrim's Guide was the first translation into English and is the only one available in English at this time. His copious notes, gazetteer, and hagiographic register are a compendium of useful information. The Guide itself is rather short, comprising pages 83-133, a mere fifty pages in Melczer's 345-page book.

What was in the 1940s, 1950s, and 1960s primarily a scholarly revival of attention to the pilgrimage road contributed to the burgeoning interest in the road as also a road to walk. This interest was encouraged by the activities of dedicated people such as Elías Valiña Sampedro in the tiny village of Cebreiro. As a result, the bibliography of the pilgrimage route has been enriched with abundant numbers of guides to the road (or roads) to Compostela: guides for hikers and bikers, many taking their basic format not only from the logical geographical structure, but also from the divisions found in the twelfth-century LSJ Guide. Now there are guides for various routes in their entirety as well as guides for specific sections of the trek. Valiña's first guide, for example, published in 1971, was a mere ninety-six pages. It was republished, greatly expanded to 180 pages, in 1985 and has become one of the three or four basic guides to the route. Other guides, like that of Millán Bravo Lozano, follow a similar format.

163. An unidentified group, perhaps from the area of the Garonne.

164. An unidentified group, possibly the Goths of eastern France.

165. It is not certain if the author intends Angles or English; Bretons or British.

166. From the modern Savoy. This area is mentioned again in Miracle 13. See n. 613 below.

167. Originally the Roman province north of the Danube River, presently Romania. But, according to Grabois (*Encyclopedia* 253), this nomenclature was "erroneously used during the Middle Ages to designate Denmark and other Scandinavian provinces" and by the twelfth century the term "Dacia" included all of Scandinavia. Dacia is referred to once again in this sermon to talk about the various routes to the saint's tomb, in the last paragraph, and in the opening letter to Book II.

168. Norwegians is one possibility for the Latin *Noroequi*; another possibility is Noricans, who lived between the Alps and the Danube.

169. The Latin is *Ioranti*; possibly from the noun *Hierapolis* or the modern Königsberg or Kaliningrad.

170. The portion "Greeks, Armenians, Dacians, Norwegians, Russians, Prussians, Nubians" was added in the margin.

171. From Sardis, the ancient capital of Lydia.

172. The Latin is *Esclavoni*; because of the specificity of this list, "Slovenians" from the area of modern Croatia and Slovenia, seems more likely than the more generic "Slavs."

173. The Latin *Mauri* could indicate Mauritanians, sometimes used in synecdoche for Africans, or, less likely in this context, Moors, depending on the author's intentions.

174. The text reads *peregrinantum* rather than the more usual *perigrinantium*; here and elsewhere the *-ium* ending is replaced with simply *-um*, apparently indiscriminately.

175. A psaltery is a kind of stringed instrument. For information on medieval musical instruments and their depiction on

the Pórtico de la Gloria, see the works by López-Caló and Villanueva and the video produced by Caldwell and Enrico.

176. Psalms 18:4.

177. The Latin of the manuscript is *assidue.* It could be used to mean either "assiduous vigils" or "heard assiduously."

178. Cf. Miracle 18, in which the count of Saint-Gilles is denied permission to stay the night in the cathedral in vigil since the oratory doors are locked. This may point to different policies at different times.

179. At this time and in this context, it is unlikely that the word *praesul* is used in its original sense of "dancer." Maigne d'Arnis gives "bishop" as a translation.

180. The word *sua,* "their things," is added interlinearly.

181. See Miracles 14 and 22.

182. This use of *copia,* or saying things in an abundance of different ways, is typical of an age dominated by the dictaminal writers.

183. John 15:16.

184. Source for this quote is unknown. It may be an attempt to complete the apparent aposiopesis of the preceding statement.

185. The text here is ambiguous. The "passion" may be that of St. James or that of Jesus Christ. By using standard English capitalization we have opted for meaning the passion of Jesus Christ.

186. John 20:23.

187. *Iacobi* is added interlinearly.

188. The manuscript reads *postes* for *postea*; Whitehill 150 corrects it.

189. Whitehill 150 transcribes *suffragia* (accusative case) as *suffragiis* (ablative case).

190. See Table 3, pp. liv-lv, and the maps, pp. lxxiv-lxxv. The miracles took place over a large area and are well distributed geographically: Jerusalem, at sea, on the Iberian Peninsula, the cathedral, France, and Italy. Eleven miracles occur on route to Compostela or in Compostela itself. This list of miracles continues the enumeration begun three (long) paragraphs earlier.

191. See Miracles 9, 12, 13, and 21.

192. See Miracles 1, 11, 14, 20, and 22.

193. Whitehill 150 has *fecnnditatem,* where the first *u* was probably set upside down producing two *n*'s.

194. See Miracle 3.

195. The Latin, *liberatio,* "release" or "acquittal," used here in the sense of delivery of birth. Such a miracle does not occur in the Book II collection.

196. See Miracles 7, 8, 9, and 10.

197. The Latin *reditum* indicates the fact but not the manner of the return. The simple word "return" does not, however, ring sufficient for English. See Miracles 5, 6, and 17.

198. See Miracle 6.

199. See Miracles 3 and 5, and especially 16 and 17.

200. See Miracles 6 and 16.

201. See especially Miracle 1, as well as 11, 14, and 20.

202. See Miracles 11, 14, and 20.

203. Such a miracle is not found in the collection.

204. See Miracle 9; possibly also Miracles 7, 8, and 10.

205. Possibly Miracles 7, 8, and 10.

206. See introduction, n. 78, and n. 20 above about fire and miracles.

207. See Miracles 5 and 6.

208. See Miracles 2, 3, 18, and 20, and possibly 13 and 15.

209. This situation is common to most of the Book II miracles, although there is no instance of a pagan being saved.

210. Here the author addresses the issue of location of miracles directly.

211. The word *sine,* "without," is added interlinearly.

212. The Latin *Veritas* is used for the Bible, God, or as here, Christ.

213. John 16:7.

214. Passage from the *Dialogues* of St. Gregory I, the Great, 2.38 (PL 66:204). For brief information on St. Gregory, see n. 34.

215. This attempt at inclusion of the eastern peoples is somewhat ironic, following a paragraph in which there is reference to the Holy Spirit proceeding from the Father *et Filio,* "and the Son." Although normally worded with the alternate *Filioque* form, the notion of the Holy Spirit proceeding from both the Father and the Son was one of the causes of the East-West schism.

216. This poem, somewhat modified as noted here, is found in Venantius Fortunatus, *Miscellanea,* 10:7-12 (PL 88:332). It was written to Childebert the king and Brunhilda the queen about St. Martin of Tours. The poet is a favored source for Calixtus, who quotes from his works in many of the other Book I sermons and exhortations, for example, in chapters 2, 6 (for the mass of July 25), and 30, the last the mass for the saint's December 30 feast day. He is also quoted in the Turpin Chronicle (Book IV chapter 21). St. Venantius Fortunatus lived from c. 540 to 600. He was born in northern Italy and studied at Milan and Ravenna. He befriended the Merovingian kings of France and ultimately became the bishop of Poitiers in 599. His religious works in prose and poetry, including several saints' lives and an exposition of the Catholic faith, are found in PL 88:59-597.

See Moralejo Laso for further insights into the importance of Fortunatus' works in the CC.

217. Venantius' verb *pertendit* has been changed to *protendit*, but without a significant change in meaning.

218. Line 10 in Venantius reads, "It is the honor of Martin by which the world holds these places."

219. Line 12 in Venantius reads, "That he may be a surety for all, he has canvassed the route of the world."

220. The author begins to focus on the specific activities of pilgrimage, beginning with the symbolic value of the activity and its physical symbols before turning to the biblical origin of pilgrimage.

221. The Latin *relevatio* is not used here with its standard meaning of "relief" or "lightening," but in the sense of "restitution" or "amelioration" as found in Maigne d'Arnis.

222. The word *census* seems to have a special meaning in this sermon: one's listing or inventory of goods. It appears that it may also indicate an official list of assets, which could be used as a kind of collateral in times of need. We have rendered it with "inventory" with this in mind. See n. 266 for other legal concerns.

223. The word *limina*, "threshold," or *ad limina*, literally "to the threshold," are recurring synecdoches for the basilica of St. James at Compostela and to making the pilgrimage. Here it is used as well for the shrines of other saints.

224. Maigne d'Arnis gives *pera* as "purse." See illustration, p. 169.

225. Whitehill 152 transcribes *merearis* as *mearis,* or "deserve" as "go."

226. The common Latin prayer ending *per omnia saecula saeculorum,* literally "through all the ages of ages," alternates in the CC with *infinita saecula saeculorum.* We render these phrases into English with "world without end." A third, simpler, form *in saecula saeculorum,* is also used, and we translate it with the familiar English "for ever and ever."

227. The blessing for the staff and purse is common to medieval Catholic liturgy. For examples and analyses, see Brundage and Romano Rocha. For the text of the blessing and the pilgrimage mass in English, see Legg.

228. According to Maigne d'Arnis, *scarcella* is Latin for "purse." The modern Italian for the same word is *scarsella.*

229. Maigne d'Arnis gives *sportella* as meaning *châsse* (French), or "reliquary." We have not found it as a Provençal word. There is also an Old French word *esport* meaning "basket."

230. The word *ysquirpa* is related to the ancestor of the modern French *écharpe,* "scarf," and *escarcelle,* "purse."

231. The Latin is *orator* or "the one praying."

232. For an example of such a false apparition, see Miracle 17. The banner of the Holy Trinity is reminiscent of the "Pauline armor" of Ephesians 6:13-17.

233. The Latin term is *crusillas*. It is the same word used in the Pilgrim's Guide (Book V chapter 9) to describe the mementos of the Santiago pilgrims. In Book II's Miracle 12, a pilgrim's shell is also referred to as *crusillam*. One finds the Old French word *crusilles* with the same meaning. See Hohler, "Badge," about the scallop as pilgrimage symbol. See nn. 145 and 149 about the palm.

234. The modern Galician *vieira*. See Melczer (58) and Rees for discussions of this type of mollusk.

235. We have not found this word.

236. Whitehill 153 transcribes *Deum* (accusative case) as *Deus* (nominative case).

237. Cf. Matthew 22:37-39, Mark 12:29-31, and Luke 10:27.

238. The *q* of *quia* has three dots under it in the manuscript, although the *q* is necessary here. When it was impossible to make an actual erasure, scribes ordinarily indicated a deletion by placing dots under the letter or letters to be disregarded.

This sentence, set within the discussion of the physical symbols of pilgrimage, begins a new motif, that of the duties of the pilgrim and the faulty actions he should avoid as he travels.

239. The text reads *veram*, giving the name of the fish, rather than the word "shell."

240. The word *es*, "you have," is added interlinearly.

241. Whitehill 154 transcribes the word *es* as *est*, causing a change in person.

242. The next four paragraphs give a good synopsis of the theological bases for pilgrimage and allude to the various kinds of pilgrimage, from the exile of Adam to the penitential pilgrimage imposed by one's priest. See the introduction, xxvii-xxix.

243. See Miracle 17.

244. Genesis 12:1.

245. The story is found in Genesis 25-35.

246. This is the first direct reference to the earthly evils that await the pilgrim on the road to Santiago, a theme to which the author has alluded in the Introductory Letter and which is exemplified in Miracles 5 and 6. After the author concludes his thought about the bad ways to go on pilgrimage, he will discuss extensively the various kinds of fraud and travails along the route, "what shall I say about evil innkeepers...?" (34).

247. Luke 24:18. Christ as the Emmaus pilgrim is a fairly popular theme in the Middle Ages. He is represented in a twelfth-century sculpture in the cloister at the monastery of Silos, with a scallop shell as well on his purse. See illustration, p. lxxviii.

248. Whitehill 155 transcribes *pascit,* "feeds," as *pascitur,* "is fed."

249. Psalms 40:2.

250. Matthew 10:9-10. See also Luke 9:3. There is an irony evident here between the admonition of the Gospel and the ceremony of bestowing on the pilgrim exactly what was admonished against in that Gospel. The author strives to displace the apparent irony in stressing charity. This is a controversial point in later medieval literature. For example, Guillaume de Deguileville discusses this irony in his *Le pèlerinage de la vie humaine,* c. 1330.

251. Whitehill 156 transcribes *ait,* "he says," as *sit,* "he may be."

252. Matthew 19:21; also Mark 10:21 and Luke 18:22.

253. The manuscript originally read *damnentur* (plural) but was corrected to *damnetur* (singular) by dotting under the line. This correction was not respected by Whitehill 156.

254. See Acts 5:1-11.

255. Maigne d'Arnis gives *trosellus* as a synonym for *fasciculus,* "small bundle."

256. The Latin is *felicitatum,* "of happinesses." This figurative use does not carry well into English.

257. The Latin is *vestimentis duplicibus* in reference to Christ's injunction about taking a second tunic, mentioned above. Cf. Matthew 10:9-10.

258. Whitehill 156 transcribes *deliciosis* (ablative or dative case) for *deliciosos* (accusative case).

259. The first references to Rome and Jerusalem as pilgrimage centers vying in importance with Compostela. Rome was an important pilgrimage center by the fourth century. Guides that spoke to both classical and Christian monuments existed from the third century, and at least one, *The Marvels of Rome,* was written in the twelfth century. Pilgrims went to revere St. Paul in S. Paolo fuori le mura and the martyrs in the catacombs and to view the many relics in the churches, but St. Peter and the Vatican, the basilica covering his grave, were most important. Since it was also the center of church business as well as the center of classical history, motives for visiting Rome were often multiple, including pilgrimages to request special penance from the pope for a committed sin. The pilgrimage to Rome was apparently so popular that it soon degenerated into worldly celebrations, something which this sermon writer must have known in order to make this comparison. See Sumption and Stopani.

260. This section of the sermon refers to various pilgrimage centers in France, all three mentioned in Book V as sites to visit. Saint-Gilles was probably the most important pilgrimage center on the southern route to Compostela. The saint or his town

are mentioned six times in this sermon, indicative of their popularity. Although there is a tenth-century *vita,* giving much of the legend, it is probably a false document. The legend recounts that Giles (feast day Sept. 1) came to Marseilles to be a hermit. He convinced a king of the Goths, named either Wamba or Flavius, to build an abbey, located in the department of Gard in Provence. He died c. 725. Two strong motives for the forged documents were to free the abbey and its monks from control by the bishop of Nîmes and to counteract the strong attraction of Compostela and Rome to pilgrims. The cult of St. Giles enjoyed a considerable group of followers and several miracles are told, one similar to Book II Miracle 2. Giles is the patron of cripples, lepers, nursing mothers, and blacksmiths. In Book V, the Pilgrim's Guide, the author knows no end of praise of this saint. In chapter 8 we are told about various miracles of St. Giles, given a succinct *vita,* and subjected to an item-by-item description of the sumptuous casket (which has disappeared). Information can be found in AASS, Sept. 1:284-304, the *Liber miraculorum S. Aegidii* in MGH 12:316-23, the *Analecta Bollandiana* 9:393-422, BHL 93-98; see also the *New Catholic Encyclopedia.* There are also several modern studies about this saint.

261. St. William, duke and later monk, died in 812. His feast date is May 28. He is mentioned only once in this sermon. Like St. Giles, he is listed in the Pilgrim's Guide, Book V chapter 8 (Melczer 102-3) as a saint meriting a visit (his remains are in Toulouse, on the same route as Saint-Gilles), but there is nearly no information about him. See BHL 8916-18.

262. St. Leonard is referred to only once more in this sermon, although he apparently was a popular saint in France during the Middle Ages. His feast date is November 6. His eleventh-century *vita* is probably false, but legend has it that he was a hermit and founded a monastery in the diocese of Limoges at Noblat (or Noblac), on the Vézelay route to Compostela. There is no trace of a cult of St. Leonard prior to the eleventh century. His popularity may be due to the fact that Bohemond of Antioch credited to this saint his release from a Moslem prison in 1103 (Farmer 244). He is the patron of pregnant women, captives and prisoners of war: the last similar to the cult of St. James. The Pilgrim's Guide, Book V chapter 8 (Melczer 105-7) also talks about the importance of St. Leonard, in considerably more detail than for St. William. There is a brief *vita,* concentrating on the privations in his life as a hermit and a long passage on the true location of his remains, with an interesting description of *furta sacra.* The writer is impressed with the miracles that Leonard works and informs us that many, many shackles and chains from former prisoners — thankful pilgrims — decorate

his walls. The standard references are found in AASS, Nov. 3:139-209, *Analecta Bollandiana* 21 (1912):24-44, and BHL 4862-79.

263. Whitehill 157 transcribes *caelibe* (ablative case) for *caelibem* (accusative case).

264. While the Latin *census* actually implies inventory, as previously mentioned (n. 222), the term simply would not work here in English, and "goods" was chosen to fit the context.

265. The Latin *adripere* is literally to "seize upon," here used to express the immediacy with which the pilgrim might take up a pilgrimage.

266. Here the sermon writer enumerates the duties of the pilgrim before beginning the journey. Many of the legal concerns were codified in the thirteenth century in Title 24 of the First Partida of the Spanish legal code, *Las siete partidas*, patronized by Alfonso X el Sabio (1221-84), king of Castile and León. This code defines "pilgrims" and regulates their treatment and the treatment of their estates. See Wohlhaupter for specific cases regarding this legislature. For juridical concerns outside of Spain, see Garrison.

267. Whitehill 157 transcribes *fugit,* "he flees," as *fugat,* "he chases."

268. Whitehill 157 transcribes *festivis,* "feast," as *festius,* "more festively."

269. Psalms 118:54.

270. See n. 260.

271. We interpret the manuscript's *castellum novum* as a common noun, as did Whitehill 158. Although there are over a dozen places called Châteauneuf with various spellings, none is sufficiently close to Saint-Gilles to warrant being a reference point. Périgueux is also quite distant from the named site.

272. The source of this aphorism has not been found.

273. The source of this aphorism has not been found.

274. 1 Corinthians 3:3.

275. Ephesians 4:26 and Psalms 4:5.

276. Ephesians 4:26-27.

277. See Acts 15:36-40.

278. Mark 10:44. See also Mark 9:34 and Matthew 20:26. Ironically, it is James and his brother John, the sons of Zebedee, who wished to appear greater by asking to sit on Jesus' left and right when He ascends to the kingdom of heaven.

279. Ecclesiasticus 32:1. Not an exact quote.

280. While the Latin *districtio* usually means "hindrance," Maigne d'Arnis gives "judgment" as a possibility.

281. The source of this aphorism has not been found.

282. Whitehill 159 transcribes *fortem* (accusative case) as *forte* (ablative case).

283. The source of this aphorism has not been found.

284. Cf. the story in Genesis 9:20-27, where Noah becomes drunk and naked and is observed and mocked by his sons. Whitehill 159 transcribes this as *verenda suam*; however, the *m* seems to have been deleted in the manuscript by dotting under the line. The literal meaning is "his things to be feared." However, "his shame" seems to be the idea from the context of the biblical story.

285. Isaiah 5:22.

286. Isaiah 5:11-12.

287. Whitehill 159 transcribes *omnes* (plural) as *omnis* (singular).

288. Joel 1:5.

289. Ecclesiasticus 19:2.

290. Ephesians 5:18.

291. Whitehill 159 adds *sed culpa vini*, "but the fault of the wine," before continuing on with *sed culpa bibentis*, "but the fault of the one drinking."

292. Proverbs 23:31-32. The word *regulus* means "basilisk," but its description in the twelfth-century bestiary does not mention the animal's bite, only its smell, hiss, and stare, all of which can kill (White 168-69). Rowland (28) refers to Pliny's description of the death of a horseman, caused by the basilisk's venom having traveled up the man's spear and killed the horse and the rider. Later descriptions and beliefs of the basilisk modified with time until it was confused with the cockatrice. It may be that the writer wished to refer to the adder instead, since authorities like Aelian asserted that the adder's poison penetrated the body, although the Latin term would then be *vipera*.

293. Whitehill 159 fails to transcribe the word *momordit*, "has bitten."

294. See Romans 13:13.

295. The title nearest to the one referred to here is *El Libro de los doze sabios o Tractado de la nobleza y lealtad*, but it dates from 1237, commissioned by Ferdinand III of Castile. No corresponding passage was found in that work. Neither has the "Basil" mentioned here been located in this work or others of its type.

296. Venus, whose Greek counterpart was Aphrodite, was the goddess of love.

297. Bacchus, whose Greek counterpart was Dionysus, was the god of wine and revelry.

298. Cupid, whose Greek counterpart was Eros, was the son of Venus and is usually represented as holding a bow and arrow, which he is thought to shoot into the hearts of humans to provoke desire. *Cupido* in Latin means "desire."

299. The Latin *saepe ciet* was given as one word *sepeciet* in Whitehill 160.

300. The town that was the epicenter of the Trojan War between the Greeks and the Trojans.

301. A god associated with, if not another name for, Dionysus or Bacchus.

302. A mythological people who dwelled in the mountains of Thessaly.

303. Bacchus' surname.

304. The concerns expressed by the LSJ author about fair treatment and fair pricing are echoed in Compostela legal codes for the same century. The *Historia compostellana* lists the decrees of Diego II from the 1113 council meeting. They include attention to crimes, robbery, disposal of goods of a deceased person, and the safety of merchants and pilgrims (Book I chapter 96). Twenty years later, a decree dated 1133 established guidelines regulating a variety of details of the economic life of the city of Compostela. The decree set prices for bread, wine, and cider; governed the sale of spices, fish, and meat; decreed that false coins and weights were prohibited to many including innkeepers and moneychangers (*Historia compostellana* Book III chapter 33) See Stokstad and Biggs for discussions and English translations of parts of parts of these documents.

305. The manuscript reads *esset*. We interpret it as the plural *essent* by context.

306. *Sicera* is Latin for both alcoholic cider and liquor in general. If it means "cider" here it shows the author's acquaintance with an Iberian drink.

307. Whitehill 160 transcribes *mutatum*, "changed," as *matutum* (non-existent word).

308. While *triduanam* exists in standard Latin for "three days," *biduanam* was not found in standard Latin, although DuCange and Maigne d'Arnis both give it as meaning "a fast of two days."

309. We have not located the term *marsicias*.

310. Isaiah 32:7. An exact quote, but one in which the subject in the biblical verse is knaves, not innkeepers.

311. The Latin *tunella* is not found in Maigne d'Arnis and DuCange; the meaning is obvious: a "small barrel" for wine, from *tunna* plus the diminutive ending.

312. The Latin *pacca* was not found. Its meaning is clear from the context, and it is probably related etymologically to the modern verbs *pagar* in Spanish and *payer* in French, which come ultimately from the Latin *pacare*, "to pacify" by handing over money.

While the values of medieval coins cannot be converted exactly into comparable modern money equivalents, contemporary documents can reveal their relative values. Stokstad's study of the twelfth-century documents relating to life in Compostela allowed an insight into the financial organization of the economy. Her conclusions (106) are that "the basic unit of money...was the silver mark" equivalent to two-thirds of a pound of silver. "The mark was divided into [twenty] sueldos to the pound of silver. The sueldo...consisted of twelve dinarios or ten nummo."

313. The Latin *nummus* means "coin." However, its use in the next few lines requires translation as a specific coin of an arbitrary value, here "farthing," to fit the context of the passage. It is difficult to pin down the specific value of this or the various other medieval coins.

314. The obolus was a coin of very small value in the Middle Ages.

315. We have not found the Latin word *gurlum*. The translation is hypothesized from the context. Moralejo et al. (215) suggests this translation.

316. Whitehill 161 transcribes *in quo,* "in what," as *iniquo,* "iniquitous."

317. The word *ductileus* is not found at all in Maigne d'Arnis, and is found only as an adjective in DuCange, and even there not with this meaning. We translate by context.

318. The word *cafhit* is not found as such, but Maigne d'Arnis gives the forms *caffium, caficium,* and *cafisa* as measures.

319. The manuscript has *arroa,* but probably should be *arroba,* which is a Spanish term (from the Arabic) for a dry weight measure of about twenty-five pounds.

320. The solidus, which is related to such words as the English "soldier" and the Spanish "sueldo," was a coin, authorized by Charlemagne to be worth 12 *denarii,* which has its origin in the idea of a solid or compact method of carrying coins. It was originally "solid gold" fit to be carried by a "soldier."

321. Whitehill 161 transcribes *praesaepiis* (ablative case) as *praesaepii* (nominative or genitive case).

322. Minean Bridge or Portomarín (*Pons Mineae*), in Lugo in Galicia, was an important site for pilgrims: a Roman bridge crossed the Miño River there. The bridge was destroyed in the early twelfth century in the battles between Alfonso I el Batallador and his wife Urraca, but was reconstructed in 1120. It is mentioned in Book V chapters 5 and 6. The original town was flooded during the construction of the Belesar Dam between 1956 and 1962.

Between Palas del Rey (Pallatium in this sermon, Pallatium Regis in the Pilgrim's Guide Book V chapters 2 and 3), in Lugo in Galicia, and Santiago there are approximately 63 kilometers. It lies one day's walk west of Portomarín, approximately twenty-three kilometers.

323. The Latin *ab omnibus depraedandae nasibusque verecundandae,* literally means "to be plundered by all and to be shamed with their noses." In actuality it probably indicates that

their noses would be disfigured as a sign of punishment that they would have to bear. A similar punishment is mentioned in the *Chançun de Willame*. Whitehill 161 transcribes it *nasibusque* as *nasibu-que*, leaving out the -s-.

324. This paragraph is the only place in the sermon that deals with women, and they all epitomize aspects of evil and deceit. It is interesting to note that women were apparently innkeepers, or at least in charge of various activities at inns. Also note that the prostitutes mentioned are located at specific sites.

325. This was literally "with a tricky platter"; in a sort of metonymy; in other words he uses the free meal or platter as an inducement to buy the overpriced candles.

326. That is, four solidi.

327. The text "or cooked or boiled broadbeans" is interlinear.

328. See earlier in this sermon (pp. 12-13) for examples of the false tales.

329. Whitehill 162 transcribes *huc* as *hu.*

330. Barbadello, also mentioned in the Pilgrim's Guide Book V chapter 3 (Melczer 87), is in the province of Lugo and has a church named for the saint. It is located on the road between Sarria (not mentioned in the Pilgrim's Guide) and Portomarín, approximately 5 kilometers west of Sarria. That would make it approximately four days' walk from Compostela.

331. Triacastela, which lies east of the villages of Barbadello, Sarria, and Portomarín, also has a church named for the saint. It is the beginning point of the twelfth travel "stage" (Palas del Rey is the ending point of that stage) mentioned in the Pilgrim's Guide. That stage contains approximately 58 kilometers. Triacastela is approximately 17 kilometers east of Sarria. It is an old city, having a monastery dedicated to Sts. Peter and Paul that dates from about the middle of the ninth century. In 922 Ordoño II donated this monastery to the Compostela church. Melczer mentions that there are remains of "various" hospitals and of a pilgrim prison, among other things (300-301). See illustration, p. xx.

332. Whitehill 162 transcribes *invenerit* as *tinvenerit*, a non-existent word.

333. Whitehill 162 transcribes *salutavit,* "he greeted," as *salutaverit,* "he may have" or "will have greeted."

334. The mark was another coin, which is the etymological ancestor of the modern Deutsche Mark.

335. Whitehill 163 transcribes *adivendendum,* for the manuscript *ad vendendum.* Here the *i* of the manuscript had been deleted by dotting under the line.

336. Maigne d'Arnis gives *reva* as "toll." Here it obviously means "unjust commission" or "cut."

337. Maigne d'Arnis gives us *passum* as yet another word for "toll." It is not difficult to see how in the broader sense the idea of a toll, as money that is charged to someone for a service, could be interpreted as a commission. The present context indicates that a particular amount of money is intended.

338. The sermon writer unites these saints again later in the sermon: the Mother of Christ, two apostles, and three very popular French saints. It might be better to say along the "routes" to St. James, because these saints' altars span various roads in France. Leonard and Mary Magdalene are along the Vézelay route (*via lemovicense*); Giles and William shared the Toulouse route, and St. Peter's shrine in Rome can be considered the eastern extension of this southern route (*via tolosana*); Martin's shrine at Tours (*via turonense*) and the Virgin Mary's shrine at Le Puy (*via podense*) represent the other two routes through France. For St. Giles, see n. 260; for Leonard, n. 262.

339. This is the first mention of Martin of Tours (316-97), but not the last. He was born in Pannonia (Hungary) of pagan parents, converting to Christianity sometime during his teens. The most famous of his acts, the one that has become his emblem, occurred while he was a youth in the army: he cut his cloak in half to share it with a beggar. He became a disciple of St. Hilary of Poitiers, spent time as a hermit, and was finally made bishop of Tours in 372. At this point he became committed to the dissemination of the Christian religion throughout the region and the eradication of cult and heretic practices, and he founded several monasteries in Gaul. During his work he had a complicated relationship with Priscillianists, occasionally defending their view, especially as he worked with the bishops in Spain. The Pilgrim's Guide author describes the saint's miracles and his tomb, not bothering with a *vita* (see chapter 8). St. Martin is also mentioned in Miracle 3, when discussing a saint's power to raise someone from the dead. Sources for his life are the *Vita* by Sulpicius Severus (PL 20:159-74) and the various works of Gregory of Tours (PL 71). BHL entries for Martin of Tours are 5610-66.

Tours, on the Loire River, is centrally located in France. There are records of toll collections from pilgrims as they crossed the bridge over the Loire on their way to Compostela. Because it was the site of the relics of St. Martin, Popes Urban II (1096) and Calixtus II (1119) visited there. The eleventh-century basilica was dedicated in 1108 and rebuilt after 1175. See Grabois, *Encyclopedia* 675 and the *New Catholic Encyclopedia*.

340. Le Puy, located in the French department of Haute-Loire, may predate Roman settlement, perhaps even be the site of a stone cult. It became prestigious after the tenth century, when

the cult of the Virgin became important there, although no relics were attached to Le Puy's cult until after the twelfth century. Its location as a starting point of the road to Compostela also helped its popularity. Popes Urban II (in 1095) and Calixtus II made pilgrimages there. In 1087 Raimond of Saint-Gilles, count of Toulouse, came to Le Puy to pray to the Virgin (cf. Miracle 18). See *Grande Encyclopédie Larousse.*

341. The second reference to St. Peter and Rome. Here the author wishes his audience to link Rome and its basilica directly with the Santiago route. He downplays the importance of Rome as a pilgrimage center in itself. See n. 259.

342. We have not found this word in the standard dictionaries; its meaning is obvious.

343. The Latin *acus/acum* is found only with the meaning "needle." This appears to be a retrogressive construction of a Latin word based on the French coin called the *écu.* The Latin basis for the French word is *scutum,* which became *escut* and finally *écu.* While the *écu* was officially introduced during the reign of Louis IX in the following century, this reference could indicate an earlier popular usage of the word.

344. See Numbers 16:1-33 and Deuteronomy 11:6. These passages narrate a revolt against Moses when two men (Datan or Dathan and Abiram or Abiron) joined with the Levite Korah in an insurrection. Moses ordered his people to move away from the tents of the rebels, which were then swallowed up in a great earthquake. Though the biblical quote here is accurate, it is only tangential to the subject of false innkeepers and fraudulent practices.

345. The manuscript reads *cyphum* for *scyphum.*

346. See Miracle 5.

347. The Italians are the only nationality, other than the Navarrese, to be singled out as evil as a race.

348. This entire passage repeats a portion of the sermon for July 24 (Book I chapter 2), even to the number of masses and number of coins.

349. The Latin says literally "false hypocrites," but this sort of double negative does not carry into English.

350. These vices, enumerated in order, are most likely the seven deadly sins of sloth, pride, flattery, anger, avarice, gluttony, and lust. It is the last three, the sins of the flesh, that are the author's greatest concern in this sermon.

351. Whitehill 164 repeats the word *tribuit.*

352. The Latin is *buleiis* probably for *bulbis,* "bulbs."

353. We have not found the Latin *lotuesses.* It could be a kind of lotus, although this is not certain. Corominas cites "loto" as the name of various African plants, with the Latin *loto,* from the

Greek *lotós.* Modern French has *lotus* or *lotos,* but the only Old French variant in Godefroy is simply *lote.*

354. Whitehill 165 transcribes *dimittentes,* "setting aside," as *dinitentes,* a non-existent word.

355. Maigne d'Arnis gives *scatia* as "staff, walking stick or crosier."

356. Maigne d'Arnis gives *scabellus* as "seat or stool."

357. The Latin, although difficult to decipher, is *contracti,* or "cripples." Whitehill 165 transcribes this as *contincti,* a non-existent word.

358. Whitehill 165 transcribes *viarum* as *voarum,* a non-existent word.

359. "Others...alms" is found in the margin of the manuscript in a similar, if not the same, hand.

360. Cf. Ambrose of Milan's spurious *Letters,* in this case *Epistula IV to Florian* (PL 17:750-51). This passage is not found in Isidore.

361. James 5:20.

362. Maigne d'Arnis gives "moneychanger" for *cambiator.* A concern for money and fair exchange and a resultant control mechanism existed fairly early in Compostela. The guild of moneychangers also was concerned about the weights and balances. See the introduction, xxvii.

363. The word *trebuchetum* literally means "catapult." It is obviously used here as a colorful term for a scales, which can resemble a catapult if one side is pulled down and let go quickly.

364. Whitehill 166 transcribes *amplos* as *amplios,* adding an *-i-,* perhaps on the model of *amplius,* the adverb.

365. The talent was another of the coins in use at the time.

366. The word *non* is found interlinearly.

367. Maigne d'Arnis gives *contrafactus* as "counterfeit." Whitehill 166 transcribes this as two words. In fact, the author is attempting to give a definition of a word that he probably considers unfamiliar to at least a part of his audience.

368. Whitehill 166 transcribes *in stateris* as one word.

369. Psalms 61:10.

370. Matthew 7:2 and Luke 6:38.

371. Proverbs 20:10.

372. Matthew 21:12. See also Mark 11:15.

373. The Latin is *speciariis,* a "spice dealer" or "herbalist." While it occurs only for the feminine in standard Latin, Maigne d'Arnis gives it for both masculine and feminine.

374. Maigne d'Arnis give this meaning for *bastardus.*

375. The Latin for ginger was *gingiber* according to Maigne d'Arnis. In this text we find *genebrii,* which seems to be a variant of the same word. Corrupt spice sellers were interested in the weight of pepper because during the Middle Ages its price

was much higher than many other spices, including ginger. "In the latter centuries of the medieval world...a pound of pepper represented the equivalent of two to three weeks' wages for an agricultural laborer" (Tannahill 189). Hayes (40) notes that during the Middle Ages, ginger was "second only to pepper in value." Both were popular spices: shipping records indicate that in the fifteenth century Venice imported from the East about 2,500 tons each per year of ginger and pepper, but almost that much for all other spices combined (Tannahill 236, quoting Mallett).

376. The manuscript reads *gliscem,* literally "clay." The meaning is some "substance" or "mineral."

377. The manuscript reads *plumam* accusative case, indicating a feather's weight, or a slight amount, while Whitehill 167 transcribes it as *pluma* (ablative), "with a feather."

378. The standard Latin for "sap" is *sappinus,* rather than the manuscript's *sappi.* The word is of probable Germanic origin and related to the English word.

379. The Latin is *terram,* "earth," here again with the meaning of "earth element" or "mineral" or "substance."

380. Maigne d'Arnis gives *vinum* or "wine" as an option for *Graecum;* perhaps here in the sense of "wine-colored."

381. Maigne d'Arnis gives *vermilius* as "red."

382. Maigne d'Arnis gives *azurus* as "blue or sky-colored." Here it appears to refer to a type of blue dye.

383. Blaise gives *elactuarium* as "electuary."

384. Blaise gives *syropus* with this meaning, while Maigne d'Arnis gives *syroporius* as one who prepares *syropos,* although he has no entry for the word "syrop" itself.

385. For the Latin *alna,* Maigne d'Arnis gives "measuring stick."

386. The word *et,* "and," was added interlinearly.

387. The Latin is *bragarios,* etymologically related to "breeches" and originally of Celtic origin. Maigne d'Arnis gives *braca* and *bracae* for "breeches." While the Latin of the manuscript would indicate *bracarius* or "maker of breeches," the context indicates "breeches."

388. See n. 340 for Le Puy.

389. See n. 260 for Saint-Gilles.

390. See n. 339 for Tours.

391. Piacenza is an ancient city in Lombardy, northern Italy, on the Po river between Milan and Parma. From 1000 on it was an important ecclesiastical center. From a council held there in 1095 with Pope Urban II attending, came the idea of a crusade. See Grabois, *Encyclopedia* 587.

392. Lucca is mentioned only in this passage about fraud. It is a town in Tuscany in northwestern Italy, which may have been

Christianized in apostolic times. Legend has it that Paulinus, a disciple of Peter, may have been the first bishop there, and Lucca perhaps was the earliest Christian town in Tuscany. There was apparently a religious revival during the eleventh, twelfth, and thirteenth centuries, with concomitant increased building of churches. Lucca lies on the ancient Via Cassia; and to its east is Pistoia, a town that favored the Compostela pilgrimage. See the *New Catholic Encyclopedia*.

393. See n. 259 for Rome.

394. Bari is one of two important seaports on the east coast of Italy. It is the capital of the southeastern Italian region of Apulia. It is the seat of the archdiocese of the area, established in the fourth century, and became a metropolitan see in 1025. In addition to its strategic location — it was one of two ports for travel to and from Jerusalem — and the resulting commercial importance, Bari became a significant pilgrimage site when, in 1087, sailors brought the relics of St. Nicholas of Myra to it. The basilica housing the relics was finished in 1108. See n. 402 for St. Nicholas, and Porter for comparisons of Romanesque style in Bari and Compostela.

395. Barletta is an Italian port on the Adriatic Sea in the Apulia region. It is the northernmost seaport city in the Bari province.

396. The passage "O crafty cupidity...of all fraud" is added in the margin in a similar, if not the same, hand as the main text.

397. This is the second occasion that the writer links the Virgin Mary with apostles and popular French saints. Here he adds Mary Magdalene, John the Baptist, and Sts. Michael, Bartholomew, and Nicholas, the last two having important cult centers in Italy.

398. In a combination of myth and legend St. Mary Magdalene, a disciple of Christ, was generally considered in the Middle Ages to have been a repentant sinner. She was popular very early in Christianity, by at least the fifth century. Later additions to her legend make her, her brother Lazarus, and her sister Martha the evangelists of Provence. Although she was originally buried in Ephesus, Vézelay (Burgundy) claimed her relics from early in the eleventh century, perhaps brought from Provence. By the time of Abbot Geoffrey (c. 1037) Vézelay had become a pilgrimage center. In 1058 Abbott Boniface convinced Pope Stephen IX to validate the relics; that same year Cluny took control of the monastery. In 1146 Bernard of Clairvaux preached the Second Crusade there. Vézelay's importance declined in the thirteenth century when the Magdalene's relics were "rediscovered" in Provence. Book V (chapter 8) gives a short *vita* and discusses how the relics arrived in Vézelay. See BHL 5439-513 (her feast day is July 22), AASS Iul 5:187-225, Grabois, *Encyclopedia* 510, 695.

399. John the Baptist, honored at Saint-Jean-d'Angély in France, was a very important figure in the medieval Christian church. The location of his head [after it was severed in the Herod and Salome episode (Matthew 14:6-11)] is disputed. Several churches in France claim it, and the *Colegiata* in León, Spain claimed his lower jawbone (Melczer 179 n. 257), but many believed that the head was in Saint-Jean-d'Angély, on the Paris-Tours road to Compostela. The author of Book V, the Pilgrim's Guide, tells pilgrims that they should visit the relic and tells something of the *translatio,* but gives no biography of the saint. John the Baptist has BHL entries 4290-315 (his feasts are June 24 and August 29).

400. The Latin, *Michaelem marinum,* must refer to Mont-Saint-Michel, located on the coast of Normandy. The church is a result of several dreams that eighth-century bishop St. Aubert had in which Michael the Archangel ordered him to build a church on the rock. It soon became a site for pilgrimage; among others, St. Louis IX, king of France, visited there. St. Michael is often portrayed as a warrior saint, but during the Middle Ages he was also popular as the saint who received the souls of the dead, and occasionally was imbued with classical mythology as the saint who helped the dead cross the river of death. He is also the patron saint of Norman mariners. See BHL 5947-56 (his feast days are May 8 and September 29).

401. Bartholomew of Benevento, according to the Synoptic Gospels, was an apostle, although other sources name him Nathaniel. He supposedly traveled to India and Armenia, where he was martyred. His relics were first transferred to the island of Lipara, near Sicily, then to Benevento, and finally to Rome. In the eleventh century an arm bone was given to Canterbury. See AASS Aug. 5:7-108, PL 116:31-4, BHL 1001-14 (his feast day is August 25).

Benevento lies in south-central Italy, on the road between Bari and Naples, a secondary Italian road that could lead pilgrims toward Santiago.

402. St. Nicholas of Bari is also called St. Nicholas of Myra. Nicholas (d. 345 or 352) may have been a bishop in Myra, a seaport in Lycia, in southwest Turkey, in the first half of the fourth century, but there is really no reliable historical evidence about him. However, his cult seems to have been in place by the sixth century. Methodius (d. 847) wrote a fictitious biography in the ninth century, and the cult was thriving by the middle of the tenth century. The oldest authentic evidence of his legends comes from an eleventh-century manuscript now in the Karlsruhe (Germany) Library. In 1087, when the Muslims conquered Myra, Italian soldiers stole the saint's body and took it to Bari. The saint is famous for supplying dowries for three penniless women,

and thus he has become the saint of giving, of Christmas gifts, and of pawnbrokers. According to other information, a heavenly substance, "manna" or "myrrh," emanated from his shrine at Bari, and therefore he is also the patron of perfumiers. See Farmer 292 and the *New Catholic Encyclopedia*. Nicholas' feast is December 6, and BHL entries are 6104-221.

403. The manuscript reads *ingecerunt* for *infecerunt*, a scribal error. Whitehill 168 does not correct the text.

404. Psalms 27:4-5.

405. Psalms 54:16.

406. Whitehill 168 transcribes *hoc*, "this," as *haec*, "these."

407. Isaiah 65:12-15.

408. The standard Latin meaning of *adunare* is "to unite." Maigne d'Arnis gives "to collect," and here the context seems to require "to amass."

409. Whitehill 169 transcribes *ultimum* as *ultimim*.

410. Ecclesiasticus 34:27.

411. Luke 9:25. See also Matthew 15:26 and Mark 8:36.

412. 1 Timothy 6:10.

413. The Latin of the manuscript is *visuer~t*, not a recognizable form, although the stem seems to be from *vis-*, "to see, aim"; the translation here is from context.

414. Isaiah 5:8 and 18-23.

415. See Acts 15:36-40.

416. Isaiah 5:14.

417. Isaiah 29:8.

418. Isaiah 1:14-15.

419. Jeremiah 30:15.

420. This is a second comparison to Datan and Abiron; see n. 344.

421. Maigne d'Arnis gives *portagerus* as "collector at a gate." "Toll" has been added here to fit the context.

422. Saint-Jean and Saint-Michel are French villages near each other along the Nive River, at the foot of Cize Pass. Saint-Michel is named in Book V, the Pilgrim's Guide, as the beginning point for the northern route across the Pyrenees (chapter 3). Pilgrims from the three northern routes (Paris, Vézelay, and Le Puy) would meet in Ostabat and proceed a few kilometers southwest to enter Saint-Jean Pied-de-Port and then begin the climb of the Pyrenees. The Pilgrim's Guide warns pilgrims that those who collect tolls at Ostabat, Saint-Jean, and Saint-Michel are evil and may beat and search pilgrims for their money. This is the beginning of the section about what chapter 7 of the Pilgrim's Guide describes as the repulsive Basques.

423. Isaiah 58:1.

424. Whitehill 171 transcribes *coronam gloriae*, "crown of glory," as *coronam gloriam*, "crown, glory."

425. Whitehill 171 transcribes *omnes,* "all," as *omnesque,* "and all."

426. The author begins an address to the people of Spain in this rhetorical use of apostrophe.

427. The word *ingratiosa* was not found; the meaning is clear: *in,* "not," plus *gratiosa,* "filled with grace."

428. The manuscript reads *dō4,* which Whitehill 172 transcribed as *domorum,* "of the houses," rather than *daemonum* or *daemoniorum,* "of the spirits."

429. See Miracle 19 in which St. James is compared to Titan.

430. Churches dedicated to St. James were built throughout Europe during the Middle Ages. González Sologaistúa notes that in the thirteenth century there were nearly 500 churches dedicated to the saint in Germany, 400 in the British Isles, and nearly the same number in Italy, France, Switzerland, and the Low Countries. Jacomet ("Santiago") traces devotion to Santiago in France in the form of churches and towns dedicated to the saint. Stuckelberg does the same for Switzerland.

431. The word *eius* is added interlinearly.

432. Psalms 18:6.

433. See Malachia 4:2. Not an exact quote of the Vulgate.

434. Habacuc 3:11. Not an exact quote of the Vulgate.

435. Whitehill 172 transcribes *unum* (accusative case) as *unus* (nominative case).

436. Whitehill 173 transcribes *in strata,* "in the street," as one word.

437. Luke 1:78.

438. Luke 1:79.

439. Whitehill transcribes *descripsi te* as one word.

440. The manuscript reads *ubi,* "where," for *tibi,* "yours." Our translation follows the Vulgate here.

441. Isaiah 49:16-26.

442. See Matthew 13:44.

443. See Matthew 13:45.

444. Whitehill 174 gives *omnis* (singular) for *omnes* (plural); the manuscript reads *om~s.*

445. This quote from Venantius Fortunatus, *Miscellanea,* 5:3:1-2; 5-6; 17-34; 43-4 (PL 88:184-5). For more about Venantius and Book V, the Pilgrim's Guide's use of the poet's works, see n. 216. This text was originally addressed to the people of Tours and concerned their bishop, Gregory.

446. Venantius' text reads "happy people" rather than "people of Galicia." Whitehill 174 transcribes *Gallaeciae,* "of Galicia," as *Gallaecia,* simply "Galicia."

447. Venantius' text reads "holding vows" rather than "songs for Christ."

448. Venantius' text reads " leader's arrival" rather than "coming of James."

449. Whitehill transcribes *regantur*, "are ruled," as *regnatur*, "he is ruled," and built on a different verb.

450. Venantius' text reads "May He govern" rather than "He governs."

451. Venantius' text in the PL reads "those who served" rather than "those sleeping," although the latter is given as a variant reading.

452. Venantius' text reads "florid" rather than "flowering."

453. Lines 29 and 30 of Venantius' text appear to be of doubtful clarity. The PL version gives two major variants for them. The LSJ author's reworking departs even further from the original.

454. Venantius' text reads "they may" rather than "he may."

455. Whitehill 175 gives *duodeciman*, non-existent, for *duocecimam*.

456. The sermon ends with this prayer addressed to James.

457. Whitehill 175 transcribes *Gallaecia* (ablative case) as *Gallaeciae* (dative, genitive, or nominative plural).

458. Another list of miracles one can expect from the saint. In Book II's Miracles, we find examples of resuscitation in Miracles 3 and 17. The saint corrects his devoted from "straying" in a broad sense in Miracles 2, 13, and 22. He does not restore sight in any miracle here, although there is one case of this in the Reading Abbey miracle collection (Miracle 18, dated 1163-87; see Kemp, "Miracles").

459. Luke 8:49-56. Jairus was a synagogue leader whose daughter Jesus raised from the dead.

460. Whitehill 175 transcribes *Transfigurationem* without the second *t*.

461. Again a reference to the inclusiveness of the devotion to St. James, especially from lands outside of western Europe.

462. This verb has only a deponent form in standard Latin. Maigne d'Arnis, however, gives it as both deponent and non-deponent.

463. Tobias 13:14-15.

464. Whitehill 176 transcribes *ad*, "to," as *at*, "but."

465. Tobias 13:17-18.

466. Those from Sheba.

467. Isaiah 45:14.

468. See 2 Timothy 1:15.

469. Maigne d'Arnis gives *cunctipotentis* as a synonym for the usual *omnipotentis*, both meaning "all-powerful."

470. While the English suggests a possible etymological play on words concerning the name Compostela, i.e., *campus + stellarum*, the words chosen by the author here, *castris...in astris*, preclude such a conjecture.

471. The manuscript adds the word *est* interlinearly. Whitehill 176 transcribes it as *este*, non-existent in Latin.

472. Whitehill 176 transcribes *regnat* (singular) as *regnant* (plural).

473. The Latin is *argumentum*, "argument," but "attestation" seems best to describe this introductory section.

474. The author, although ostensibly pope, uses the first-person singular rather than the more usual first-person plural common to popes and emperors. In the next paragraph, he will mix the use of "I" and "we." This kind of vacillation is not new, having occurred in the Introductory Letter and in the "Veneranda dies" sermon. See the introduction, pp. xxxix-xl, for more commentary.

475. Either an ancient Roman province, roughly corresponding to modern Romania, or possibly a reference to the Scandinavian countries. Dacia was used as an example in the "Veneranda dies" sermon as well. See n. 167.

476. A reference to the Mediterranean Sea region: the whole sea, the Mediterranean (*mare nostrum*), and two gulfs, generally also called seas: the Tyrrhenian, or Etruscan (*mare inferum*), and the Adriatic (*mare superum*).

477. The narrator is cognizant of and concerned with the geographical sphere of the saint. This reference to wandering in various lands echoes what we have already read in the Introductory Letter and this relatively short list of countries echoes the much longer list of international pilgrims to the saint's tomb in Galicia in the "Veneranda dies" sermon. Here the first four places mentioned (Galicia, France, Germany, and Italy) are certainly the most important sites when speaking of pilgrims and the cult of St. James. Of Book II's twenty-two miracles, sixteen occurred in these four areas, and fifteen of the recipients were inhabitants of those areas.

The manuscript spells the word for "shores" as *horis* rather than *oris*; Whitehill 259 retains the *h-*.

478. The narrator seemingly relies on the tradition of *auctoritas*, in using written documents as a base for his own writing. Yet, of the following twenty-two miracles, only four are attributed to other sources (Miracles 2, 4, 16, 17). Of the eighteen others, all with Calixtus' name as author, only three indicate reliability of the information (Miracles 1, 9, and 22), the last of which says "I met the man myself."

479. The veracity of miracle reports was of concern to many shrine custodians. One registrar (in the late twelfth-early thirteenth century) at the shrine of Thomas Becket reported, "inasmuch as these [miracle recipients] have not produced witnesses, and the truth has not been perfectly sifted by us, we let their stories pass out of our ears as fast as we let them come in"

(Finucane 102, quoting from *Materials for the History of Thomas Becket*).

In the Latin, the word "true" is repeated three times here: miracles are true (*vera*), assertions are most true (*verissimis*), and people asserting are most truthful (*verissimorum*).

480. For *pergamenum*, DuCange gives "parchment."

481. The material of Books I and II are considered appropriate for reading in church, although it may be read at refectory if time does not permit its reading at services. See the Calixtine Introductory Letter, 3-4, for more information on this observation.

482. The only title in which the apostle is not mentioned.

483. These titles are more like plot summaries, especially when compared to the actual heading of each miracle, which gives only authorship. A later hand has inserted the corresponding folio number for each miracle after its title. We have not reproduced this information.

484. The chapter designations appear to have been added later in the margin of the manuscript by a different hand from that of the main text.

The twenty-two miracles, as is the case with the rest of the CC manuscript, are written in black ink. Preceding each miracle is a short chapter designation, truly not a title, for each one of the designations gives only an attribution of author. These chapter designations are written in red ink, but apparently were written at the time of the composition of the maniscript. At some later time another hand inserted margin chapter indications (e.g. "cap. iiii." in the manuscript.

The Latin consistently refers to Pope Calixtus with the Latin Dominus whenever a miracle is attributed to him. The modern form of reference is "His Holiness" for a pope, but we have settled on "Excellency" as a compromise between "Holiness" and "Lord."

485. The Latin is simply *passionis,* "suffering." However, the context indicates and history confirms that this refers to his martyrdom inflicted by Herod Agrippa in Jerusalem. See Acts 12:2.

486. A water image, a kind of reference that the writer has made in the "Veneranda dies" sermon. The imagery continues in the next sentence with allusions to, perhaps, the legend about the cloth that Veronica gave to Jesus Christ to wipe his brow, followed by a "pouring" of powers, reminiscent of baptismal cleansing.

487. The Latin *rationi* can be interpreted in several ways. Here, "in its properly accounted place among the other miracles" fits most appropriately. The AASS has the reading *notitiae* here, which would indicate the idea that it was told "for the knowledge of his followers." *Notitia* might well represent a *lectio facilior*

(when the scribe chose an easier word) for the more ambiguous Latin *ratio.*

488. Alfonso VI of Castile and León (1065-1109) was the strongest of the peninsula's Christian rulers at that time, and he named himself *"imperator totius Hispaniae,"* probably to free himself from the efforts of Pope Gregory VII (1073-85) to gain some controls in the peninsula, including some power over the efforts of the Reconquest. The miracle's author does not use the exact terminology that Alfonso had, preferring instead *"regis Adefonsi in Hispaniae partibus."* Another aspect of the battles between King Alfonso and Pope Gregory revolved around the substitution of the Roman liturgy for the Mozarabic, and during the conflict the pope managed to make Bernard de Sauvetot, a Cluniac, the abbot in Sahagún, on the road to Santiago. For more of the history of this epoch see O'Callaghan 200-215.

489. Moralejo et al., based on David, identifies him as the count of Urgel, Ermengol IV (1065-92) or V (1092-1102). Urgel is a province in northeast Spain in Lérida, part of Cataluña. It was recaptured from the Moors in the eighth century. The reconquest of the area of Lérida is credited to Ramón Berenguer, the count of Barcelona in 1149 (see n. 726 about Berenguer's role in the reconquest of Almería).

Lérida also has a tradition that Santiago stepped on a thorn while entering the city. Since he could not remove it, he prayed to the Virgin, who sent down angels to remove it for him. At least two chapels were built in the area to commemorate this miracle. See Ortiz y Estrada.

490. Alfonso VI was so successful in his reconquest efforts, that the Moors in Seville, Granada, and Badajoz realized that they needed help to maintain control of the southern part of the peninsula. They called on a faction in North Africa, the Almoravids. This group was an ascetic warring group, which, when it arrived in Spain, dampened severely the successes of the Christians. It took about eight years, but by 1094, "the Almoravids had restored the unity of al-Andalus and confronted Christian Spain with the most serious threat since the days of Almanzor" [1000 AD] (O'Callaghan 211). Thus the paragraph's opening sentence referring to the increased "fury" of the Saracens.

The Latin text uses the word *Moabitarum,* "Moabites," in reference to this group. The term is also used in Book IV, the Turpin Chronicle (chapter 1), along with many others in the same sentence, to refer to various Moslem groups ("Saracens, Moors, Ethiopians, Turks, Africans, Persians"). Moab, in the area of Jordan, was the site of the ancestry of Ruth (Ruth 1:4). It is used here, perhaps, to indicate a tribe that has come from far away, contrasted with the Moors that were living on the Iberian Peninsula.

491. Literally, "surrounded."

492. The Latin is *invincibilis pugnae*, "of an invincible battle"; "of certain victory" seems clearer.

493. This is an interesting variant of litotes, in which the author essentially implies rather than says "he did not triumph" to indicate "he was defeated."

It was because of the Almoravid invasion that Alfonso VI had to leave his siege of Zaragoza and go south to fight the new group. The reconquest of Zaragoza was thus delayed for about twenty years.

494. Zaragoza lies in the northeast portion of Spain and is the capital of Aragón, but it is not on the main road to Compostela. There were probably several Moorish prisons there. One possible candidate that still remains is the famous Aljafería in the western part of the city, founded by Aben-Alfaje (864-89). It was the castle-palace of the Moorish rulers until 1118 when Alfonso el Batallador of Aragón (the second husband of Urraca), who had reconquered the city, gave it to a religious order. Zaragoza has long identified itself with the cult of Santiago.

Part of the saint's legend relates that, as he was returning to Jerusalem, the Virgin Mary appeared to him in what is now Zaragoza, asking him to build a church there. To prove that it was she (this may be her only miracle before death) and that her request was important, she brought the pillar on which Jesus had been flagellated. Thus the name of the church: La Virgen del Pilar, and, subsequently, the popularity of the feminine name "Pilar" in Spain.

495. In this collection of miracles, this is the only time a priest must encourage the petitioners to call to St. James.

496. The Latin is *inauditae*, literally "unheard-of."

497. The Latin is *succincti*, literally "girded."

498. We have not located the Latin *visceratenus*. The standard Latin adverb *visceratim* means piecemeal. However, Blaise gives *viscerate* with the meaning of "deeply." This word appears to mean the same thing with the adverbial *-atenus* of such words as *nullatenus*, rather than *-e* ending.

499. See Miracle 18 where the cathedral's gates also open because of the apostle. In this sentence, the narrator uses the contracted forms of the perfect *ministrarunt* and *reformarunt*, leaving out the usual *-ve-* indicator.

500. The Latin does not identify the subject. It is supplied here by context.

501. That is, going on pilgrimage to the saint's tomb in Compostela. See n. 223.

502. December 30, the feast date for which the "Veneranda dies" sermon was written. This is the first reference to the saint's

translatio in the Miracles. See the introduction, xxx, for information about the saint's feast days.

503. This prayer-like conclusion to the miracle is a formula and is used in most of the miracles. Only in a few is this phrasing changed: Miracles 16, 17 (these two miracles attributed to Anselm), 18 (this miracle also a part of the Anselm collection), and 22. See n. 226 for the phrase "for ever and ever."

504. The Venerable Bede was an English monk, historian, and saint. He was born c. 673 and was educated by monks, first at the monastery of St. Peter in Wearmouth and then at St. Paul in Jarrow, from which he seems never to have left. Devoted to learning and the religious life, he authored several large works, the most famous the *History of the English Church and People,* completed c. 731. He also wrote a *Lives of the Abbots,* several lives of saints, and hymns and poems. He was careful to check sources, and he combined much information in his historical writings. He was translating the *Etymologies* of Isidore of Seville into the vernacular when he died in 735. His feast day is May 29 (see BHL 1067-76, PL 90-95, Attwater, and Bede).

Based on his biographical dates and the date of discovery of St. James' tomb in Compostela, his authorship of this story is impossible. It is possible that he believed that St. James preached in Spain, for Isidore (or perhaps an eighth-century interpolation in Isidore's works) mentions this aspect of the saint's legend. Aldhelm of Malmesbury (who died in 709) attributes to St. James the conversion of people in Spain. Two of Bede's sermons are in Book I's liturgies: the first opens the first book with a sermon for July 24, the other is chapter 8, a homily for July 25. In the latter piece, Bede speaks about the saint's life and martyrdom, but does not refer to Spain. Moralejo, citing David, indicates that, given the faulty dating, the mention of these two names (Bede, Teodomiro) may be symbolic for "in ancient times" (340).

505. Teodomiro was the bishop at Iria Flavia at the time of the discovery of the saint's burial place in Compostela, c. 830. His tomb, or at least a tombstone with his name on it, was found under the Compostela Cathedral during mid-twentieth-century excavations.

506. The word *schedula* is difficult to translate since English has scarcely any word that does not indicate the type of material on which one has written. Parchment seems too important. Paper was probably really not in use at the time. We have used "note" to avoid naming the type of material on which it was written.

507. The scribe placed the word *ante* before *altare* and then deleted it by dotting under it. Whitehill 262 did not respect the deletion and reproduced it as a part of the text. This passage

indicates that the basilica of St. James allowed the pilgrims access to the altar.

508. This may be used literally to mean the "first hour," although this might be reference to "at or near the time of the prime service." It is unlikely that the pilgrim approached the altar during a ceremony, especially since the bishop wondered how the note had been placed there when he found it.

509. July 25. In the first two miracles the author has managed to refer to both important feast-day celebrations of the saint. See discussion of these days in the introduction, xxx.

510. Teodomiro was actually the bishop of Iria Flavia. The episcopal seat was not moved to Compostela until the twelfth century.

511. The word *ad* is added interlinearly.

512. Again, this could be simply "at the third hour" or a reference to terce and the morning mass, which generally occurred at about 8:00 AM. Either way, two hours would have passed between the sinner's having placed the note and the bishop's finding it.

513. The Latin is merely *cedulam* for *schedulam*, here and at the next occurrence of the word "note" at the end of this paragraph. The non-existent word *cedulam* was transcribed without comment by Whitehill 262.

514. There is a curious marginal notation at this point reading *Non Dei miraculum*, or "Not a miracle of God." This miracle is similar to one attributed to St. Giles. According to one legend, Charlemagne could only confess his most heinous sin by writing it down on paper. The information, having to do with the parentage of Roland, magically disappeared at the behest of St. Giles. For more information on this French saint, see n. 260.

515. It is unusual in this collection to find a part of the formulaic closing located within the body of the text. It suggests a scholarly discussion of intercession appended to, perhaps, an earlier version of this miracle.

516. There is some ambiguity here: it could be on the "sixth day (Saturday) following that" or on simply whatever day happened to be the sixth after the day on which he gave the order to fast.

517. Here and elsewhere the author actually says "In the year of Our Lord's Incarnation." At times this technicality in dating was taken seriously to mean that one should start counting years from March, nine months before the Lord's birth.

518. The Latin *promereri* is really "to deserve to get," "to earn"; *interpellavit* bears a persistent, almost annoying connotation.

519. The Montes de Oca are located east of Burgos between Villafranca and Atapuerca. See Book V, the Pilgrim's Guide, chapters 3 and 7. Although the Latin text here terms it *montem,*

"mountain," this area is really a forest, and as such it is called *nemore*, "grove," in the title index and the Pilgrim's Guide.

520. Literally, "breathed out his soul."

521. The Latin is *arreptitiorum*. DuCange gives the translation "delirious" for this word.

522. Whitehill 264 transcribes *his* (ablative) as *hos* (accusative).

523. This is an impressive threat to a saint. Although in a plea to a saint there may be quite strong demands for action, we are unaware of any other miracle that has potential suicide as a part of the supplication.

524. That is, from the third hour on Saturday until the ninth hour on Sunday.

525. Here the narrator uses the word *tramitem* rather than the usual *viam*.

526. Whitehill 264 transcribes *suavius* (neuter comparative) as *suavis* (masculine positive).

527. The first instance of this rhetorical question of the author. This phrase will appear twice more, in Miracles 9 and 22.

528. This is the standard conclusion to the miracles, but here, for the second time, the narrator theorizes in a final paragraph.

529. *Res nova* means "new" in the strongest sense, almost, if not, "revolutionary."

530. See n. 339 for information on Martin of Tours, to whom the author refers here. While Melczer (176 n. 243) believes the number three is symbolic, the *Vita* by Sulpicius Severus recounts two resurrections (chapters 7 and 8) and a third is in Severus' *Second Dialogue* (chapter 4). In the first instance, the man revived two hours after Martin lay across his body. The second instance is the resuscitation of a slave who had hanged himself. The last example occurred in Vendôme, where Martin was preaching to pagans. A woman approached with her dead infant son in her arms. After Martin prayed over the body, the baby revived and the town was converted to Christianity. See Sulpicius Severus. The idea that Martin had raised three dead persons was widely held. In addition to Sulpicius Severus' work above, we find mention of the fact in his "First Letter to Eusebius" (PL 20:175). Bernard of Clairvaux also made note of this (PL 183:495). Gregory of Tours in his *Historia Francorum* 1.36 (PL 71:180) asserts that Martin raised three people from the dead. In addition, Gregory tells the story of a small boy resuscitated in his *De Miraculis Sancti Martini* 2.43 (PL 71:960-61), another small child in 3.8 (PL 71:972-73), and there is passing mention of a resuscitated monk in 3.50 (PL 71:970).

531. The three people raised from the dead by Jesus were Lazarus (John 11:1-44), the daughter of Jairus (see n. 459) and the son of the widow of Nain (Luke 7:11-15).

532. Actually *leguntur*, "are read...."

533. Whitehill 264 in all three instances transcribes *suscitare* (active infinitive) as *suscitari* (passive infinitive).

534. John 14:12.

535. Mark 9:23.

536. Besançon lies about 380 kilometers southeast of Paris. Guy of Burgundy, known as Pope Calixtus II, was born there. There is evidence of a Humbert, archbishop of Besançon; for example, a letter in PL 180:1465, dated 1155. The name is also seen in the indices of PL volumes 180 and 182. Vincent of Beauvais (36.32) attributes this miracle to Hubertus Sibuntinus while Voragine (Graesse 426) ascribes it to Ubertus Bysuntinus.

537. This is the first of several times that Galicia is referred to as a specific geographical entity. It is mentioned as such once more in this miracle, and once each in Miracles 7, 8, 9, 11, 12, 14, 16, 17, 22: all of these references use "Galicia" as a point of reference for the pilgrimage goal. It is also referred to in the "Veneranda dies" sermon and elsewhere in Book I of the LSJ.

538. Cf. Ecclesiastes 5:4.

539. The province in northeastern France, named after Lothaire, Charlemagne's grandson, who ruled over the central strip of land in the empire. By the eleventh century its rule had passed to Alsace.

540. Gascogne, the southwestern province of France. We have not located "Porta Clusa," but by its name, one suspects a difficult or high place. It cannot be in the Pyrenees, since the men walk a five-day distance in fifteen days before reaching the Cize Pass at the border of Spain in the Pyrenees. Therefore, one might posit a difficult place, perhaps in a forest, such as in the vicinity of Mont-de-Narsan.

541. The mountain pass in the Pyrenees between the French Saint-Michel and the Spanish Roncesvalles (see previous note and n. 422 about its location. The two men do not reach the summit, however.

542. The manuscript reads *hopus* for *opus*. Whitehill 265 transcribes it was *hopus* without comment.

543. Saint-Michel and Saint-Jean Pied-de-Port are the two French villages at the base of the pass. See n. 422 for more information.

544. Whitehill 265 transcribes *esset*, "he would," as *es et*, "you are and."

545. The Latin is *Basclorum*. Whitehill 265 transcribes *Baclorum*, leaving out the *-s-*. In Book V, the Pilgrim's Guide (chapter 7, Melczer 90-96) also singles out the Basques as particularly barbarous. In the "Veneranda dies" sermon the Navarrese are similarly maligned.

546. Here, as in Miracle 19, the saint is visible in his militant imagery.

547. An illustration in a fourteenth-century manuscript of the Parma (Italy) confraternity shows this scene exactly. See the cover of *Santiago: La Europa del peregrinaje* (Caucci) for a reproduction of this miniature.

548. Twelve days is the appropriate amount of time for travel between Cize and Compostela, according to Book V, the Pilgrim's Guide.

549. The mountain top called the Monte de Gozo is about five kilometers east of Compostela. From there, pilgrims could, and still can, see for the first time the cathedral of Compostela.

550. Whitehill 266 transcribes *praefati*, "of the aforementioned one," i.e., "saint," as *praefatae*, making it agree with basilica, which was not "aforementioned."

551. The correct city according to the number of days' journeys in Book V, the Pilgrim's Guide.

552. We translate the Latin *ultra quam dici fas est*, "beyond what is allowed to be said," into English with "indescribable."

553. This is probably the most popular of the St. James' miracles throughout time. Versions have been created in prose, poetry, sculpture, and painting through the nineteenth century, in England, France, Germany, Portugal, and Switzerland. Along the way the site changes to Santo Domingo de la Calzada and, as proof of the son's innocence, two roasting chickens spring to life, complete with feathers, in the mayor's house. Two live chickens reside in the Santo Domingo church to commemorate the miracle. The bibliography on this miracle is extensive. We suggest the following: Auriol, Boschung, Ciril, Ferreiro, Gaiffier, Jacomet ("Miracle"), Lima, *Ludus,* Piccat, Southey. See illustration, p. lxxx, for the seventeenth-century frieze of the miracle in Tafers, Switzerland. David mentions similarities of this miracle with one attributed to St. Giles, written by Pierre Guillaume (10:17-18 and 11:161-64, 182).

554. The "Veneranda dies" author speaks forcefully against pilgrims who carry an abundance of riches on their pilgrimage unless it should be for distribution to the needy (pp. 24, 28-30).

555. DuCange gives this meaning for *debriatus.*

556. The word *abscondidit* is repeated in the margin.

557. Whitehill 267 transcribes *convinceret,* "he would convict," as *conviceret* (non-existent).

558. The first but not the last evil innkeeper on the route in the Miracles. See the cautions and curses in the "Veneranda dies" sermon, 34-37, as well.

559. Whitehill 267 transcribes *iudicium* as *udicium* (non-existent).

560. Whitehill 267 transcribes *indictae* (genitive case) as *indicta* (nominative case).

561. Whitehill 267 transcribes *apostolico* (ablative case) as *apostolici* (genitive case).

562. It was customary to leave the bodies of convicted felons hanging on the gibbet so that passers-by could be reminded of the penalties of crime.

563. The "Veneranda dies" sermon, 44-48, speaks to appropriate punishments for evil innkeepers. Here, as in Miracle 6, the curses are effective, and the writer takes two more opportunities to sermonize against those who take advantage of the pilgrims.

564. Whitehill 268 transcribes *proximos* (accusative plural) as *proximus* (nominative singular).

565. William IX, count of Poitiers and duke of Aquitaine, was born in 1071. He is well known for his literary compositions.

566. Louis VI the Fat was king of France c. 1108-37. Philip I was king in the year 1100. One solution to the contradiction in dates is to translate the Latin *principante* as "while he was still prince." The other is to consider this an anachronism.

567. A city in northeast Spain on the route that uses the Saint-Jean Pied-de-Port to Roncesvalles route across the Cize Pass. It is east of Puente la Reina in Navarra. The Pilgrim's Guide chapters 2, 3, and 7 mentions the town several times but gives no details about it.

568. Whitehill 268 transcribes *anxietates* (accusative plural) as *anxietatis* (genitive singular).

569. Note the cautions in the "Veneranda dies" sermon, p. 37, about accepting gifts from strangers.

570. Here is the first of three references to the basilica's being open at night. See also Miracles 18 and 19.

571. Whitehill 269 transcribes *gloriosissimus* as *gloriossimus*.

572. Whitehill 269 transcribes *revertaris* as *revertans* (non-existent).

573. See Introductory Letter, p. 28, and the "Veneranda dies" sermon, p. 36, where the author clearly voices his concern about evil innkeepers and the dispersal of a pilgrim's goods.

574. Whitehill 269 transcribes *damnantur* (plural) as *damnatur* (singular).

575. The name "Frisonus" is reminiscent of several references to Frisians throughout the CC. Here the word is clearly used as a proper name, possibly to imply a northern European.

576. The only specific geographical clue is Jerusalem, the others are generic ("sea," "port"); we can only assume that this miracle occurred somewhere in the Mediterranean.

577. As both Moralejo et al. (351) and David (165) point out, the names "Avitus" and "Maimon" appear in the CC version of the Turpin Chronicle (chapter 8), but what they do not make

clear is that they appear separately. "Avitus" is listed as the king of Bougie, and Maimon as king of Mecca. Both of the names and kingdoms have multiple variant forms in the other manuscripts.

Dozy (410) identifies a group, the Beni-Maimón, as admirals for the Almoravid invaders (end of the eleventh century) who plagued the Christian coast, even battling Compostela Archbishop Gelmírez's ships off the northwest coast. Several historical texts, including the *Historia compostelana,* mention this group.

578. See n. 490 for information about the Moabites.

579. The Latin is *galeam.* It is unlikely that the author intends "helmet" here as a type of synecdoche for armament; thus the translation "galleon" or "ship" with the later Latin usage of *galea.*

580. This is the first occasion in which St. James holds a conversation with someone other than the beneficiary of a miracle.

581. Travel to the Holy Land was popular during the Middle Ages. Since the area was held by the Moslems until the First Crusade (and again after the fall of the Latin Kingdom in the late thirteenth century), the expeditions were more dangerous because of the possibility of being taken prisoner for ransom. See Grabois ("Anglo-Norman") for information about the traditions of Anglo-Normans visiting the Holy Land through the twelfth century and Wilkinson et al. for translations of nineteen texts of pilgrimage narratives between 1099 and 1185.

582. It is uncertain if this could be the "god of the sea" of mythology or a reference to the Christian or Saracen God. But it is clear in St. James' answer that the saint is referring to the Christian God.

583. The Latin is *borum,* a non-existent word. It should probably read *bordum* or "edge." Vincent of Beauvais 36.34 has *oram* here while the AASS text also corrects this to *bordum.*

584. The psalter is an alternative name for a book containing the Psalms.

585. The Latin gives *Thetis,* the mother of Achilles and wife of Peleus, used here as a sort of metonymy for the sea.

586. Again, the sea.

587. This is the second time the saint directs his words to someone who is not the beneficiary of the miracle.

588. Whitehill 271 transcribes *gloriosissimum* as *gloriossimum.*

589. The first of the nine tones of Gregorian chant.

590. The text of this responsory is found in Book I chapter 23, where it is noted that the author was a certain bishop returning from Jerusalem.

591. The usual concluding phrase, "And it is miraculous in our eyes," is separated from the closing prayer by the author's story of the composition of the responsory. The formulaic

ending is interrupted in other miracles, but this is the longest separation of the parts.

592. Probably the modern Teverya, in ancient times Tiberias, on the western shore of the Sea of Galilee. The Latin is *Thabariam.*

593. Here "Turks" is a general name for the infidels.

594. The Latin is *mendax,* "a liar." The context requires a softer connotation, however.

595. It is interesting that James uses an intercessor of sorts in the form of the shieldbearer, who instructs his master on how to be cured again directing himself to someone other than the miracle recipient.

596. See the "Veneranda dies" sermon, pp. 23-24, for information about and the blessing for the pilgrim's items.

597. Whitehill 272 transcribes *irruentibus* as *irreuentibus* (nonexistent).

598. These apparently were Holy Land pilgrims returning to Europe.

599. The manuscript reads *vele* for *velae* rather than the needed *veli.* We have interpreted the literal "bent" to mean "loosened" here.

600. Whitehill 272 transcribes *usus est,* "had occasion," as *visus est,* "appeared."

601. This is the first physical description of the saint, albeit generic. Other descriptions occur in Miracles 19 and 20.

602. Apulia is a region in southeast Italy. Bari and Brindisi were two medieval ports there, Bari being the more important one. Bari is mentioned, along with its patron St. Nicholas, in the "Veneranda dies" sermon, p. 44. Apulia is also mentioned in Miracle 12. See n. 394.

603. This is probably a euphemism similar to "relieving himself."

604. Probably a leather shield instead of metal, in which case there would be greater likelihood of its floating.

605. The Latin is *Corsanum,* normal for Cosa, now Ansedonia, on the west-central coast near Orbetello in southwestern Tuscany. This is too far from Modena, however, to have been in the same diocese.

606. Whitehill 273 transcribes *adligatus,* "bound," as *adlegatus,* "sent."

607. This is the phrase Jesus uses in Mark 10:21 when responding to the rich man who wished to know how to inherit eternal life.

608. Second instance of this rhetorical question. See Miracles 3 and 22.

609. The word "Amen" is repeated here in the manuscript.

610. For Apulia, see nn. 394 and 602.

611. The Latin reads *uter,* literally "udder."

612. The Latin term used is *crusillam*. Although this is the only mention of the shell in the Miracles, the author talks about its importance and use in the "Veneranda dies" sermon, pp. 24-25, and refers to Compostela shell-vendors in the Pilgrim's Guide (chapter 9, Melczer 122), where the term is *crusillae piscium* (see introduction, n. 17, and n. 233). The Latin *crusilla* was literally "small crosses," but it is clear that the medieval writer was referring to the conch shell.

613. Chavannes is located in the French department of Drôme, south of Vienne. This area was formerly in the province of Dauphiné. The Latin *Allobrox* or *Allobros* represents roughly the modern areas of Savoy and Dauphiné, the area between the Rhône and Isère rivers, in the province of Vienne, where Calixtus had been archbishop. This group of people is one of several mentioned in the "Veneranda dies" sermon, p. 18.

614. Whitehill 274 transcribes *iniuste*, "unjustly," as *iniusto* "unjust."

615. Whitehill 274 transcribes *in gena*, "on the cheek," as one word.

616. It is unclear in the Latin how much time has passed. It is unusual to be absolved by more than one priest.

617. The word "Amen" is repeated in the manuscript. The chapter index at the beginning of Book II says of Miracle 13 only that the apostle brings Dalmatius "to justice," but the importance of the miracle is the subsequent forgiving of Dalmatius' actions.

618. Whitehill 275 transcribes *instinctu* (ablative case) as *instinctum* (accusative case).

619. The word *et* is added interlinearly. Whitehill 275 omits the word.

620. Whitehill 275 transcribes *e laesione* as one word.

621. In recent conversations, Compostela scholars and custodians of the Cathedral Treasury assured us that there are no extant chains anywhere in the Compostela Cathedral, but the practice of leaving signs of having been freed from imprisonment or illness (e.g., chains, canes, and crutches) is ancient and still continues. See illustration, p. lxxvii.

622. "Amen" is repeated in the manuscript.

623. The "league" varies in its equivalents from country to country and from epoch to epoch, but may be from four to six and one half kilometers (3933 meters to 6620 meters) (*Enciclopedia universal ilustrada*). Although the description is not specific, St. James does have a militant aspect because he covers the man with his shield.

624. See the discussion of money in the "Veneranda dies" sermon, pp. 37-42, and corresponding notes.

625. There is a hole in the manuscript with the *f* of *factum* supplied from context. Whitehill 276 apparently used the AASS to fill in here.

626. Anselm was born c. 1033 in Burgundy, became bishop of Caen in 1063, and became archbishop in Canterbury in 1093. He died in 1109. This miracle and the next are chapters 21 and 22 of Anselm's *De miraculis,* but the PL places them in his *Spuria* (PL 159:335-38) and signaled them as being from a *Codex Sangermanensis.* See Ward and also Southern and Schmitt about the provenance of Anselm's *De miraculis.* His feast date is April 21 (see BHL 525-35) and his works are in PL 158-59.

627. The Latin is *Dumzeii.* In conjunction with Lyon, two possibilities arise: Donzy-le-National and Donzy-le-Pertuis, both to the north of Lyon and both located in the department of Saône-et-Loire. There is also the town of Donzy in the department of Nèvre, but this is far removed from Lyon. The next miracle in this collection is also attributed to Anselm and concerns Giraldus, who lived in a village near Lyon. Lyon lies some 470 kilometers southeast of Paris.

628. The Latin reads *saculo*; both the woman and the sack are consistently found with a diminutive ending in this miracle. The "Veneranda dies" sermon, p. 24, gives a fairly elaborate description of the bag that the pilgrim should carry, including translations of the Latin word into Provençal and Italian.

629. According to strict Latin grammar *suis* should refer only to possessions of the subject, here the woman; in this case, however it is clear from context that it does not refer to her. In fact, we see the influence of what was to become the norm: *su/sus* (Spanish) used without a necessarily reflexive meaning.

630. According to the Book V, the Pilgrim's Guide, this would put the soldiers in Viscarret.

631. Latin *baculum.* The "Veneranda dies" sermon, p. 24, describes the type and uses of the pilgrim's staff. See n. 227.

632. Whitehill 277 transcribes *decubuit* as *descubuit* (non-existent).

633. There is a lacuna here with *ut s[ua]* left out. We have supplied from meaning and from AASS.

634. The lacuna also obscures this word, *petere,* "to seek," which we added from context and the AASS. Whitehill 277 did not emend here, transcribing *pete,* "seek" (an imperative).

635. The word *ago* is added interlinearly.

636. Whitehill 277 transcribes *spirituum* (genitive plural) as *spiritum* (accusative singular).

637. The manuscript reads *poterim* (non-existent) probably for *poteram.*

638. Whitehill transcribes *et,* "and," as *ei,* "to him."

639. Translated literally from the Latin *sanctae communionis viaticum*; viaticum is the final Holy Communion.

640. David (169) offers some information about this person, apparently not an imaginary character.

641. This miracle does not end with the formula statement "It is miraculous in our eyes."

642. See n. 626. This miracle is not original to Anselm. Benton points to an eleventh-century poem by Guaiferius of Salerno, *De miraculo illius qui seipsum occidit* (PL 147:1285-88), whose conclusion cites the miraculous cure "near Cluny in the time of Abbot Hugues" [sic]. What is most interesting is that "the theme of sexual mutilation is absent from the poem..." (Benton 218 n. 2). Another early eleventh-century version of this miracle, in prose and with castration as part of the story, is recounted by Guibert of Nogent in his *Monodiae* (*Memoirs*), chapter 19, written c. 1125. This miracle is found in Anselm's *Spuria* (PL 159:337-40).

643. Maigne d'Arnis gives *pellezarius* and DuCange gives *pelletarius* as "having to do with pelts."

644. Maigne d'Arnis gives *caritativus* with this meaning.

645. Whitehill transcribes *quis sim* (indirect question in subjunctive) as *qui sum* (relative in indicative). This follows the version of the AASS. From this point on, the influence of the AASS text on the Whitehill text is quite evident.

646. Whitehill 279 transcribes *tuam* (feminine) as *tuum* (masculine).

647. This type of moral sermon is not typical of others in this collection of saint's miracles. It is somewhat ironic that such sound advice should come from the mouth of the devil who is busily deceiving the pilgrim. The devil's speech does, however, confirm the "Veneranda dies" warning about taking care when preparing to leave on a pilgrimage.

648. Maigne d'Arnis gives *pleniter* as a synonym for the usual *plene.*

649. Whitehill 279 transcribes *vivere*, "to live," as *vivero* (non-existent).

650. The Latin is *non habens certitudinem*, "not having certainty." Blaise gives *certitudo* as meaning "certainty."

651. Whitehill transcribes *advocat* (here a singular for the collective family) as *advocar* (non-existent).

652. Labicum was a town located about fifteen miles southeast of Rome near Valmontone, on the *via labicana*. It is now Colonno.

653. Whitehill 280 transcribes *insecutus* (masculine singular) as *insecutos* (accusative plural).

654. The third description of the saint. See Miracles 9, 19, and 20.

655. See Puy Múñoz for a study of the theme of St. James as advocate and lawyer in the LSJ.

656. Whitehill 281 transcribes *lumina*, "gaze," as *limina*, "threshold."

657. Whitehill 281 transcribes *super* as *supra*, an alternative reading found in AASS.

658. Whitehill omits this word.

659. Whitehill 281 transcribes *tenuerant* (plural) as *tenuerat* (singular).

660. Whitehill 281 gives *Iacobi* for *Apostoli*, apparently again from AASS.

661. Whitehill 281 transcribes *minantur* (deponent form) as *minant* (non-deponent form).

662. Whitehill 282 transcribes *enarraverant* (past perfect) as *enarraverunt* (present perfect).

663. St. Hugh, abbot of Cluny, died in 1109. His feast is April 29; BHL 4007-15. His works are in found in PL 159. See n. 642.

664. Blaise gives *annuatim* as "yearly."

665. This is October 3 in the modern calendar. See the introduction, p. xxx, for discussion of the saint's feast days.

666. The text from "and we give the order..." to "...miracles of St. James" is found in the margin of the manuscript.

667. This miracle does not end with the formula "and it is miraculous in our eyes."

668. This miracle, like the previous two, is found in Anselm's *De miraculis*. It forms chapter 23 of Anselm's collection. The first sentence is a direct quote, which accounts for the lack of a formulary opening sentence typical to the other miracles ascribed to Calixtus. See Southern, "English."

669. The town of Saint-Gilles is in the department of Gard in France. St. Giles is a favorite saint of the author. The saint and the town bearing his name are cited several times in the "Veneranda dies" sermon. See n. 260.

670. Pontius was count of Toulouse, as well as other places, from 1037 to 1060/1061 (Southern and Schmitt 208 n. 3; Chevalier).

671. See Conant and the annotated edition of Conant by Moralejo Alvarez for the architecture of the cathedral.

672. The Latin is *pro suo libitu*. Blaise gives *libitus* as either a second or fourth declension noun with this meaning.

673. Whitehill 282 transcribes *carere*, "to lack," as *carcere*, "from prison."

674. Traveling in groups was necessary and typical. Noble pilgrims often had a retinue with them.

675. Whitehill 282 omits *per*.

676. Whitehill 282 transcribes *Apostole Dei Iacobe* as *Iacobe Apostole Dei*.

677. Whitehill 282 transcribes *faciamus* (subjunctive) as *facimus* (indicative).

678. See Jacomet for a miniature, from a fifteenth-century copy of Vincent of Beauvais' *Speculum historiale*, which shows this scene.

679. The manuscript reads *obserebantur*, "were shown," for *obserabantur*, "were locked." Whitehill corrects without comment.

680. Whitehill 283 transcribes *laetificati* as *laetifacti* (non-existent).

681. Whitehill 283 transcribes *quem* (relative masculine or feminine) as *quam* (various possibilities).

682. The closing sentence is only part of the formulaic termination of these miracles, omitting the phrase "and it is miraculous in our eyes." The narrator takes advantage of the moral lesson just taught by adding his own brief prayer addressed to St. James in closing, asking for guidance in this life. These byways into sermons and reminders of more abstract and heavenly goals appear only a few times in these miracles. Compare with other short sermons in Miracles 1, 2, 3, 4, 5, 6, 17, and 22.

683. This miracle is connected to a specific historical event. The conquest of Coimbra and the saint's part in it were first related in the *Historia silense*. See Díaz y Díaz *Visiones* for a careful comparison and transcriptions of the two narrations. Also important are the edition of the *Historia silense* by Santos Coco, and the later chronicle version found in Alfonso X, *Primera crónica general de España*. See Sicart Giménez for two serious discussions of the development of St. James' military imagery from *caballero* to "Matamoros."

684. Maigne d'Arnis gives *episcopium* with this meaning.

685. Whitehill 283 transcribes *Beati Iacobi videlicet* as *Beati videlicet Iacobi*.

686. Whitehill 284 transcribes *vocaverunt* as *vocarent*, and alternate form.

687. Whitehill 284 transcribes *cum*, "when," as *quod*, "that."

688. Here used in reference to Titan's embodiment as the sungod from Greco-Roman mythology. His clothing thus shone brighter than the sun.

689. Although the saint has appeared in most of the miracles, he is described in few, and this is the most detailed instance in which he is specifically dressed as a soldier of God. This identification is not new to this miracle. The narrator has already called him as such previously: in Miracles 4 and 18 and in Book I chapter 7, a sermon for his feast day on July 25, referring to 2 Timothy 2:4.

The actual word intended here in Latin is *athletam*, which, through probable scribal error, is actually *aht-* in the manuscript. Whitehill 284 corrected this without comment.

690. Whitehill 284 gives *autem* for *enim*.

691. Whitehill 284 transcribes *sim* (subjunctive) as *sum* (indicative).

692. Coimbra, Portugal was captured by Ferdinand I of Castile, mentioned in the next sentence, in July 1064. Perhaps the feast referred to earlier in the Miracle is July 25.

693. A brief attempt to broaden the meaning of this miracle to encompass not only physical battle but the spiritual battle as well.

694. Whitehill 285 transcribes *invigilans* as *invigilians* (non-existent).

695. Whitehill 285 gives *suscepit* for *accepit*, an alternate form used in the AASS version.

696. Whitehill 285 omits this word.

697. The Latin is *Fontis Calcariae* for *Fori Calcarii* or *Foricalcariensis* for the town of Forcalquier, located in the department of Alpes-de-Haute-Provence, formerly Basses-Alpes.

698. The Latin *spiculator* usually means "scout" or "spy." DuCange gives this meaning of "executioner."

699. Whitehill 285 gives *eoque*, "and he," for *eo*, "he."

700. Whitehill 285 gives *dixit ad eum*, "said to him," for *ait*, "says."

701. The fragrant scent and the "magical" light surrounding a saint's appearance is typical in medieval hagiographic and other tales. In other descriptions of St. James, light or brightness is a factor (e.g., Miracle 1), but this is the only mention of a fragrant scent surrounding James.

702. Whitehill 286 gives *ipsius* for *eius*, a variant form from AASS.

703. Whitehall 286 gives *enarret* for *enarravit*, a variant form from AASS.

704. Interlinear in the manuscript.

705. Note the abrupt beginning of this miracle, and that this miracle, unlike most of the others in the collection, does not have a specific date attached to it. "In our time," just as Miracle 20's similar nonspecific phrasing, brings the miracle closer to the audience's era.

706. Melczer (225, n. 587) describes the Hospital del Apóstol Santiago, "on the north side of the north parvis of the cathedral." Moralejo et al. (379) also gives information, including that it was designated for poor pilgrims. See López Alsina for good maps and descriptions of the evolution of Compostela's physical space.

707. Whitehall transcribes *eius ecclesia* as *ecclesia eius*, a transposition found in AASS.

708. The Latin *proprio ore*, "with his own mouth." The use of the number thirteen is interesting, for it will appear again in Miracle 22 when the man is made prisoner thirteen times.

709. The second miracle for a resident of the Iberian Peninsula. Barcelona is the capital of Cataluña, in the northeast portion of the peninsula. It is mentioned in passing in the Pilgrim's Guide (chapter 7, Melczer 95). During the twelfth century Barcelona and Cataluña were strongly expanding their roles and

strength in resettling the reconquered lands to the south in the peninsula and in the Mediterranean, as part of growing sea power. It is quite in keeping with the commercial role that Barcelona was beginning to play that this citizen should travel to Sicily.

710. Sicily lies at the southernmost tip of Italy. It was part of Moslem-controlled lands from the early ninth century until the mid-eleventh century as bit by bit the island fell to the Normans, under the leadership of the Hautevilles. Although the Norman groups conquered much of southern Italy, the power of the Saracens in the Mediterranean Sea was not completely quashed.

711. The third appearance of this rhetorical question. See Miracles 3 and 9.

712. The Latin *conterente* literally means "wearing them down."

713. The Latin reads *Corociana*. This area has not been located. One possibility is Corsica. This list of thirteen sites circumscribes a nearly perfect circle around the Mediterranean from east back to the west.

714. The Latin reads *apud urbem Iazeram in Esclavonia*. This is probably the town of Zadar or Zara, in modern Croatia, as Croatia and Slovenia were often a single political unit. Slavic pilgrims to Compostela were not unknown in the Middle Ages (see Ciril).

715. The Latin reads *Blasia*. This area has not located. The closest contender may be *Bleisa* for Pleis in Germany.

716. The Latin reads *Turcoplia*. This area has not been located, but it is likely that it has some relationship to Turkey.

717. The Latin reads *in Perside*. Persia was under Arab control from the seventh century to the thirteenth century.

718. The Latin reads *India*. The general eastward journey ends here.

719. The Latin reads *Aethiopia*, located to the south of Egypt on the east coast of Africa.

720. The Latin reads *Alexandria*, located in the north of Egypt.

721. The Latin reads *Africa*. While Africa, as a broad designation, may signify land under Saracen control, this may well represent the area to the west of Egypt on the North African Mediterranean coast.

722. The Latin reads *Barbaria*, which could be a reference to the Barbary Coast or to the Berber area of the African coast, in the area of Libya.

723. The Latin *Beserto*, probably for the more standard Latin *Bescera / Bescerensis*, the modern Biskra in Algeria.

724. The Latin reads *Bugia*. It was used either for Bougie or for Bugeaud in Algeria. The twelfth-century Arabic geographer al-Idrisi mentions a town named Bugia as a four-day sea trip

due south from Barcelona on the central coast of Africa. He defines (206) a day's sea trip as 100 miles. Bugia is linked with Avitus and Maimon. See n. 577.

725. For *tredecimus* Maigne d'Arnis gives the possibility "thirteenth."

726. The Latin reads *Almaria*. It is the capital city of a province of the same name in the extreme southeast of the Iberian Peninsula. It was held by the Saracens until 1147, when Alfonso VII and other Christians, including Ramón Berenguer of Barcelona, reconquered it. The Christians held the area only ten years. The Moors reconquered the land in 1157 and held it strongly until 1310. Almería is a fitting site to close these twenty-two miracles, which opened with the saint's freeing captives after a battle against the Moors in the northern part of the same peninsula.

727. Whitehill 287 gives *tui* for *tibi*, again from AASS.

728. Whitehill 287 transcribes *solutus* (nominative) as *solutis* (dative).

729. This is the only thing that the apostle has touched that the miracle recipients keep. The "magic" is transferred to something that the saint has touched, although not owned, a third-class relic (a second-class relic is an article used by the saint, and a first-class relic is an actual body part). This is also the only mention of the saint protecting a pilgrim against wild beasts.

730. The only miracle in which the narrator personally attests to having met and talked with the beneficiary.

731. This should be the formulaic closing of the miracle, just as in all others. But here, as it is the last miracle, the narrator closes with a sermon to the audience. The saint indeed has saved many others from physical harm and given to the sinner his own earthly heir (Miracle 3), but, perhaps because this is the last miracle of the collection it is incumbent upon the compiler to reinforce the heavenly, eternal aspects of Christian life.

732. The Latin is *exempla,* clearly meaning just this chapter and miracle, in Book II, but the moral is applicable to almost all of the miracles in the book.

733. The Latin *census,* literally "inventory." See n. 222 on this word.

734. Maigne d'Arnis gives *proficuum* as a noun.

735. It is interesting that two different words are used in Latin for "necessity": *necessaria* for the body, and *iura* or "rights" for the soul. Whitehill 287 gives *vita,* "life," for *iura,* "rights."

736. Whitehill 287 transcribes *similia* (neuter plural) as *similis* (masculine/feminine singular).

737. "Amen" is repeated in the margin of the manuscript.

BIBLIOGRAPHY

Ac-ta Sanctorum. Ed. Iohannes Bollandus, et al. Paris: Victor Palmé 1863-1919.

Alfonso X el Sabio. *Primera crónica general de España.* Ed. Ramón Menéndez-Pidal. Fuentes cronísticas de la historia de España 1. 1955. 2 vols. Madrid: Gredos, 1977.

———. *Las siete partidas.* Rpt., Madrid: Atlas, 1972. 1:497-500.

Analecta Bollandiana. Brussels: Société des Bollandists (1882-).

Anselm, St. See Southern and Schmitt.

Aronstam, Robin Ann. "Penitential Pilgrimages to Rome in the Early Middle Ages." *Archivum historiae pontificiae* 13 (1975). 65-83.

Attwater, Donald. *The Penguin Dictionary of Saints.* Baltimore: Penguin, 1965.

Auriol, Achille. "Une illustration d'un épisode toulousain des miracles de Saint Jacques." *Mémoires de la Société archéologique du Midi de la France* 19 (1935): 1-4.

Azner, Fernando. *El Camino de Santiago: Peregrinos en la Europa Medieval.* Madrid: Anaya, 1990.

Bartolini, Domingo, trans. *Apuntes biográficos de Santiago el Mayor.* Rome: Tipografia Vaticana, 1885.

Bede, Venerable. *A History of the English Church and People.* Trans. Leo Sherley-Price. Baltimore: Penguin, 1975.

Bell, Adrian. "New Departures." *New Statesman & Society* 3.82 (5 Jan. 1990): 28.

Benton, John F., ed. *Self and Society in Medieval France: The Memoirs of Abbot Guibert of Nogent.* Trans. C. C. Swinton Bland. New York: Harper & Row, 1970. Medieval Academy Reprints for Teaching 15. Toronto: University of Toronto Press, 1984.

Berlière, Ursmer. "Les pèlerinages judiciaires au moyen âge." *Revue benedictine* 7.1 (Nov. 1890): 520-26.

Bibliotheca Hagiographica Latina. 2 vols. Brussels: Société des Bollandists, 1898-99.

Biggs, Anselm Gordon. *Diego Gelmírez, First Archbishop of Compostela,* Washington, DC: Catholic University of America, 1949.

Blaise, Albert. *Lexicon Latinitatis mediae aevi.* Corpus Christianorum. Turnholt: Brepols, 1977.

Blecua, José Manuel. "Libros de caballería." *Diccionario de literatura castellana.* Ed. German Bleiberg and Julián Marías. Madrid: Revista de Occidente, 1964, 456a.

Boschung, Moritz, Jean-Pierre Dewarrat, Edouard Egloff, et al. *Chemins de Saint-Jacques en terre fribourgeoise.* Repères fribourgeois 4. Fribourg: Meandre, [1992].

Bravo Lozano, Millán. *Guía práctica del peregrino: El Camino de Santiago.* León: Everest, 1993.

Brundage, James. "'Crucesignari': The Rite for Taking the Cross in England." *Traditio* 22 (1966): 289-310.

Bull, George. *Harmonia apostolica, seu, Binae dissertationes: Quarem in priore, doctrina D. Jaccobi de justificatione ex operibus explanatur ac defenditur. In posteriore consensus d. Pauli cum Jacobo liquido demonstratur.* Early English Books, 1641-1700 n. no. London: Sumptibus Guliel. Wells & Robert Scott..., 1670.

Caldwell, Susan, and Eugene Enrico. *"And They Sang a New Song": Twenty-four Musical Elders at Santiago de Compostela.* Oklahoma City: OK Foundation for the Humanities, 1989.

Carro Otero, José. "El reconditorio que ocultó los restos del Apóstol." *El Correo gallego* (July 31, 1994): 32.

Castro, Américo. *España en su historia: Cristianos, moros y judíos.* Buenos Aires: Losada, 1948.

Caucci von Saucken, Paolo, ed. *Santiago: La Europa del peregrinaje.* Barcelona: Lunwerg, 1993.

———. "La tematica jacopea nelle 'Sacre Rappresentazioni' italiane del cinquecento e dei seicento." *Actas del Coloquio internacional. Teoría y realidad en el teatro español del siglo XVII: La influencia italiana.* Salamanca: Europa Artes Gráficas para el Instituto Español de Cultura de Roma, 1981, 471-84.

Chançun de Willame. Ed. Nancy V. Iseley. Studies in the Romance Languages and Literatures 35. Chapel Hill: University of North Carolina Press, 1967.

Chaucer, Geoffrey. *Canterbury Tales.* Eds. A. Kent Hieatt and Constance Hieatt. New York: Bantam, 1964.

Chevalier, Cyr Ulysse Joseph. *Répertoire des sources historiques du moyen âge.* 2 vols. Paris: A. Picard, 1903-5.

Ciril, Mejac. "Galicia en los romances eslovenos." *Cuadernos de estudios gallegos* 3.9 (1948): 81-92.

Conant, Kenneth. *The Early Architectural History of the Cathedral of Santiago.* Cambridge: Harvard University Press, 1926.

Connolly. See *Miraglos.*

Constable, Giles. "Opposition to Pilgrimage in the Middle Ages." *Studia Gratiana* 19 (1976): 125-46.

Corominas, Joan. *Breve diccionario etimológico de la lengua castellana.* 2d rev. ed. Madrid: Gredos, 1967.

Dalyrymple, William. "Pilgrimage to Galicia." *Conde Nast Traveler* (Aug. 1992): 11-26.

David, Pierre. "Études sur le Livre de Saint-Jacques attribué au pape Calixte II." *Bulletin des études portugaises et l'Institut français au Portugal* 10 (1945): 1-41; 11 (1947): 113-85; 12 (1948): 70-223; 13 (1949): 52-104.

Davidson, Linda, and Maryjane Dunn-Wood. *Pilgrimage in the Middle Ages: A Research Guide*. Garland Medieval Bibliographies 16. New York: Garland, 1993.

Díaz y Díaz, Manuel. "Literatura jacobea hasta el siglo XII." *Il Pellegrinaggio a Santiago de Compostela e la Letteratura Jacopea*. Perugia: Università degli studi di Perugia, 1985, 225-50.

———. *Visiones del más allá en Galicia durante la alta edad media*. Bibliofilos gallegos. Biblioteca de Galicia 24. Santiago de Compostela: Xunta de Galicia, 1985.

———, Manuel, María Araceli García Piñeiro, and Pilar del Oro Trigo. *El Códice Calixtino de la Catedral de Santiago: Estudio codicológico y de contenido*. Santiago de Compostela: Centro de Estudios Jacobeos, 1988. [Referred to as Díaz y Díaz et al.]

Digital Chart of the World. Data Dictionary. New York: Environmental Systems Research Institute, 1993.

Dioscorides. See Goodyear.

"Do You Believe in Miracles?" *Life* (July 1991): 28-41.

Dozy, Reinhert. *Recherches sur l'histoire et la littérature de l'Espagne pendant le moyen age*. 3 ed. Paris: n.p., 1881.

DuCange, Charles DuFresne. *Glossarium ad scriptores mediae et infimae Latinitatis*. 2 vols. Frankfurt-am-Main: Zunneriana, 1710.

———. *Glossarium ad scriptores mediae et infimae Latinitatis*. Rpt., Graz: Akademische Druk, 1954.

Dunn, Maryjane, and Linda Davidson. *The Pilgrimage to Santiago de Compostela: A Comprehensive, Annotated Bibliography*. Garland Medieval Bibliographies 18. New York: Garland, 1994.

Enciclopedia universal ilustrada europeo-americana. 70 vols. in 72. Barcelona: Espasa Calpe, 1907-30.

Erce Ximenez, Miguel de. *Prveva evidente de la predicacion del Apostol Santiago el Mayor en los Reinos de España: Doctrina, Que aviendo satisfecho al Santissimo Padre Vrbano Octavo la puso afirmativamente en el Breviario Romano por estudio, I diligencia*. Madrid: Alonso de Paredes, 1648.

Farmer, David Hugh. *Oxford Dictionary of Saints*. Oxford: Clarendon, 1978.

Ferreiro Alemparte, Jaime. "El milagro del ahorcado y su representación iconográfica en el portal románico de s. Leonardo en Francfort." *Compostellanum* 34.3-4 (July-Dec. 1989): 297-309.

Finucane, Ronald C. *Miracles and Pilgrims: Popular Beliefs in Medieval England*. Totowa, NJ: Rowman and Littlefield, 1977.

Fletcher, Richard A. *Saint James's Catapult: The Life and Times of Diego Gelmírez of Santiago de Compostela*. Oxford, Clarendon, 1984.

Gai, Lucia. "El camino italiano de Santiago." In *Santiago: La Europa del peregrinaje*. Ed. Paolo Caucci von Saucken. Barcelona: Lunwerg, 1993, 299-320.

Gaiffier, Baudouin de. "Un thème hagiographique: Le pendu miraculeusement sauvé." *Revue belge d'archéologie et d'histoire de l'art* 13 (1943): 123-48.

García Alvarez, Manuel Rubén. "El monasterio de San Sebastián del Picosagro." *Compostellanum* 6.2 (Apr.-June 1961): 5-48.

Garrison, F. "À propos des pèlerins et de leur condition juridique." In *Études d'historie du droit canonique dédiées à Gabriel de Bras*. Paris: Sirey, 1965, 2:1165-89.

Gerson, Paula. "Spain on Five Nummus a Day: A Medieval Travel Guide." *Topic: A Journal of the Liberal Arts* 35 (Fall 1981): 3-10.

Godefroy, Frédéric. *Dictionnaire de l'ancien français*. 10 vols. Paris: F. Vieweg, 1881-1902.

——. *Lexique de l'ancien français*. Paris: Honoré, 1971.

González Sologaistúa, Benigno. "La influencia económica de las peregrinaciones a Santiago de Galicia." *Economía española* 2.13 (Jan. 1934): 77-93; 2.14 (Feb. 1934): 39-57.

Goodyear, John, trans. *The Greek Herbal of Dioscorides*. Ed. Robert T. Gunther. Rpt., New York: Hafner, 1959.

Grabois, Aryeh. "Anglo-Norman England and the Holy Land." *Anglo-Norman Studies VII: Proceedings of the Battle Conference, 1984*. Ed. R. Allen Brown. Anglo-Norman Studies 7. Woodbridge: Boydell, 1985, 132-41.

——. *Illustrated Encyclopedia of Medieval Civilization*. New York: Mayflower; London: Octopus, 1980.

Graesse, Johann Georg Theodor, and Friedrich Benedict. *Orbis Latinus: Lexikon lateinischer geographischer Namen des Mittelalters und der Neuzeit*. 3 vols. Ed. Helmut Plechl and Sophie-Charlotte Plechl. Braunschweig: Klinkhardt & Biermann, 1972.

La Grande Enciclopédie Larousse. Paris: Larousse, 1975.

Gregory of Tours. *Miracles of St. Martin*. See Van Dam.

Guerra Campos, José. "Excavaciones en la catedral de Santiago." *Ciencia tomista* 87.273 (Jan.-Mar. 1960): 97-169; 87.274 (Apr.-June 1960): 269-324.

Guibert of Nogent. See Benton.

Guillaume de Deguileville. *The Pilgrimage of the Lyfe of Manhode*. Ed. Avril Henry. EETS 288, 292. 2 vols. 1985. London: Oxford University Press, 1988.

Hämel, Adalbert. *Uberlieferung und Bedeutung des Liber Sancti Jacobi und des Pseudo-Turpin*. Sitzungsberichte, Philosophisch-historische Klasse 2. Munich: Bayerischen Akademie der Wissenschaften, 1950.

Hayes, Elizabeth S. *Spices and Herbs: Lore & Cookery*. 1961. New York: Dover, 1980.

Henggeler, Rudolf. "S. Jacobus Major und die Innerschweiz." *Spanische Forschungen der Görresgesellschaft* Reihe 1:

Gesammelte Aufsätze zur Kulturgeschichte Spaniens 20 (1966): 283-94.

Herbers, Klaus. *Der Jacobsweg. Mit einem mittelalterlichen Pilgerfuhrer unterwegs nach Santiago de Compostela.* Tübingen: Gunter Narr, 1986.

——. *Der Jacobuskult des 12. Jahrhunderts und der "Liber Sancti Jacobi": Studien über das Verhältnis zwischen Religion und Gesellschaft im hohen Mittelalter.* Historische Forschungen 7. Wiesbaden: F. Stiner, 1984.

——. "The Miracles of St. James." *The Codex Calixtinus and the Shrine of St. James.* Ed. John Williams and Alison Stones. Jakobus-Studien 3. Tübingen: Gunter Narr, 1992. 11-35.

Historia compostellana. Ed. Emma Falque Rey. Corpus Christianorum, Continuatio Medievalis 70. Turnhout: Brepols, 1988.

Historia silense. Ed. Francisco Santos Coco. Junta para ampliación de estudios e investigaciones científicas. Centro de estudios históricos. Madrid: Rivadeneyra, 1921.

Hitt, Jack. *Off the Road: A Modern-Day Walk down the Pilgrim's Route into Spain.* New York: Simon & Schuster, 1994.

Hohler, Christopher. "The Badge of St. James." In *The Scallop: Studies of a Shell and Its Influences on Humankind.* Ed. Ian Cox. London: Shell Transport and Trading Co., 1957, 49-70.

——. "A Note on the Jacobus." *Journal of the Warburg and Courtauld Institutes* 35 (1972): 31-80.

Huidobro y Serna, Luciano. *Las peregrinaciones jacobeas.* 3 vols. Madrid: Instituto de España, 1951.

Iacobus de Voragine. *Legenda aurea.* Ed. Johann Georg Theodor Graesse. Wroclaw Köbner, Rpt., Osnabrück: Otto Zeller, 1969.

——. *The Golden Legend of Jacobus de Voragine.* Trans. William Granger Ryan and Helmut Ripperger. 2 vols. London: Longmans-Green, 1941.

——. *The Golden Legend: Readings on the Saints.* Trans. William Granger Ryan. Princeton: Princeton Univ. Press, 1993.

al-Idrisi. *Geografía de España.* Trans. Eduardo Saavedra. 1881. Ed. Antonio Ubieto Arteta. Textos medievales 37. Valencia: Anubar, 1974.

Isidore of Seville, St. *De ortu et obitu Partum.* Ed. trans. César Chaparro Gómez. Paris: Société d'Editions "Les Belles Lettres," 1985.

Jacomet, Humbert. "Un miracle de Saint Jacques: Le pendu dépendu." *Archeologia* [Brussels] 278 (Apr. 1992): 36-47.

——. "Santiago: En busca del gran perdón." In *Santiago, Camino de Europa: Culto y Cultura en la Peregrinación a Compostela.* Catalog eds. Serafín Moralejo Alvarez and Fernando López Alsina. Santiago de Compostela: Fundación Caja de Madrid; Xunta de Galicia, Consellería de Cultura e Xuventude,

Dirección Xeral do Patrimonio Histórico e Documental; Arzobispado de Santiago de Compostela, 1993, 55-81.

Kaydeda, *see Liber Sancti Jacobi.*

Kemp, Brian. "The Miracles of the Hand of St. James." *Berkshire Archaeological Journal* 65 (1970): 1-19.

——. "The Hand of St. James at Reading Abbey." In *Saints and Saints' Lives: Essays in Honour of D.H. Farmer. Reading Medieval Studies* 16 (1990): 77-96.

Kendrick, Thomas Downing. *St. James in Spain.* London: Methuen, 1960.

King, Georgiana Goddard. *The Way of Saint James.* 3 vols. Hispanic Notes and Monographs, Peninsular Ser. I. New York: Putnam's, 1920. 2nd ed., 1930. Rpt., New York, 1980.

Legg, J. Wickham, ed. *Sarum Missal Edited from Three Early Manuscripts.* Oxford: Clarendon, 1916.

Leo XIII, Pope. "*Omnipotens Deus.*" November 1, 1884. *Acta Leonis XIII.* Rome: Typographia Vaticana, 1885, 4:159-72.

——. *Roma y Santiago. Bula "Deus Omnipotens" de S.S. Leon XIII sobre el Cuerpo del Apostol Santiago.* Intro. and notes, José Guerra Campos. Compostela: Cabildo de la Catedral, 1954. Rev. ed., *Roma y el Sepulcro de Santiago. La bula "Deus Omnnipotens" (1884).* Santiago: Ed. del Excmo. Cabildo de la S.A., 1985.

Liber miraculorum S. Aegidii. Ed. P. Jaffei. MGH Scriptores 12 (1861): 316-23.

Liber Sancti Jacobi. Photostat reproduction of the Vatican ms. Codex C 128 in the archives of the chapter of St. Peter.

Liber Sancti Jacobi: Codex Calixtinus. Ed. Walter Muir Whitehill, Germán Prado, and Jesús Carro García. 3 vols. Santiago: CSIC: Instituto Padre Sarmiento de Estudios Gallegos, 1944. [Referred to as Whitehill.]

*Liber Sancti Jacobi: Codex Calixtinus.*Trans. A. Moralejo, C. Torres, and J. Feo. Santiago: CSIC: Instituto Padre Sarmiento de Estudios Gallegos, 1951. [Referred to as Moralejo, et al.]

Liber Sancti Jacobi: Codex Calixtinus de la Catedral de Santiago de Compostela. Madrid: Kaydeda, 1993. [Referred to as Kaydeda.]

Liber Sancti Jacobi. Liber de vita, passione et miraculis S. Jacobi, Galleciae patroni, partium ex Hieronymi, Ambrosii, Augustini et aliorum scriptis compilatus et in v. libros distributus. Photostat reproduction of British Museum Add. M.S. 12213.

El Libro de los doze sabios o Tractado de la nobleza y lealtad. Ed. John K. Walsh. Madrid: Anejos del Boletín de la Real Academia Española, 1975.

Lima, Fernando de Castro Pires de. *A lendo do senhor do galo de Barcelos e o milagre do enforcado.* Prolog, Ramón Otero Pedrayo. Lisbon: Fundaçao nacional para a alegria no trabalho; Gabinete de etnografia, 1965.

López Alsina, Fernando. *La ciudad de Santiago de Compostela en la alta edad media.* Santiago: Ayuntamiento de Santiago de Compostela; Centro de estudios jacobeos; Museo nacional de las peregrinaciones, 1988.

López-Aydillo. See *[Os] Miragres.*

López-Caló, José. *La música medieval en Galicia.* La Coruña: Fundación "Pedro Barrie de la Maza," 1982.

López Ferreiro, Antonio. *Historia de la Santa [Apostólica] M[etropolitana] Iglesia de Santiago [de Compostela].* 11 vols. Santiago: Seminario, 1989-1909.

Ludus Sancti Jacobi: Fragment de mystère provençal. Ed. Camille Arnaud. Marseille: Arnaud, 1858.

Maes, Louis-Théo. "Les pèlerinages expiatoires et judiciaires des Pays-Bas Meridionaux à Saint-Jacques de Compostelle." *Boletín de la Univeridad de Santiago de Compostela* 51-52 (Jan. 1948): 13-22.

Maigne d'Arnis, W.H. *Lexicon manuale ad scriptores mediae et infimae latinitatis.* Paris: Garnier, 1890.

Mâle, Emile. *Religious Art in France of the Thirteenth Century.* Trans. Dora Nussey. New York: Harper & Row, 1972.

Mandach, André de. *Naissance et développement de la Chanson de Geste en Europe. I: La Geste de Charlemagne et de Roland.* Geneva: n.p., 1961.

The Marvels of Rome (Mirabilia Urbis Romae). Ed. and trans. Francis Morgan Nichols. 2nd ed. Ed. Eileen Gardiner. New York: Italica Press, 1986.

The Mass of St. James (Solemn Mass for the Feast of the Passion of St. James of Compostela according to the Codex Calixtinus). Ed. Paul Helmer. Musicological Studies 49. Ottawa: Institute of Medieval Music, 1988.

Melczer. See *Pilgrim's Guide.*

Menaca, Marie de. *Histoire de Saint Jacques et des ses miracles au moyen-âge (VIIIème-XIIème siècles).* Nantes: Université de Nantes, 1987.

Mitchell, R. J. "Robert Langton's *Pylgrimage.*" *Library,* ser. 5, 8.1 (March 1954): 42-45.

Los Miraglos de Santiago (Biblioteca Nacional de Madrid MS 10252). Ed. Jane E. Connolly. Textos recuperados 5. Salamanca: Universidad de Salamanca, 1991.

Miragres de Santiago. Ed. José L. Pensado. Revista de Filología Española Anejo 68. Madrid: CSIS, 1958.

Os miragres de Santiago: Versión gallega del códice latino del siglo XII, atribuído al papa Calisto II. Ed. Eugenio López-Aydillo. Valladolid: Castellana, 1918.

Monumenta Germaniae Historica. Scriptores. 32 vols in 34. Hannover: Hahn, 1826-1934. [Referred to as MGH.]

Moralejo. See *Liber Sancti Jacobi.*

Moralejo Alvarez, Serafín. *Arquitectura románica de la Catedral de Santiago de Compostela: Notas para una revisión crítica de la obra de K.J. Conant.* Santiago: Colexio de Arquitectos de Galicia, 1983.

Moralejo Laso, Abelardo. "Las citas poéticas de S. Fortunato en el Códice Calixtino." *Cuadernos de estudios gallegos* 4.14 (1949): 349-66.

Murphy, Jerome J. *Rhetoric in the Middle Ages.* Berkeley: Univ. of California Press, 1974.

New Catholic Encyclopedia. 16 vols. New York: McGraw-Hill, 1967.

O'Callaghan, Joseph F. *A History of Medieval Spain.* Ithaca: Cornell Univ. Press, 1975.

Ortiz y Estrada, Luis. "Santiago pasó por Lérida." *Misión semanario del hogar* Year 7. 197 (24 July 1943): 11.

Oxea, Hernando. *Historia del glorioso Apóstol Santiago Patrón de España: De su venida a ella, y de las grandezas de su Yglesia, y Orden militar.* Madrid: Luis Sánchez, 1615.

Patrologiae cursus completus: Series latina. Ed. Jacques Paul Migne. 221 vols. Paris: Migne, 1844-64.

Peake, Harold. "Santiago: The Evolution of a Patron Saint." *Folklore* 30.3 (1919): 208-26.

Pensado. See *Miragres de Santiago.*

Peregrino. Revista del Camino de Santiago. Ed. José Ignacio Díaz. Santo Domingo de la Calzada, La Rioja, Spain.

Pérez de Urbel, Justo. "El antifonario de León y el culto de Santiago el Mayor en la liturgia mozárabe." *Revista de la Universidad de Madrid* 3.9 (1954): 5-24.

Pérez de Villagrá, Gaspar. *Historia de la Nueva México, 1610.* Trans. and ed. Miguel Encinias, Alfred Rodríguez, and Joseph Sánchez. Albuquerque: Univ. of New Mexico Press, 1992.

Piccat, Marco. "Il miracolo jacopeo del pellegrino impiccato: Riscontri tra narrazione e figurazione." In *Il Pellegrinaggio a Santiago de Compostela e la Letteratura Jacopea.* Perugia: Università degli studi di Perugia, 1985, 287-310.

Piel, Joséph M., and Fermín Bouza Brey. "Una opinión valiosa sobre el origen del topónimo 'Compostela.'" *Compostellanum* 5.4 (Oct.-Dec. 1960): 431-32.

———. "El topónimo Compostela." *Compostellanum* 7.2 (Apr.-June 1962): 163-66.

The Pilgrim's Guide to Santiago de Compostela. Ed., trans. William Melczer. New York: Italica Press, 1993. [Referred to as Melczer.]

Plötz, Robert. "Lazo espiritual y cultural entre América y Europa: Santiago de Compostela." *Galicia, Santiago y América.* [Santiago]: Xunta de Galicia, [1992], 57-74.

Portela Pazos, Salustiano. *Origen del topónimo Compostela.* Santiago de Compostela: Tipografía del Seminario, 1958.

Porter, Arthur Kingsley. "Compostela, Bari and Romanesque Architecture." *Art Studies*. Spec. issue of *The American Journal of Archaeology* 1 (1923): 7-21.

Puy Múñoz, Francisco. "Santiago abogado en el 'Calixtino' (1160)." *Pistoia e il Cammino di Santiago*. Perugia: Edizione scientifiche italiane, 1984, 57-92.

Quevedo y Villegas, Francisco de. "Su espada por Santiago, solo y único patrón de la [sic] Españas." *Obras completas. I: Obras en prosa*. 5th ed. Mardid: Aguilar, 1961, 400-445.

Rahtz, Philip, and Lorna Watts. "The Archaeologist on the Road to Lourdes and Santiago de Compostela." In *The Anglo Saxon Church*. Ed. L. A. S. Butler and R. K. Morris. *Papers on History, Architecture and Archaeology in Honour of Dr. H. M. Taylor*. Research Report 60. London: Henry Ling at Dorset, 1986, 51-73.

Rees, W. J. "The Living Scallop." In *The Scallop: Studies of a Shell and Its Influences on Humankind*. Ed. Ian Cox. London: Shell Transport and Trading Co., 1957, 15-32.

Remuñán Ferro, Manuel. "Gremios compostelanos relacionados con la peregrinación Jacobea." In *Il Pellegrinaggio a Santiago de Compostela e la Letteratura Jacopea*. Perugia: Università degli studi di Perugia, 1985, 109-34.

Robert, Ulysse. *Bullaire du Pape Calixte II*. 2 vols. Paris: Imprimerie Nationale, 1891. Rpt., Hildesheim: G. Olms, 1979.

——. *Histoire du pape Calixte II*. Paris: Alphonse Picard; Besançon: Paul Jacquin, 1891.

Romano Rocha, Pedro. "El Peregrino a Santiago y la oración de la iglesia." In *Santiago, Camino de Europa: Culto y Cultura en la Peregrinación a Compostela*. Ed. Serafín Moralejo Alvarez and Fernando López Alsina. Santiago de Compostela: Fundación Caja de Madrid, 1993, 17-35.

Rowland, Beryl. *Animals with Human Faces: A Guide to Animal Symbolism*. Knoxville: University of Tennesse Press, 1973.

Santiago, Camino de Europa: Culto y Cultura en la Peregrinación a Compostela. Catalog ed. Serafín Moralejo Alvarez and Fernando López Alsina. Santiago de Compostela: Fundación Caja de Madrid; Xunta de Galicia, Consellería de Cultura e Xuventude, Dirección Xeral do Patrimonio Histórico e Documental; Arzobispado de Santiago de Compostela, 1993.

Santiago e America. [Exposition at the Monastery of San Martín Pinario, Santiago de Compostela, 1993. Santiago]: Xunta de Galicia. Consellería de Cultura e Xuventude, 1993.

Sebold, Russell. "Enlightenment Philosophy and the Emergence of Spanish Romanticism." In *The Ibero-American Enlightenment*. Urbana: University of Illinois Press, 1971, 111-40.

"El Sepulcro del Apostol Santiago" *Galicia diplomática* 1.3 (23 July 1882): 17-19.

Sicart Giménez, Angel. "La iconografía de Santiago ecuestre en la Edad Media." *Compostellanum* 27.1-2 (Jan.-June 1982): 11-32.

——. "La figura de Santiago en los textos medievales." In *Il Pellegrinaggio a Santiago de Compostela e la Letteratura Jacopea.* Perugia: Università degli studi di Perugia, 1985, 271-86.

Southern, R. W. "The English Origins of the Miracles of the Virgin." *Mediaeval and Renaissance Studies* 4 (1958): 188-90, 205-13.

——, and F.S. Schmitt, eds. *Memorials of St. Anselm.* Auctores britannici medii aevi 1. London: British Academy, Oxford University Press, 1969.

Southey, Robert. "The Pilgrim to Compostela: Being the Legend of a Cock and a Hen to the Honour and Glory of Santiago." *The Poetical Works of Robert Southey.* London: Murray, 1829.

Stalley, Roger. "Sailing to Santiago: The Medieval Pilgrimage to Santiago de Compostela and Its Artistic Influence in Ireland." In *Settlement and Society in Medieval Ireland: Studies Presented to F.X. Martin, O.S.A.* Ed. John Bradley. Kilkenny, Ireland: Boethius, 1988, 397-420.

Stanton, Edward F. *Road of Stars to Santiago.* Lexington: University of Kentucky Press, 1994.

Stokstad, Marilyn. *Santiago de Compostela in the Age of Great Pilgrimages.* Centers of Civilization. Norman, OK: University of Oklahoma Press, 1978.

Stones Alison. "Four Illustrated Jacobus Manuscripts." *The Vanishing Past: Studies of Medieval Art, Liturgy and Metrology Presented to Christopher Hohler.* Ed. Alan Borg and Andrew Martindale. BAR International Series 3. Oxford: Bar, 1981, 197-222.

Stopani, Renato. *Le grandi vie di pellegrinaggio del medioevo: Le strade per Roma.* Florence: Centro Studi Romei, 1986.

Storrs, Constance Mary. *Jacobean Pilgrims from England to St. James of Compostella from the Early Twelfth to the Late Fifteenth Century.* Prepared for press by Angus Wold and David MacKenzie. Foreword by Brian Tate. Compostela: Consellería de Cultura & Direccíon Xeral de Promoción do Camiño de Santiago, 1994.

Stuckelberg, E.A. "Schweizerische Santiagopilger." *Basler Jahrbuch* (1903): 190-96.

Sulpicius Severus. "Writings." "Life of Saint Martin, Bishop and Confessor." "The Second Dialogue." Trans. Bernard M. Peebles. In *The Fathers of the Church.* Ed. Roy Joseph Deferrari. New York: Fathers of the Church, 1949, 7: 101-40, 201-24.

Sumption, Jonathan. *Pilgrimage: An Image of Mediaeval Religion.*Totowa, NJ: Rowman and Littlefield, 1975.

"Suplemento." *Peregrino* 41 (Feb. 1995): 1-8.

Tannahill, Reay. *Food in History.* New York: Stein and Day, 1973.

Ulrich, Jakob. "Drei romanische Fassungen der beiden Jakobsbrüder." *Romanische Forschungen* 19 (1906): 595-632.

Valiña Sampedro, Elías. *El Camino de Santiago: Guía del Peregrino.* León: Everest, 1985.

Van Cauwenbergh, Etienne. *Les pèlerinages expiatoires et judiciaires dans le droit communal de la Belgique au moyen âge.* Université de Louvain, Recueil de Travaux 48. Louvain: Ceuterick, 1922.

Van Dam, Raymond. *Saints and Their Miracles in Late Antique Gaul.* Princeton: Princeton Univ. Press, 1993.

Van Herwaarden, Jan. "Saint James in Spain up to the 12th Century." In *Wallfahrt kennt keine Grenzen.* Ed. Lenz Kriss-Rettenbeck and Gerda Mohler. Munich: Schnell & Steiner, 1984, 235-47.

Vázquez de Parga, Luis, José María Lacarra, and Juan Uría Riu. *Las peregrinaciones a Santiago de Compostela.* 3 vols. Rpt., Pamplona: Iberdrola, 1992.

Villanueva, Carlos, ed. *El Pórtico de la Gloria: Música, Arte y Pensamiento.* Santiago: University Press, 1988.

Vincent of Beauvais. *Speculum Maius.* 4 vols. Douay: Baltazar-Beller, 1624. Rpt., Graz, Austria: Akademische Druck und Verlagsanstalt, 1964-65.

Ward, Benedicta. *Miracles and the Medieval Mind: Theory, Record and Event, 1000-1215.* Philadelphia: University of Pennsylvania Press, 1982.

Werf, Hendrik van der. *The Oldest Extant Part Music and the Origin of Western Polyphony.* 2 vols. N.p.: [the author], 1993.

White, T. H., ed. *The Bestiary: A Book of Beasts.* New York: Putnam's, 1980.

Whitehill, Walter Muir, see *Liber Sancti Jacobi.*

Wilkinson, John, Joyce Hill, and W.F. Ryan, ed. and trans. *Jerusalem Pilgrimage, 1099-1185.* Hakluyt Society, ser. 2, 167. London: Hakluyt Society, 1988.

Williams, John W., and Alison Stones, eds. *The Codex Calixtinus and the Shrine of St. James.* Jacobus-Studies 3. Tübinger: Gunter Narr, 1992.

Wilson, Stephen, ed. *Saints and Their Cults: Studies in Religious Sociology, Folklore and History.* Cambridge: Cambridge University Press, 1983.

Winchester, Simon. "The Long, Sweet Road to Santiago de Compostela." *Smithsonian* 24.11 (Feb. 1994): 65-75.

Wohlhaupter, Eugen. "Wallfahrt und Recht." *Wallfahrt und Volkstum in Geschichte und Leben.* Ed. Georg Schreiber. Forschungen zur Volkskunde 16-17. Düsseldorf: L. Schwann, 1934, 217-42.

ABBREVIATIONS

AASS	*Acta Sanctorum*
BHL	*Bibliotheca Hagiographica Latina*
CC	*Codex Calixtinus*
Díaz y Díaz et al.	Díaz y Díaz, Manuel, María Araceli García Piñeiro, and Pilar del Oro Trigo. *El Códice Calixtino de la Catedral de Santiago: Estudio codicológico y de contenido.* Santiago de Compostela: Centro de Estudios Jacobeos, 1988.
Kaydeda	*Liber Sancti Jacobi. Codex Calixtinus de la Catedral de Santiago de Compostela.* Madrid: Kaydeda, 1993.
LSJ	*Liber Sancti Jacobi*
Melczer	*The Pilgrim's Guide to Santiago de Compostela.* Ed., trans. William Melczer. New York: Italica Press, 1993.
MGH	*Monumenta Germaniae Historica*
Moralejo et. al.	*Liber Sancti Jacobi: Codex Calixtinus.*Trans. A. Moralejo, C. Torres, and J. Feo. Santiago: CSIC. Instituto Padre Sarmiento de Estudios Gallegos, 1951.
PL	*Patrologiae cursus completus: Series latina*
Whitehill	*Liber Sancti Jacobi. Codex Calixtinus.* Ed. Walter Muir Whitehill, Germán Prado, and Jesús Carro García. 3 vols. Santiago: CSIC: Instituto Padre Sarmiento de Estudios Gallegos, 1944.

Pre-Christian burial site under the cathedral, Santiago de Compostela.

INDEX

163

Pilgrim with staff and purse at Last Judgment, Convent of Santa Bárbara, La Coruña, Spain.

*This Book Was Completed on April 5, 1996 at
Italica Press, New York, New York. It Was
Set in Palatino & Charlemagne. It Was
Printed on 60 lb Natural Paper
by Stanton Publication
Services, St. Paul,
Minnesota,
U. S. A.*
* *

*